COSTING THE EARTH

COSTING THE EARTH

The Challenge for Governments, the Opportunities for Business

Frances Cairncross

Environment Editor, *The Economist*

Harvard Business School Press
Boston, Massachusetts

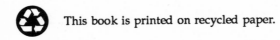 This book is printed on recycled paper.

First published in Great Britain by Business Books Ltd, an imprint of Random Century Ltd, in association with The Economist Books Ltd. Copyright © 1991 The Economist Books Ltd; Text copyright © 1991 Frances Cairncross; Charts and diagrams copyright © 1991 The Economist Books Ltd.

Harvard Business School Press edition published by arrangement with The Economist Books Ltd.

Printed in the United States of America

96 95 94 93 92   5 4 3 2 1

The paper used in this publication meets the requirements of the American National Standard for Performance of Paper for Printed Library Materials 239.49–1984.

Library of Congress Cataloging-in-Publication Data

Cairncross, Frances.
Costing the earth: the challenge for governments, the opportunities for
   business / Frances Cairncross.
        p. cm.
    Includes bibliographical references and index.
    ISBN 0-87584-315-8
    1. Environmental policy.   2. Social responsibility of business.
3. Marketing—Social aspects.   4. Marketing—Environmental aspects.
I. Title.
    HC79.E5C27 1992
    363.7'056—dc20   91-33750
                                                              CIP

Contents

Acknowledgments

For *The Economist* to give space to the environment startles some of its readers. The subject, in the minds of many businessmen, has long been firmly linked with woolly beards and woolly thinking. So my first debt is to Rupert Pennant-Rea, the magazine's editor, for having the imagination to see that *The Economist* could make an original and mind-clearing contribution to environmental issues by approaching them from an economist's standpoint, and for giving me the job of trying to do so.

As *The Economist*'s first environment editor, I am aware of boarding a bandwagon that has been rolling for some time. But I have been astonished by the generosity of those already aboard in sharing their ideas and knowledge with newcomers. Among those who have helped me most are people who began to work on green issues early in the 1970s and who went on doing so when that early period of green excitement came to an end. Their persistence has paid off: environmental argument is better informed today than it was 20 years ago.

Although I have acknowledged some of my intellectual debts in the pages that follow, many people who have helped me with facts or (more important) ideas go unnamed. Some, working in governments or in large companies, may be relieved, but to the others I apologize. I am constantly astonished at and grateful for the willingness of busy people to spend time educating journalists. Several people have read all or part of this book, and to them I have a special debt. They include Rob Stavins, of the John F. Kennedy School of Government at Harvard; David Pearce, of

University College, London; John Elkington, of SustainAbility; Scott Barrett, of the London Business School; Nigel Haigh, of the Institute for European Environmental Policy; and Nico Colchester and Peter Haynes, two of my colleagues at *The Economist*.

The research department at *The Economist*, under Carol Howard and Peter Holden, has saved me from many howlers; Pauline Cuddihy, the systems manager, has rescued me from computer illiteracy; and at Economist Books, Stephen Brough has been a cheerfully encouraging editor. At Harvard Business School Press, Carol Franco and her colleagues have shown a professionalism rare among publishers.

Most encouraging of all, though, has been my household. Collin Hawkins has kept us calm and well fed. My daughters, Isabella and Alex, have plied me with hard questions about the mess they see the adult world making of the planet. Above all my husband, Hamish McRae, has provided me with good ideas, disentangled muddled arguments, and kept the show on the road. This book is for him, with love.

COSTING THE EARTH

Introduction

Something extraordinary happened toward the end of the 1980s. People in many countries began to feel unhappy about the way the human race was treating its planet. They began to complain more noisily about filthy air and water, about the destruction of the rain forest and the disappearance of species, about the hole in the ozone layer and the buildup of greenhouse gases. Politicians realized that there were votes to be lost by appearing not to care about the environmental issues that preoccupied voters. In America the proportion of those who thought that environmental improvements must be made "regardless of cost" rose by a quarter in a matter of months. Green parties won two dozen seats in elections to the European Parliament in the summer of 1989. In Britain 8,000 people deluged ministers with letters protesting the devastation in the Amazon area. In Eastern Europe, as the summer wore on, discontent with tottering Communist governments centered on green issues: a belching steel works in Poland, a grandiose dam in Hungary. In Bulgaria the main opposition movement called itself "Eco-glasnost."

The environmental whirlwind swept through boardrooms, too. Shoppers who had never worried about the origin or the final fate of their purchases began to ask awkward questions about both. Chief executives who once would have dismissed environmentalists as long-haired radicals found that their profits depended on knowing whether their products were recyclable or biodegradable, and why it mattered. Environmentalists were in the line at the check-out, asking disturbing questions about whether the tuna was caught with drift nets or whether the disposable diapers contained dioxins. In Britain the proportion of people who said they had bought a product because it was environmentally friendly more than doubled within a year.

Now, the first outburst of environmental fervor in many countries has subsided. Some of the environmental hysteria of 1988 and 1989 has abated. More conventional issues—unemployment, taxes, housing, education—have begun to preoccupy voters. This does not mean that the pressures for change on governments and companies will vanish. Although public interest in green issues may ebb and flow, politicians and managers will find some environmental pressure irresistible and lasting. Some of this pressure has noble origins: as people grow wealthier, they will worry more about the world they will pass on to their children. Some of it will be selfish: once an environmental bureaucracy is in place, it seeks out new work to do. Each outbreak of green passion leaves standards higher, and government policy tougher, than before.

Environmental issues will not go away. Politicians who hope that they will win green votes, though, may be disappointed. The environment is what public-opinion pollsters call a "consensual" issue: one that a politician can lose votes by being against but not gain votes by supporting. Moreover, those politicians who try hardest to appear "green" will often be the very ones picked out by environmental lobbying groups and upbraided for not being even greener. Environmental issues pose immensely difficult questions for politicians.

An Environmental Resurgence

For some rich countries, the United States among them, this is not the first time that voters have become worried about environmental issues. A previous tide reached highwater mark in the early 1970s. Toward the end of the 1960s, Rachel Carson's *Silent Spring* alerted Americans to the dangers of indiscriminate use of pesticides. In 1970, Earth Day gave a focus to American environmentalism. The year 1972 saw the publication of a grim review of the threats to output from pollution and the exhaustion of raw materials, under the title *The Limits to Growth,* by a team from the Massachusetts Institute of Technology.[1] That year, too, saw the publication in America of *The Population Bomb* by Paul Ehrlich, predicting that a quarter of mankind would starve to death between 1973 and 1983; and in Britain of E.F. Schumacher's *Small Is Beautiful*, a plea for technology with a human scale. The world's first nationwide green party was founded in 1972, in New Zealand; and the Stockholm conference on the environment, the largest international negotiations on the theme the world had ever seen, took place that year.

The concerns of environmentalists in the early 1970s differed from those that have come to the fore two decades later. Then, issues of domestic pollution were important. Countries worried about dirty air, dirty water, toxic waste. In the United States, those issues were addressed in a series of important pieces of national legislation: the Clean Air Act of 1970, the Resource Conservation and Recovery Act of 1976, and the Clean Water Act of 1977. These measures shared some common features: they dealt with pollution by extensive regulation, and they were drawn up with little concern for the cost of implementing them.

Two decades later, environmentalism has re-emerged in a different guise. First, it has become clear that many environmental issues are international or even global. Sometimes those harmed by a country's environmental degradation will be its neighbors. Dirt travels across borders. The gases from America's power stations may shrivel Canada's trees; the sewage dumped into the Rhine by the Germans washes onto Dutch shores. This sense of ecological interdependence is perhaps less vivid in the United States than in other parts of the world: in Europe, where two dozen countries huddle cheek by jowl on a landmass smaller than the United States and Canada together, sharing rivers, land-locked seas and winds, the sense of a shared environmental fate is powerful. In tight-packed Asia, it will grow. But the discovery of a damaged ozone layer, the threat of species extinction and of the loss of great rain forests, and worries about global warming have all drawn public attention to the extent to which environmental issues involve the entire planet.

The policies of a few countries may determine the fate of the rest. As a result, environmental issues will increasingly vie with defense as the staple of international negotiations. Diplomats will learn to argue about whether sulphur dioxide or nitrogen oxides cause acid rain, rather than about warheads and troop deployments. Not only do the intractable environmental issues increasingly tend to be international, they often involve irreversible damage. This was not true of many of the sorts of pollution that preoccupied people in the early 1970s. Clean up the Hudson and the fish come back. It may take centuries for the hole in the ozone layer to repair itself or the oil in the sea to degrade or the greenhouse gases in the atmosphere to fall to levels that no longer threaten global warming.

The end of the 1980s saw a growing anger at the apparently relentless increase in pollution. In many countries, this anger was entirely justified. In developing countries and Eastern Europe, economic growth without environmental concern has produced some horrific consequences. A mammoth survey conducted in the first half of 1988 by Louis Harris and Associates in 14 countries, nine of them poor, found high levels of alarm about pollution of drinking water and of the air and land; in almost every country majorities of people and leaders thought that pollution would get worse; and in all countries large majorities saw a direct link between environmental quality and public health. In Argentina, 76% of those surveyed thought their environment was deteriorating; in Kenya, 69% expected air pollution to become a very serious problem over the coming five years; and in India, 81% of those polled considered deforestation to be a major cause of environmental damage. Given that the grisliest environmental horror stories come from third world countries, that may not be surprising: the air is filthier in Mexico City than in Los Angeles, and in Shenyang than in Düsseldorf.

In rich countries, by contrast, 20 years of environmental policies has brought some results. On some measures, rich countries have undoubtedly grown cleaner in the two decades since the first Earth Day. Cars are quieter, houses better insulated, and machines more energy efficient. Several big countries, including the United States, West Germany, and Japan, have cut their output of sulphur dioxide. Once-filthy rivers such as the Hudson and the Tiber carry more oxygen than they did 15 years ago; airborne lead in the United States is less than one-tenth the level of 1975.

Yet this is not the public perception. Most people in rich countries believe their environment is continuing to deteriorate. Certainly, there are ways in which this is true. The 1980s, like the 1960s, was an era of rapid economic growth and (from 1986) of falling real energy prices. As growth has accelerated, with more countries and more people joining in, so have its environmental side effects increased. Falling energy prices have encouraged people to use coal, oil, and gas less frugally. The consequence, inevitably, is more pollution, even if the most unpleasant kinds of pollution have been curbed in the richer countries. Growth has also brought a continued erosion of natural habitats, although in the richer countries, the pace has probably slowed since the 1950s and 1960s.

The public has also become more aware of environmental disasters. The ten years after the *Amoco Cadiz* spilled its oil on the shores of Brittany brought Seveso and Bhopal, which put the spotlight on the chemical industry; Three Mile Island and Chernobyl, which increased hostility to nuclear power; and the *Exxon Valdez*, the most expensive environmental accident ever to befall a company. People have become more willing to see such disasters as the result of bad environmental policies. They have also become more eager to find links between changes in nature and human activities. The drought of summer 1988 made Americans believe in the greenhouse effect; dying seals in 1988 made the British worry about the muck they were dumping in the North Sea; wilting forests persuaded the West Germans to reverse their opposition to curbing acid rain. People especially protest about what they can see in their own back yards, and what affects their own lives. And as people grow richer, they want higher environmental standards. As science becomes better at measuring minuscule quantities of pollution, more pollutants have become frightening.

The Need for Intervention

Anxious to respond to public concern, many politicians seized on the environment as an attractive platform in the final years of the 1980s. They often leapt before they looked. Environmentalism involves dangerous issues for politicians. Margaret Thatcher can hardly have thought through the telling metaphor she used in her speech to the Conservative party conference in October 1988 that marked her transition from Iron Lady to Green Goddess. "No generation has a freehold on the earth," she said. "All we have is a life tenancy—with a full repairing lease." The implications are enormous. For up to now, no generation has carried out its fair share of planetary repairs. Each has ignored the costs that accrue to future generations. To demand that this generation should undertake repairs means making people pay for something that they have previously regarded as free. Yet only government can ultimately set the terms of that "full repairing lease."

Environmental policy is inevitably interventionist. Without government intervention, the environment cannot be fully protected. That was clearly anticipated over a century ago by John Stuart Mill. "Is there not the Earth itself, its forests and waters, above and below the surface?" he asked in his *Principles of Political Economy.* "These are the inheritance of the human race. . . . What rights, and under what conditions, a person shall be allowed to exercise over any portion of this common inheritance cannot be left undecided. No function of government is less optional than the regulation of these things, or more completely involved in the idea of a civilised society."

This intrinsic need for intervention makes environmentalism difficult for political radicals to accept, especially after the 1980s' fashion for deregulation. An eloquent exposition of the free-marketer's case for environmental intervention was made by one of Mrs. Thatcher's closest political allies, Nicholas Ridley, while he was British environment secretary:

> Pollution, like fraud, is something you impose on others against their will so that you can perhaps gain financial advantage. It is an ill for which the operation of the free market provides no automatic cure. Like the prevention of violence and fraud, pollution control is essentially an activity which the State, as protector of the public interest against particular interests, has to regulate and police.[2]

Harder yet for many governments to accept, environmental issues are frequently about justice, too. Allocating rights and determining conditions drags government, willy-nilly, into nasty questions of winners and losers that politicians usually prefer to avoid. The winners and losers may live in the same town. But the gainers may be rich and powerful, the losers poor and weak. The losers may even be foreigners, if one country's environmental damage harms the citizens of another. Or they may be the weakest of the weak: generations yet unborn. "Why should I care about posterity?" Groucho Marx is supposed to have said. "What's posterity ever done for me?" Posterity has no votes; yet caring for the environment is often a matter of changing the habits of today's voters for the benefit of future generations. Heating our homes would cost far more if we used only wind power and solar energy, in order to avoid putting into the atmosphere the carbon dioxide that may well cause global warming. Why should politicians ask us to bear such costs? After all, alarming though the speed of global warming may be in terms of the history of evolution, by the time today's politicians retire, its results will still be barely noticeable.

Even within a country, environmental issues may raise awkward questions of justice and rights which only government can protect. For it is only government that can decide how much society should value the environment, and how that value should be inserted into economic transactions. The market, that mechanism that so marvelously directs human activity to supply human needs, often has no way of putting a proper price on environmental resources. "Free as the air" is all very well, but it means that factories pay nothing to belch smoke from their stacks. It is easy to put a price on a tree as timber. But that price will take no account of its value as a mechanism for preventing soil erosion, or as a home for rare birds or insects, or as a store of carbon dioxide that might otherwise add to the greenhouse gases in the atmosphere.

To talk of trees in the language of economics seems odd to many environmentalists. The very idea that values can be attached to natural beauty is an affront to those who think that it is beyond price. Yet to think of the environment in economic terms is a useful way of understanding environmental problems.

In particular, it is a helpful approach for politicians and managers who are familiar with using economic concepts to analyze policy decisions. Some environmentalists have grasped this, and realize that governments and companies may become more concerned with environmental issues if they see them as benefiting their economic interest.

Because the market does not set prices on environmental resources, the economy is skewed in favor of those things that can be developed and marketed and against those that cannot. A developer who wants to put up a factory in a beauty spot can easily calculate the gain in terms of jobs and production. Those who want to protect the beauty spot have no such numbers. The undeveloped spot has no "output" to set against the products of the factory. It is never easy to argue that the gain to those generations who can enjoy its views will be greater, over the years, than the hard cash that the developer thinks can be earned.

Why are environmental goods so often unpriced or underpriced? Sometimes the reason is cultural: in Muslim countries, many of which are dangerously short of water, people have strong religious objections to paying for a gift from God. More often, the reason is that the resource is owned by everybody and therefore by nobody. People take less care of what is theirs than of what is owned collectively; and the ozone layer, the oceans, and the atmosphere are all common property.

This point was made by Joan Robinson, a distinguished British economist, in a famous question: "Why," she asked, "is there litter in the public park, but no litter in my back yard?"[3] In primitive societies, people frequently have long-established customs for ensuring that common property is managed to the maximum benefit of all. Herdsmen accept limits on the number of cattle they can graze on a common field. Yet such traditions are vulnerable. An individual herdsman can always do better by grazing more cattle on the land. Once the common restraint goes, all will be tempted to overgraze until the common field is bare and all are worse off than before. This dilemma was described as "The Tragedy of the Commons" in a famous article by Garret Hardin.[4] In fact, property owned in common is more likely to escape tragedy than property that is accessible to all. That is the position of most environmental resources.

No one owns the sea or the sky; therefore no one charges those who overfish the sea or fill the air with ozone smog. Nobody owns quietness; therefore nobody can set a price on nasty noises. Where no one owns an environmental resource, the market will not give its usual warning signals as that resource is used up. In the early 1970s, some environmentalists fretted terribly about the imminent exhaustion of oil, iron, and copper, which, they rightly pointed out, were nonrenewable. Once all the oil was burned, that was that. They reckoned without the oil-exporting countries, which behaved like any cartel with limited supplies of a product in great demand and jacked up the price. Result: much investment went into energy conservation and into searching for oil in places like the North Sea and Alaska where it would not previously have been profitable.

We will never pump the last barrel of oil. We may well, however, kill the last elephant, for as that mammal becomes more scarce, so the rewards for catching it increase. In fact the true limits to growth are not the earth's stocks of natural resources such as coal, oil, and iron, which are bought and sold at prices that will rise to reflect their increasing scarcity. The limits are the capacity of the environment to deal with waste in all its forms and with the "critical" resources—such as the ozone layer, the carbon cycle, and the Amazon forest—that play no direct part in world commerce but that serve the most basic economic function of all, which is to enable human beings to survive. It is these two kinds of resources, long treated as free goods, that have been most dangerously overexploited.

Making Markets Work

Because the forces of unfettered markets can destroy the environment, environmental lobbyists have wanted to replace markets with government. If private enterprise chops down forests, the argument runs, put the forests in the hands of the state. This extreme faith in the benign green role of the state has faded, thanks in part to growing realization of the scope of environmental catastrophe in the state-run lands of Eastern Europe. Many examples show that bad government policies may make even more of a mess of the environment than the unfettered market.

A better starting point is to look for ways to improve markets. Clear rights of ownership for natural resources may sometimes improve the way they are managed. If ownership of environmental assets is clearly established, then polluters and the polluted will be able to bargain over a reasonable price for allowing pollution to take place. Sometimes such solutions work. If people have fishing rights in a river that they can rent out to others, they will have a strong interest in seeing that their bit of the river is not overfished. They will also be able to bargain with other owners to prevent the whole river from being overexploited. But often—think of the ozone layer—it is simply not possible to use private enterprise in this way. Establishing ownership is too difficult; the number of polluters and of those affected by pollution is too great for bargaining to be practical.

Another way to improve the working of the market is to make sure consumers and producers pay the true costs of the environmental damage they cause. Markets work best when prices reflect as accurately as possible the costs of production. So the price of a gallon of gas ought to reflect the damage caused by exhaust gases, while the cost of running a bath should incorporate the environmental harm caused by water extraction and sewage disposal. The main ways in which economists urge politicians to pass such information into pricing is through taxation.

But making polluters pay is easier advocated than done. Once a politician pauses and wonders, "Right: but how much?" another set of problems appears. It is impossible to estimate exactly the price that a green government should exact from polluters. If the developer who wanted to build a factory in a beauty spot had wanted, instead, to build it where a housing estate now stands, the price of the site would have reflected the price at which houses are bought and sold. There is a housing market, but there is no beauty market. So if government is to make sure that the beauty spot is properly valued, it has to put a price on loveliness. Economists have thought up ways to do this, such as asking people what they would be willing to pay to keep the spot undeveloped. But none has the real-world quality of the price of a house. Besides, faced with a powerful developer, only a very rash politician would become involved in a fight over the social value of undeveloped land.

Simply because environmental costs are so hard to estimate is no argument for abandoning the effort, for two reasons. First, setting a rough value may be a better basis for policy than none at all. Only by groping for values for environmental resources can governments think sensibly about costs and benefits. Scientists who are alarmed by the prospect of global warming tend to argue that carbon emissions must be halted at any price. Wise governments will first ask what the costs of global warming are likely to be, and then will want an estimate of the costs of slowing the buildup of greenhouse gases. Both figures will be wobbly and widely disputed. But without some grasp of costs and benefits, governments are likely to do either too much or—worse—too little.

Most governments, far from making polluters carry the costs of environmental damage, do precisely the opposite. So a second reason for trying to put values on environmental goods is to discourage such perversity. Many governments subsidize polluting activities. In particular, many third world countries hold down electricity prices. That drives up demand. Generating electricity to supply this demand produces more gases, sulphur dioxide and carbon dioxide, both harmful in different ways. It may mean building more dams for hydro power. It may encourage a country to develop polluting industries.

Such folly is not confined to the poor world. Most rich countries subsidize agriculture. That encourages monoculture—usually more polluting than mixed cropping—and increases the demand for fertilizer and pesticides. America subsidizes the logging of its ancient forests. Britain subsidizes company cars. Germany subsidizes coal mining. Each country has its green madness, often as economically perverse as it is environmentally damaging. Such perversities survive because powerful lobbies back them. Governments, in democracies at least, can rarely do more than their electors want. If this generation of electors is not prepared to foot the bill for that "full repairing lease," governments will find it hard to make them.

To rely exclusively on the force of the market, however ingeniously harnessed, to clean the environment is as naive as relying solely on government intervention. For one thing, markets need information. If polluters are to pay, governments will need to measure pollution. Government will need to punish polluters who cheat. Monitoring, measurement, and enforcement are all jobs that cannot be done voluntarily. They require a legal frame-work and the sanction of the state.

Governments may sometimes need to make the market work better in other, more subtle ways. If a market does not exist in the first place, giving it green signals will be pointless. The countries of Eastern Europe had elaborate systems of fines and charges to discourage pollution; but, as the fines were rarely collected and the charges were carried by monopolies, pollution simply continued unabated. It is important to worry about cre-ating a market in the first place—getting, say, someone in the Soviet Union to worry about leaks of natural gas or someone in America to care about water lost from pipes—before building elaborate schemes to ensure that polluters carry the full costs of environmental damage.

This is important because a characteristic of many of the activities that most affect the environment—energy supply, the provision of water, transport—is that they are highly regulated by the state. Power lines, sewage works, roads, and airports are frequently monopolies or near-monopolies. It may therefore be difficult to rely on pricing alone, or on market forces harnessed in other ways, to influence the supply of and demand for these services. Raising the price of electricity may encourage consum-ers to turn off their lights, or it may simply leave them with less cash to spend on other things. Only gradually will it encourage them to buy more efficient central heating or to install double glazing. It may be faster and less painful—and politically eas-ier—if governments also boost conservation in more direct ways.

A New Alliance

One reason this new wave of environmentalism may have more lasting effects than that of the early 1970s is a greater confluence of ideas between moderate environmentalists and well-run companies. This has been encouraged by a more broad-minded approach to economic growth. During the last outbreak of environmental concern, which reached its peak in 1972, some environmentalists argued fiercely that economic growth was incompatible with wise environmental policies. The hostility to growth among radical greens sent environmentalism up a blind alley. Faced with a stark choice between growth and greenery, most people, in most countries, would go for growth.

In the late 1980s, the environmental movement embraced the influential concept of "sustainable development." This is a convenient phrase, meaning different things to different people. It was popularized in a report, *Our Common Future*, by an international commission set up under Gro Harlem Brundtland, then prime minister of Norway.[5] Its virtue is that it allows people to think of compromises: of ways to temper the impact of growth without sacrificing it entirely.

Many people hope that economic growth can be made environmentally benign. It never truly can. Most economic activity involves using up energy and raw materials; this, in turn, creates waste that the planet has to absorb. Green growth is therefore a chimera. But green*er* growth is possible. The history of technology has been about squeezing more output from the same volume of raw materials. Governments can dramatically reduce the environmental harm done by growth if they create incentives for companies to use raw materials more frugally. That means harnessing the inventive energy of industry.

If effective environmental policies are to be combined with vigorous economic growth, policies must be designed with an eye to their cost-effectiveness. As people grow richer, and want higher environmental standards, the cost of attaining them will rise. Compliance with federal environmental laws and regulations in the United States already costs over $100 billion a year.[6] Almost two-thirds of that bill falls on private business. That has made politicians pause, when lobbied by environmentalists, and wonder who will pick up the tab. At the same time, it is increasingly clear in the richest countries that well-run companies are now reaching a stage where becoming cleaner will cost much more. The first steps in pollution control are inevitably the cheapest. The best companies have already taken most of these. Subsequent measures will cost more with each succeeding step. Diminishing returns will set in.

Plenty remains to be done, of course, to bring the worst companies up to the standards of the best. But further advances in pollution control may involve changing not what companies do, but how individuals behave. To take just one example, for the same number of dollars far more could be achieved to remove nitrous oxides from California's air by changing the cars individuals drive and the ways they drive them than by fitting more exotic bits of machinery to the smokestacks of the state's electricity utilities.

Such realizations have created among many governments a new interest in the potential for harnessing the forces of the market to help clean up in more cost-effective ways. In America in December 1988 an influential study sponsored by two senators, a Republican and a Democrat, and drawing on industry's experience and university brainpower, set out a shopping list of 36 ways in which market forces might be swung behind problems as various as indoor radon and wetland conservation.[7] In Britain a report commissioned by the Thatcher government from a group of academics grabbed the headlines in August 1989 with its recommendations for "green taxes" and other market-based mechanisms.[8] By 1991 many industrial countries were studying or adopting green taxes or charges.

This book is intended to encourage the intelligent use of markets. Its first half looks at the challenges that environmental policy poses for government. It examines what might be called the "political economy of environmental mismanagement" and the policies that make good sense environmentally and politically. Many of those policies involve the sensible application of economic ideas. An underlying belief is that sound economics and sound environmental policies go hand in hand. Inflation, subsidies, and a failure to charge people the true costs of their activities all breed weak economies; they also breed environmental damage. Similarly, sound economics dictates that policies should put as little burden as possible on society to achieve their goal. Environmental policies that harness market forces meet that test.

The second half of the book goes beyond the requirements of policy to look at the implications for companies. It explores the incentives for companies to introduce greener products and greener ways of making them. Only by enlisting the help of companies, it argues, can governments hope to combine economic growth with good environmental stewardship. Electors will not welcome greener policies if those deliver what they perceive to be a lower standard of living. Government will be able to pursue better environmental policies only if companies find ways to give people the level of comfort to which they have become accustomed, in less environmentally damaging ways. Companies are more likely to help politicians if politicians take their proper responsibilities seriously.

Government must establish environmental priorities and determine what information (as a minimum) needs to be put before the public. It needs to set clear rules and work out how true environmental costs are to be reflected in costs of production. These are not responsibilities for companies. Their role is to respond, energetically and inventively, to the framework that government sets out. The better that framework is designed, and the more imaginatively companies use it, the more electors will support environmental policies.

There is an important lesson here for environmental lobbyists. Many of them feel uncomfortable when companies approach them, as now sometimes happens, asking them to put down their placards, abandon their boycotts, and come into the boardroom with constructive advice. If environmentalists are to campaign effectively for a cleaner world, they need to understand how companies can help. If they talk the language of wealth creation, of incentives, of efficiency, of market opportunities, they are more likely to be listened to by politicians and by managers. To say "We want a green world and to hell with who pays for it" may be good television, but it is ultimately bad politics. By harnessing technology through the deft application of market forces, companies, governments, and environmentalists stand the best chance of jointly building a cleaner environment.

1

Growth and Sustainable Development

Politicians anxious to prove their environmentalism like to tell voters that taking better care of the environment is good for economic growth. Some of them add a rider: poverty is the worst pollutant, and wealth makes it easier to clean up. The implied conclusion is that the richer a country becomes, the better care it will take of its environment. Therefore, growth is good for the environment. Campaigning environmentalists disagree. Slower growth, or no growth, would be better. Some of them add: in time, the environment will take its own revenge on growth. The world will run out of the resources it needs—oil, coal, minerals. Both sides agree on one point: the right goal is sustainable development.

Many questions of environmental policy boil down to one: how to treat the future. For most people, this is an ethical issue. Seeing posterity as their own children, they want to make sure that the world they bequeath will be as good, or better, than the one into which they were born. Optimists hope that economic growth will provide the cash and the technology to protect the environment better. Pessimists worry that the ravages of growth mean there will be nothing left to protect.

The Environmental Limits to Growth

Environmental problems arise largely because the prices paid by people for goods and services do not fully reflect the costs that their provision, use, and disposal impose on the environment. Left to themselves, factories would pollute rivers as if the rinsing waters flowed past them for free. Power stations would burn coal without charging customers for the effects of acid rain or global warming. The bill would be left for others to pick up, including other countries and future generations. In practice, the market frequently fails, and the bigger the market, the bigger the consequences of its failure. In other words, the faster the economic growth, the greater its potential to harm the environment.

The harm that growth may do to the environment was an important theme of the environmentalism of the early 1970s. In 1972, the Club of Rome, in its report *The Limits to Growth*, took the view that growth would eventually exhaust the stock of natural resources. "If present trends in world population, industrialization, pollution, food production and resource depletion continue unchanged, the limits to growth on this planet will be reached some time within the next 100 years," it contended. One of its main arguments was that the stock of nonrenewable raw materials such as oil and coal already was being speedily exhausted.

That view looked silly by the mid-1970s, when the price of both oil and coal had risen dramatically and reduced the growth of energy consumption. The report had ignored the fact that reserves of energy and minerals are generally privately owned. Prospective scarcity is readily reflected in higher prices, which in turn encourage people to use a raw material more frugally, or to find other sources. Much larger problems arise when resources are owned in common, or not owned at all, as is the case with the elephant, the whale, Antarctica, clean air, the ozone layer, the view of the Grand Canyon, and quietness. Then, the market has no way of reflecting scarcity in the price. Without well-designed government intervention, economic growth will lead to dangerous depletion of all such resources.

Environmental resources, if not sustainably managed, may indeed limit economic growth. This proposition is more obvious in the third world than in the industrial countries. But everywhere, mounting evidence suggests that bad environmental policies may carry real economic costs, measurable in terms of lost production, wasted investment, or reductions in the productivity of labor.

Pulling together a smattering of representative figures (see Table 1.1), David Pearce comments: "The figures are subject to fairly wide margins of error, but I doubt if they are far wrong in telling us that the rich world is losing income equal to at least 1% of its gross national product, and maybe 5%, while the poor world is losing even more through deforestation and soil erosion, without even beginning to count the economic cost of waterborne diseases from water pollution and other environmental stresses."[1] In industrial countries, the most dramatic examples come from Eastern Europe, where the environment has been neglected for 40 years. The result is ill health, damaged buildings, and machinery corroded by polluted water. Most estimates put the total cost of environmental degradation at 10% to 15%

Table 1.1 The Costs of Natural-Resource Degradation to National Economies

Country	Nature of damage	Year	% of GNP
Ethiopia	Deforestation	1983	6.0–9.0
Burkina Faso	Biomass loss	1988	8.8
Poland	Pollution damage	1987	4.7–7.7
Germany	Most pollution damage	1983/85	4.6–4.9
Indonesia	Deforestation	1984	3.6
USA	Avoided damage due to environmental legislation	1978	1.2
Netherlands	Some pollution damage	1986	0.5–0.8
Indonesia	Soil erosion	1984	0.4
Mali	Soil erosion	1988	0.4

Source: David Pearce, "Global Environmental Change: The Challenge to Industry and Economic Science," 35th Fawley Foundation Lecture, University of Southampton.

of national income, although that is almost certainly too high, as Gordon Hughes argues forcefully.[2] The costs of environmental damage are most evident in third world countries, where the environment is what many people live off. Typically, primary production—farming, fishing, forestry, and mining—accounts for more than a third of their GNP, more than two-thirds of employment, and over half of their export earnings. Their natural resources are their main asset. From them, they must feed a billion more mouths every 13 years. Damage to their environment means damage to their largest single source of income.

Indeed, the failure of third world countries to recognize the impact of development on the environment often renders meaningless the concept of economic growth. It profits a country nothing if it cuts down its forests to gain export earnings and extra crop land only to find that the consequences are soil erosion, shortage of wood for fuel, an increase in floods, and damage to fisheries. Moreover, most of those costs fall primarily on the poor. Economic growth that relies on destroying the environment may enrich the most powerful but impoverish the weak.

These uncomfortable truths are slowly beginning to seep into aid policies. A paper drawn up for the Development Committee of the World Bank and International Monetary Fund in 1987 pulls together some examples of the way environmental degradation threatens economic development.[3] Deforestation means that households have to walk farther to look for fuel. In Gambia and Tanzania, households already spend 250 to 300 days a year gathering wood, while in Addis Ababa fuel wood costs a household up to one-fifth of its income. Because wood is harder to find, people burn an estimated 400 million tons of animal dung each year. This in turn robs the soil of fertility and depresses each year's grain harvest by 20 million tons. The lost grain, enough to feed 100 million people for a year, would be worth about $3 billion in 1987 prices.

Deforestation brings other costs. When the trees go, soil is more easily blown or washed away. When trees are cut down along watersheds, floods are more likely: the flood-prone area in India doubled to 40 million hectares between 1970 and 1980. The eroded soil is carried by rivers and chokes harbors and dams. One set of calculations looked at 200 large dams built since 1940 and reckoned that a 1% constant rate of accumulation of sediment each year (probably a conservative figure) would cut the useful storage capacity of the dams by one-third between the mid-1980s and the end of the century.[4] By the year 2000 the buildup of sediment will have cost these dams 148,000 gw of generating capacity. To replace that with oil at the low 1988 oil price of $15 a barrel would have cost more than $4 billion. And this cost of erosion will accrue for a single year—the year 2000—alone. In each succeeding year this vast burden on poor countries will recur or grow.

Deforestation probably imposes the largest single kind of measurable costs on third world countries. But nature's nemesis takes other forms. Water pollution is an infinitely greater threat to human health in poor countries than in rich ones. Pollution of the Rimac River, on which Lima relies for its water supply, has increased the costs of chemicals and disinfectants by almost 30%. Pollution of the Isser in Algiers and the Han in Seoul have both forced municipal authorities to move water intakes upstream. In Shanghai, the cost of moving a water intake for the public supply more than 40km upstream was about $300 million.

Development economists have belatedly realized that environmental degradation may be a serious constraint to third world growth. Aid policies in the past frequently encouraged environmental damage precisely to achieve faster growth. The World Bank, which began to take the environment seriously only in 1987, reviewed the influence of its policies and accepted that it had sometimes encouraged logging as a way to boost export earnings without taking into account the impact on soil, rivers, and the livelihoods of people who lived off what the forest produced. But the bank still finds it hard to lend only to environmentally virtuous projects. It rejects the idea that all its country case studies should show how environmental damage may harm a country's growth and creditworthiness. And it finds that the sheer pressure to lend money sometimes means putting cash into projects that may cause environmental harm.

The availability of water will be an increasing environmental constraint on growth. In parts of the Middle East, the World Bank's environment department now sometimes recommends against development projects simply on the grounds that there is not enough water for them to work. The Middle East's water supplies, meager to begin with, have been reduced by the demands of rapidly growing populations. Jordan and Syria are already close to the limits of their supplies, although Syria's population will treble, and Jordan's quadruple, by 2025. Saudi Arabia and Libya squander irreplaceable fossil water from beneath the desert to irrigate crops that they would do better to pay to import.

But this is not a purely third world problem. In the midwestern and western United States, water shortage is also emerging as a barrier to development. The enormous underground Ogalalla aquifer, the great reservoir of fossil water that was discovered after the 1930s dustbowl and that helped to restore the region's farming, is likely to be pumped dry in the next 30 years. As a result, rural populations are already falling: North Dakota now has fewer people than it had in 1920. Farther west, the waters of the Colorado river are entirely committed; to squeeze another drop for new users will mean persuading some existing users to turn off their taps.

Growth and Greenery

Rapid economic growth can harm the environment; and the environment, if mismanaged, can limit economic growth. But growth also brings potential environmental benefits, of two main kinds. First, it may bring improvements in technology, which will lower the cost of preventing environmental damage. Second, higher income levels have proved in the past three decades to go hand in hand with greater environmental concern and a willingness to see a rising share of national wealth spent on environmental protection.

As countries grow richer, they become more willing to take some of the proceeds of growth and spend them on protecting the environment. The waste that economic activity creates is not necessarily polluting, unless it exceeds the capacity of the planet to absorb it. By investing in environmental preservation, it may be possible to increase this absorptive capacity. This may mean researching techniques of biotechnology for waste-disposal sites or installing proper sewage treatment in third world cities or building terraces to stop soil erosion. All these investments in environmental maintenance buy a bit of time.

Such investments inevitably have an impact on the pace of growth itself. Companies, consumers, and countries externalize costs for good reasons: if they pay as they go, polluting activities cost more. To the extent that a green economy forgoes consumption today in order to bequeath more of the world's resources and garbage-absorbing capacity to its children, it will grow more slowly than a dirty one. A decision to invest in a cleaner environment is a decision not to invest in something else. Money invested in pollution control is not available for investment in other enterprises; people who run sewage plants are not available to make widgets for export; those who spend their days working out better ways to get rid of toxic waste do not invent money-making (and perhaps life-saving) new drugs. Because low-sulphur coal costs more than the high-sulphur kind, preventing acid rain means more expensive electricity; because unleaded gas costs more to refine than the leaded sort, cleaning up city streets means larger fuel bills for motorists.

Such costs, although real enough, have so far been tiny even in the most environmentally conscious countries (see Table 1.2). France and Germany each spends about 1% of GNP on environmental protection. In the United States, where spending on environmental protection is set to double over the 1990s, the cost is still unlikely to be more than 3% of GDP. Even the Dutch, whose national environmental plan is the most comprehensive ever published, expect to spend no more than 4% of GNP by 2010. It is therefore not surprising that the effect of increasing pollution-control spending on the growth of economic output also seems to be small. An attempt by the Organization for Economic Cooperation and Development (OECD) in 1984 to estimate the effect by looking at the experience of some industrial countries found that such spending sometimes seemed to raise output (at most, by 1.5% over ten years in the case of Norway) and sometimes to depress it (at most, by 1% over 18 years in the United States). Either way, the differences were trivial.[5]

The costs may be much larger for individual industries. As the second half of this book points out, the main expense of cleaning the environment in industrial countries has fallen on relatively few industries: chemicals, energy, mining, the automobile industry, and pulp and paper. The costs may also vary over time. America devoted a much larger share of GNP to environmental investment in the 1970s, when quite a few green laws were passed, than in the 1980s. The same is true for Japan, where the brunt of environmental investment was incurred in the 1970s.

Table 1.2 Who Spends What on the Environment: Abatement Expenditure (% of GDP)

Country		1978	1985
USA	Total	1.6	1.5
	Public	0.7	0.6
Japan	Public	1.5	1.2
W. Germany	Total	1.3	1.5
	Public	0.8	0.8
France	Total	...	0.9
	Public	...	0.6
UK	Total	1.7 (1977)	1.3
	Public	0.8 (1977)	0.6
Canada	Public	1.1	0.8
Austria	Total	1.1	...
	Public	0.8	...
Denmark	Public	0.9	0.8
Finland	Public	...	0.3
Greece	Public	0.3	...
Ireland	Public	1.0	...
Netherlands	Total	1.1 (1980)	1.3
	Public	0.9	1.0
Norway	Total	...	0.8
	Public	0.8	0.5
Sweden	Public	0.8	0.7 (1986)
Switzerland	Public	1.0	...

Note: Data cover operating expenses and investment expenditure by government and the goods-producing business sector. In some cases outlays on charges and fees are also included. Coverage of data differs considerably between countries.
Source: OECD, 1990.

A second way growth may become more environmentally benign is through changes in its structure, so that it creates more human welfare from smaller quantities of natural resources. GNP measures any productive activity in which money changes hands, be it logging tropical rain forests or farming organic vegetables; buying a pack of disposable diapers or a ticket for an outdoor concert; working in a coal mine or installing a wind generator. Yet these activities have widely differing impacts on the environment. The extent to which economic growth harms the environment depends on what is growing. By setting prices right and through regulation and education, economic activity may be channeled into less damaging forms.

It will not be easy. Economists think of three factors of production: natural resources, labor, and capital. If natural resources are to be used more frugally without a reduction in conventionally measured economic growth, then one of two things must happen: either labor or capital must be substituted for the natural resources. But in rich countries labor will also be in increasingly short supply. In most industrial countries in the next century, if birth rates do not rise and immigration controls are not relaxed, labor forces will stop expanding. Then the only source of growth will be capital, which will be invested in the development and employment of ingenious new technologies to allow production to continue to expand. The companies that develop such technologies will prosper. But it will be difficult for rich countries to squeeze continued increases in GNP from an expansion in the supply of only one factor of production.

The environmentalism that comes with increasing wealth brings an enormous shift in consumer tastes. People want products that they did not want before: vegetables grown without pesticides, energy-saving refrigerators, aerosols that contain no CFCs. Such a shift in tastes is a tremendous spur to innovation at every level. It means new investment, new product development, new markets. Nothing is more exciting to industry, especially in the sated markets of the rich world. This shift in tastes may be further stimulated by tough regulations set by environmentally conscious governments. These regulations will be an incentive for industry to develop new technologies in order to comply, which companies may then find that they can export.

Japan and Germany have both built large overseas markets for pollution-control equipment by driving their own companies to meet standards well ahead of competitors'.

This source of growth will become increasingly important. Green leaders, whether they be companies or countries, will reap big rewards. But where environmentalism is fostered by regulation, there will be costs, too: dirty companies will shed jobs or close down or move abroad. Indeed, the 1984 OECD study found that the first impact of environmental spending was the most beneficial to an economy. In the short term, more investment in pollution-control equipment boosted output and activity. Only later might lower profits or higher prices erode some of these early gains. Countries may see this as one more reason for constantly tightening the screw. What balance a country strikes between gains and losses will depend on the way it has designed its regulations and on the ingenuity of its industry in turning those regulations into advantages abroad.

Sustainable Development

The idea of an accommodation between economic growth and environmental protection found expression in the phrase "sustainable development," brought into debate by the World Conservation Strategy in 1980 and the Brundtland report in 1987.[6] Mrs. Brundtland defined the idea as "development that meets the needs of the present without compromising the ability of future generations to meet their own needs." Her committee's report was anxious to extend the moral basis for development, by arguing the need for intergenerational equity (fairness to posterity) as well as for intragenerational equity (fairness to contemporaries). Part of the appeal of the concept, however, is the fact that the phrase implies so many different things to different people. Every environmentally aware politician is in favor of it, a sure sign that they do not understand what it means.

The main difference among the interpretations is the extent to which man-made assets can be substituted for natural ones.[7] Take the example of an entrepreneur cast away on a desert island that, by happy chance, lies on a busy trade route in a convenient time zone. The entrepreneur cuts down all the trees and exports them to Japan, sells off the coral for jewelry, and drills out all the oil. The proceeds are reinvested in building schools, homes, and factories for a new Hong Kong, where everybody lives prosperously ever after on the products of their brains, high technology, and imported raw materials. Is that sustainable development or not?

Certainly not, would be the reply of the three British environmental economists who wrote the Pearce Report: "We can summarise the necessary conditions for sustainable development as constancy of the natural capital stock; more strictly, the requirement for non-negative changes in the stock of natural resources, such as soil and soil quality, ground and surface water and their quality, land biomass, water biomass, and the waste-assimilation capacity of the receiving environments."[8] Professor Pearce and Anil Markandya have also argued: "Sustainability ought to mean that a given stock of resources—trees, soil quality, water and so on—should not decline."

Others would disagree. Robert Repetto of the World Resources Institute says, "This does not mean that sustainable development demands the preservation of the current stock of natural resources or any particular mix of human, physical and natural assets. As development proceeds, the composition of the underlying asset base changes."[9] Partha Dasgupta and Karl Göran-Mäler take the argument further:

> When we express concern about environmental matters we in effect point to a decline in their stock. But a decline in their stock, on its own, is not a reason for concern . . . . There is nothing sacrosanct about the stock levels we have inherited from the past. Whether or not policy should be directed at expanding environmental resource bases is something we should try and deduce from considerations of population change, intergenerational well-being, technological possibilities, environmental regeneration rates and the existing resource base.[10]

In other words, it all depends. Those who think that physical assets can indeed be substituted for natural ones tend to take a rosier view of technology than the Pearce school does. They point out that technology has steadily reduced the extraction costs of raw materials and increased the efficiency with which they can be used and recycled. Look, they say, at what happened to the gloom of Malthus or of the Club of Rome. As a natural resource becomes scarcer, its price rises, and more investment goes into conserving and finding substitutes for it.

Economists describing the limits to substitution put less emphasis on the planet's stock of oil and copper and more on its reserves of elephants and ozone. No technological fix (not even dark glasses and sun block) is a satisfactory substitute for a damaged ozone layer. Nor does it make sense to talk of substitutes for extinct species. The natural resources of concern here are not coal, timber, or fish. The limits to growth consist in the capacity of the environment to deal with waste in all its forms, and the resources that are threatened are those that play no direct part in world commerce, such as the ozone layer and the carbon cycle, critical resources whose economic function is the most basic of all—that of enabling humanity to survive.

Economists such as Kenneth Boulding at the University of Colorado and Herman Daly at the World Bank base their philosophy on the workings of the laws of thermodynamics. The second law says that there will be an increasing tendency toward entropy, a state of disorder from which nothing useful can be extracted. By implication, all recycling is inherently inefficient. To the extent that economic growth involves using up larger amounts of materials and energy, it means creating more waste. The only way to short-circuit this process is through recycling, and the second law implies that less and less of any material—or indeed of energy—can be recaptured with each recycling.

Moreover, says the more environmentally conscious economist, to use up nonrenewable natural resources is to make a decision on behalf of posterity. Even if the proceeds are invested in man-made capital, posterity may still feel the decision was the wrong one. True fairness to future generations requires that we leave our options open as far as possible. But we cannot do that if a decision to deplete resources is irreversible.

A more practical criticism of the concept of sustainable development is that, for some third world countries, the very idea of intragenerational equity may be meaningless. In a poor African country, growing food today may lead to a desert tomorrow.

Does that mean today's farmers should starve, to leave something for their children?

Indeed, to bequeath to future generations the resources to meet their needs is easier to imagine in those rich countries where populations are no longer expanding. In Western Europe, where the population in 2025 may be smaller than it is today, the phrase may have some meaning; in Kenya, which will have more than three times as many people, it does not. Ought today's 5.5 billion people assume that they leave the 10 billion of 2050 the same stock of resources in absolute terms? Or per head, which means somehow increasing it while the demands on the planet mount?

The pragmatic answer to such doubts is that the concept at least helps people to consider the stock of natural resources that will be available to future generations. Sustainable development encourages countries to think about whether they are living beyond their means. A country that is too poor to live with the concept of sustainable development is certainly too poor to live without it.

The Environment and Equity

Development economists have increasingly realized that bad environmental policies harm not just future generations but also the poor and powerless of today, while they benefit the rich and influential. When economic growth has been bought at the expense of the environment, it has often gone hand in hand with an increase in inequality. This may be hard to measure because the value of access to environmental resources may be unquantifiable. But consider a couple of examples. In rich countries, the rise in automobile ownership has brought losses that have mainly affected the poor, children, and the elderly. Public transport has become less economical to run and so has tended to be cut back; streets have become less safe for children to play in or walk along; new roads have been built through poorer areas (because house values are lower, compensation costs are less; and the poor make less fuss).

More potent examples come from the third world. When logging rights are handed to the president's friends, the resulting floods or droughts afflict peasant farmers hundreds of miles downstream. When tribal elders privatize common grazing lands, the sufferers are the poor who fed their animals there. In their essay "The Environment and Emerging Development Issues," economists Dasgupta and Göran-Mäler draw two conclusions from examples of this inequality.[11] One is that the commercial production of primary products in third world countries is often underpriced, in the sense that it imposes environmental costs that are rarely included in the market price. "Countries which export primary products do so by subsidising them, possibly at a massive scale," they comment. "Moreover, the subsidy is paid not by the general public via taxation, but by some of the most disadvantaged members of society: the sharecropper, the small landholder, or tenant farmer, the forest dweller and so on. The subsidy is hidden from public scrutiny; that is why nobody talks of it. But it is there. It is real."

A second conclusion they draw is that "during the process of economic development there is a close link between environmental non-degeneration and the well-being of the poor, most especially the most vulnerable among the poor." When common lands are privatized (or, almost as bad, taken over by the state), often by governments eager to increase productivity, it is the landless who suffer most. What looks on paper like faster economic growth may in reality be greater misery among the poorest of the poor.

Development economists have gradually become aware that it is possible to design aid projects for poor countries that meet both economic and environmental objectives. Terraces on hillsides may halt soil erosion and benefit farming; stopping industrial water pollution may improve fish catches. Above all, policies that help to reduce population growth mean a slower increase in the future pressure of people on land, and fewer people for governments to educate and care for.

Discount Rates

For economists, the environment poses particularly intriguing questions of how to deal with the future. The passage of time is responsible for many of the complexities that arise in environmental policy-making. The benefits of good environmental policies accrue over time; the bill for setting them in train usually arrives at once. The gap between the initial environmental investment and the eventual benefit may be extremely wide. A tree will take years to grow; heavy metals may pollute a river for a century before they decay; nuclear waste will far outlast those who dump it; global warming, caused by the fossil fuels we burn today, may be a problem for the grandchildren of our grandchildren. Moreover, some environmental investments are intended to avoid risk—although the risk may (as in the case of global warming) be far into the future. And some are intended to avoid consequences that may be irreversible such as the extinction of a species.

As a precept for the responsibilities of present generations toward their descendants, sustainable development is a concept that creates a special problem for conventional economists. Being fair to posterity, in the environmental sense, clashes with the usual way economists look at the concept of discount rates when valuing investments. Usually, when dealing with the future, economists assume that people today make sensible choices between spending their money now or later. A benefit today is assumed to be worth more than the same benefit enjoyed in the future. Jam today is worth more than jam on Tuesday of next week, let alone jam the year after next. To have $100 today is worth more than having $100 in ten years' time, because today's $100 can be invested and earn a return or be spent and enjoyed at once.

The level of interest rates reflects this preference, because savers require compensation for postponing consumption. The returns on an investment must be high enough to make up for spending forgone today. A business will tie up cash in building a new factory only if the return it is expected to earn when it eventually comes on stream will be greater than it could have earned by investing it today. The higher the interest rates, the greater the value of $100 today compared with the same sum in a decade's time, and the higher the discount rate applied to the value of the money ten years hence.

With this arithmetic, long-term interest rates of 10% a year mean that it is not worth paying more than $73 now to avoid an ecological loss of a million dollars expected to happen in a hundred years' time. Even if interest rates fell to 2%, costs in-curred 35 years into the future are only half as important as those suffered now. Using such logic, governments argue that it is more important to use up oil today than to keep it in the ground for future generations, and more important to sell teak forests now than to leave them standing. International aid agencies frequently demand that projects whose costs and benefits can be quantified earn a rate of return of at least 10% a year. One consequence is to rule out any project that involves conserving or replanting mature forests rather than planting fast-growing species. Trees that take a hundred years to grow make no eco-nomic sense at all.

Many other decisions with environmental consequences bene-fit people alive today at the expense of their unborn children or grandchildren. Generating electricity from nuclear power leaves posterity to solve the problem of disposing of radioactive waste; using CFCs in an air conditioner keeps people cool now, but at the expense of a hole in the ozone layer for several centuries to come. The higher the discount rates governments (or businesses) apply, the more they are willing to pass environmental costs on to posterity. Benefits today become more worthwhile, even at the expense of costs incurred tomorrow.

Faced with such problems, deeper green economists argue that the concept of discount rates applied to environmental decisions may be meaningless, or at least need to be adapted. It is silly to claim that money in the bank can ever be a substitute for—say—a rain forest or a species, as discounting appears to imply. If the concept of the discount rate is to be applied at all, then it should be an especially low discount rate.

Such economists point out that environmental investment has more in common with health or education than with investing in a new factory. The discount rate appropriate for individual consumers or companies may not be right for society as a whole. If it were, not a single school might be built, since the return on investing in a child's education would be too low compared with that on junk bonds. Indeed, many people in their personal lives work to make the world a better place for their children and grandchildren, effectively applying a negative discount rate by valuing the future more highly than the present.

Conventional economists worry that special "green" discount rates for environmental investments may lead to perverse results. They may encourage too much investment, of the wrong sort as well as the right. When governments have applied low discount rates to their own investment programs, the effects on the environment have sometimes been disastrous. Often, roads, power stations, and dams that are built by governments or nationalized companies would never have been built by a private company that had to raise its capital in the open market. Governments, which never (formally) go bust, are always able to borrow more inexpensively than everybody else. They reward themselves by accepting lower rates of return for their investments. Once environmentally beneficial decisions are made on special, low discount rates, those who want to make environmentally damaging investments may demand equal treatment.

Better, say these economists, to try to solve some of the problems of conventional discount rates. After all, society is constantly making trade-offs that imply preferences—including preferences between money in the bank and rain forests. A first step should be to improve the measurement of the value people put on the environment, through the techniques discussed in the next chapter.

Put a proper value on an environmental "good" and the balance between costs and benefits will start to look greener. Even the amount people will pay to avoid an irreversible decision may be captured. If, to take an extreme case, it would cost the world's entire GNP each year to save the African elephant, the animal would be doomed. In the same way, though with more difficulty, some provision might be made for environmental uncertainty and risk by building an insurance premium into the sums.

These adjustments may make it possible to choose among environmental projects that have their effect in the next 30 or 40 years. Indeed, the main use of discount rates in environmental investment decisions may be to clarify which course is more sensible. Should the greenhouse effect be tackled by developing solar energy or through the use of energy conservation? Should the rain forest be conserved through afforestation or extractive reserves?

But even conventional economists feel uneasy about applying such techniques to the bigger questions, of whether to try to halt the greenhouse effect or to save the rain forest. To apply discount rates to such broad questions that affect future generations means assuming that this generation can accurately predict the preferences of posterity. There is something ludicrous about discounting benefits that arise a century hence. Even at a modest discount rate, no investment will look worthwhile so far in the future; although, where an environmental decision has irreversible effects, the cost to future generations may be infinite.

On many environmental decisions, discount rates will have no bearing. Politicians will not use them to decide whether to tackle global warming or species extinction. Such decisions will be political. Most people feel comfortable with the idea that their descendants ought to enjoy the same natural inheritance as they have received. One survey found that the most important influence on the environmental thinking of corporate managers, after public opinion, was their family.[12] The best way to appreciate the concept of environmental stewardship is to remember that one's children will eventually inherit the earth.

An important corollary of the impact of discount rates on environmental investments is the consequence of inflation. Damaging for economies, inflation is lethal for the environment. The effect of inflation on discount rates helps to explain the harm. High inflation puts an enormous premium on consuming now rather than next year—let alone leaving something behind for posterity. In particular, inflation tends to drive people out of cash and into tangible assets. Most tangible of all is land, which, as Mark Twain noted, they ain't making any more. Inflation brings land grabs. In developed countries, that generally means property booms. A sharp rise in the value of property gives it an edge over the environmental value of whatever was there before, whether a street of fine old houses or a piece of woodland. The arbitrary and underdeveloped techniques of environmental valuation have not yet shown that people put higher values on conservation in periods of rapid inflation; inevitably, a property boom shifts the balance in favor of development.

The environmental impact of inflation may be much more damaging for third world countries. There, land grabs may radically change the way land is used, although the ancient use may have evolved over centuries as the one sustainable way of making the land productive. The best example is the destruction of the Amazon forest. Rain forests frequently grow on poor land, unsuitable for agriculture except in small cleared patches, which are left to recover and regenerate after growing a couple of crops. One of the most powerful forces behind tree clearance has been Brazil's stratospheric inflation. Those with cash have bought or grabbed stretches of forest and then cleared it to secure a legal title and to discourage squatters. Having cleared the trees, the land-grabber can sell the land, make a quick profit, and buy or grab another swathe. The cleared land may raise a few cattle for a year or two, but tree-felling has frequently had little to do with agriculture and everything to do with land speculation.

In a review for the World Bank of the way economic policies affect the environment, Dennis Anderson concludes: "Ecological damage is sometimes less the result of externalities than of distortions in the structure of macroeconomic policies. However well designed and executed a [development] project may be, and whatever provisions are made for its immediate environment, it is quite possible that ecological damage is unavoidable outside the project's confines, in ecologically sensitive areas, if macroeconomic policies encourage it."[13] More broadly, macroeconomic stability may be good for the environment. Tony Killick of Britain's Overseas Development Institute argues for two crucial links.[14] First, stability brings confidence in the future. This encourages government, businesses, and people to look ahead, and makes possible the environmental planning that considers both immediate and long-term issues. Second, stability in the economy as a whole brings market stability. Price signals are clearer. It therefore becomes easier to use economic measures to make sure that polluters pay for the harm they do. The economic policies that are good for economies may, by happy coincidence, frequently be the ones that are best for the environment, too.

Measuring Environmental Assets

Economic growth is conventionally measured in terms of gross national product. But as every student learns in Economics 101, conventional measures omit many things that greatly affect the sum of human happiness, or even of social well-being. They give no value to the unpaid labor of housewives, the undeclared earnings of gamblers, or the unmeasured value of clean air and pure water. Some economists now hope to find ways of measuring national wealth which will concentrate the attention of policymakers on what effect economic activity has on the environment.

One way for governments to discover whether their policies are truly sustainable is by devising national income accounts that value natural resources properly. Environmental accounts have so far developed along at least three distinct lines. One approach, pioneered in Norway and built on in France and Canada, tries to measure the stock of a country's natural resources, mainly in physical units such as acres, pounds, and gallons, and to estimate changes in that stock over time. Norway's physical accounts, which have been published since the early 1970s, show levels of stock, discoveries, depletion, and deposition of the country's main natural resources: fish, oil, forests, and so on. France has a more ambitious exercise, its Natural Patrimony Accounts, which tries to measure not only stocks and flows of physical resources, but the way they are distributed by region and the way they are used by companies, individuals, and government.

Such "satellite" accounts have certain shortcomings. If they are highly aggregated, they may lump together in a single acreage or tonnage wood from a variety of different species of trees whose ecological value is different; or they may describe in a single set of figures coal or minerals from whose mines costs of extraction vary considerably. But if the figures are disaggregated, they produce too much information to be easily used. Not surprisingly, it has proved easier to measure the quantity of physical resources than their quality.

Physical accounts are not generally intended as the basis for adjusting GNP. But they are the prerequisite for more sophisticated exercises aimed at creating a new kind of economic account. Here economists have taken two main approaches. One has been to try to extract resource depletion from GNP. If a country cuts down and sells its forests, conventional GNP figures register a rise in income, when in fact natural wealth has been depleted. The second is a broader exercise that involves trying to attach monetary values to all natural resources, whether or not the marketplace offers guide prices.

All monetary approaches have problems. To some extent, all involve putting a direct value on environmental quality or on changes in that quality. The problems with environmental valuation are formidable enough when applied to an individual bit of environmentalism. To apply them on a national scale is even more daunting. On the other side of the balance, there is the question of how to treat spending designed to prevent or cure environmental damage. The effect of the *Exxon Valdez* spill was to increase America's recorded economic growth. The money spent on cleaning up Alaska was treated as an increase in national income; the environmental damage was unrecorded. How should "defensive" expenditures such as the Exxon cleaning bill be counted? Leave them in and the result is a kind of double-counting: national income accounts record as "growth" both the rise in aircraft traffic and the sales of double-glazing firms, or the sales of both pesticides and water filters. But treat them as a negative and other questions arise, since most kinds of spending by the end user are "defensive" in some sense. As one economist put it, "Food expenditures defend against cold and rain . . . medical expenditures defend against sickness, and religious outlays against the fires of hell."[15]

Of the two main monetary lines of approach, the first is more limited but more practical. It takes its inspiration from the idea of income as defined by the late, great British economist Sir John Hicks. He argued that income was the most that could be consumed in a given period without leaving a person or a country worse off than before. On the basis of that definition, true national income is "sustainable" income. National accounts capture that concept of sustainability where investment in man-made capital is concerned through the concept of depreciation. As the value of a factory or a piece of machinery declines over time, it is written off against the value of production. If a country's man-made assets depreciate faster than they are being replaced, it is clearly living beyond its means.

No such concept applies to natural capital. As it is used up, national accounts show no charge against current income to reflect the fall in future potential production. When Britain discovered North Sea oil, its accounts did not register an enormous increase in its assets. Britain's exploitation of its oil has been measured in terms of barrels sold as an income gain, rather than a drawing down of capital. Had the national accounts treated North Sea oil as a stock of capital, they would have concentrated attention on the extent to which that asset had been drawn down to provide income or to pay for reinvestment in man-made capital.

Such a measurement would have been useful for British voters in judging where their higher incomes were coming from in the 1980s. For developing countries, largely dependent on exploiting natural resources to survive, sums of this sort are vital. National accounts that ignore their natural resources effectively ignore their main assets. Repetto sums it up: "Soils, water, forests, the gene pool, and other natural resources are economic assets, in that they can generate a flow of future income. Mistaking a decline in that wealth for a rise in income is a confusion likely to end in bankruptcy."

Repetto cites a country where this danger is a lively one. The Philippines, now struggling with unemployment and foreign debt, has chopped down 90% of its old-growth hardwood forests since 1960. It has thus wiped out a resource that could have yielded valuable income in perpetuity, had the woods been carefully replanted as they were felled. Wood exports, the country's main foreign-exchange earner in the 1960s and early 1970s, have fallen abruptly, leaving the country with the prospect of a deficit through the 1990s. On conventional measurement, the economy of the Philippines grew by an average of 5.9% a year between 1965 and 1980. Some of this growth reflects merely the destruction of a resource, which has left the country with over 12 million acres of denuded hillsides, releasing floods and silt into rivers and irrigation canals, and reducing food production and fish catches. What sort of growth is that?

Repetto and his colleagues from the World Resources Institute made a study in Indonesia to show how a developing country can start to measure what is really happening to its natural wealth.[14] Indonesia is a country where primary production accounts for more than 40% of gross domestic product, more than 80% of exports, and more than half of all employment.

Indonesia's GDP grew on average by 7% between 1971 and 1984, making it one of the most successful middle-income countries.

Look again, said the WRI. Take three natural resources: oil, timber, and soil. Put a simple market value on them, that of proven oil reserves, of standing trees, and of productive land. Look at the rate at which those resources are being depleted—by oil sales, by logging, and by soil erosion. Build that back into the accounts to produce a concept of "net" domestic product. The results appear in Figure 1.1: a sharp rise in two years of big oil finds, but otherwise a slower growth than the unadjusted figures suggest. Suitably "greened," Indonesia's 1971–1984 output growth falls to about 4%, still impressive, but more modest. For

Figure 1.1 Indonesia's GDP and "NDP" (constant 1973 trillion rupiahs)

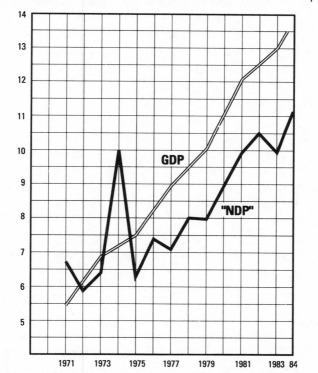

Source: R. Repetto et al., *Wasting Assets: Natural Resources in the National Income Accounts* (Washington, D.C.: World Resources Institute, 1989).

farming in particular, apparent growth has been won at the expense of future catastrophe. On overcrowded Java, where 100 million people live in an area the size of Greece or of New York State, the soil swept away every year is worth 4% of annual farm output. The capitalized losses in future productivity are some 40% of the annual value of the output from upland farms. "If erosion losses are regarded as the cost of obtaining the current year's livelihood from vulnerable upland soils, then these estimates show the bargain to be harsh," comments the WRI study. "Nearly 40 cents in future income is sacrificed to obtain each dollar for current consumption."

A great virtue of the WRI exercise is that it stays close to the marketplace. Measuring the depletion of trees and oil is relatively easy. Measuring the value of lost soil is more difficult: it involves estimating erosion rates and then trying to piece together the impact of erosion on soil productivity. But by and large the study looks at market prices to make its point. It does not try to build into the value of forests a figure for their value as a habitat for species or a nice place to walk.

One example of this approach, developed by Henry Peskin, treats environmental assets as though their contribution to economic activity were similar to that of conventional, marketed assets.[15] The environment produces inputs (such as mopping up pollution), which are consumed by other productive economic sectors (such as companies), and generates outputs, many of them recreational services (babbling brooks, bosky woods), which are consumed mainly by households. The environmental damage that so often results from consumption is set off against the output side of the accounts. This approach, although intellectually sophisticated, is less likely to be used by individual developing countries to examine the true environmental costs of economic growth. It may be more useful in developed countries, where environmental damage frequently affects people's health and happiness in more indirect, intangible ways.

The main argument for trying to keep track of how economic activity affects the environment is that, as management consultants like to say, what is not measured does not happen. Governments that learn to measure economic achievement purely in terms of GNP may make awful mistakes. The more dependent their economies are on natural resources, the worse those mistakes may be.

For poor countries good environmental statistics may be a matter of life or death; but rich countries need them too. In rich countries popular concern for the environment has in effect made the inadequacy of GNP as a measure of welfare a big political issue. If a building boom means the destruction of familiar countryside, or if increased car ownership makes towns less comfortable for pedestrians, then something unmeasured has been lost, offsetting some of the gains in measurable output. The voters in rich countries may increasingly prefer their growth to be kinder to the environment, whatever the cost to the crude statistics. Old-fashioned figures for growth—and for income distribution, too—mean nothing without an account of how environmental assets are being used, and who uses them. Before politicians make claims for the compatible merits of growth and greenery, they first need to know what is happening to their country's natural inheritance, and why.

2

Costs and Benefits

N othing so annoys environmentalists about economists as their attempt to put a price on nature's bounty. "What am I bid for one ozone layer in poor condition?" they tease. "How much is the spotted owl worth?" The idea seems ludicrous. Yet society puts prices on environmental assets all the time by deciding which policies to pursue. It is surely better to try to make sure that those prices reflect the value of the environment as accurately as possible than to pretend that they do not exist.

Most real-world decisions involve conflicts of interest. If a factory pollutes a beach, those who once swam there carry the cost. If a logging company chops down a forest, the creatures that lived in it suffer. If a view is blocked by a building, those who once enjoyed it lose, while those who rent out the building gain. In a world where money talks, the environment needs value to give it a voice.

Values are often placed on the environment almost by default. Governments implicitly judge the costs and benefits of environmental action, whether deciding to sign the Montreal Protocol on CFCs or passing laws about the permitted level of water pollution. They do implicit sums when deciding whether to run a road through a beauty spot; so do companies when carrying out an assessment of environmental impact.

Of course, political pressures are often the way governments measure environmental benefit. Newspapers, whipped up by environmental lobbyists, clamor for action; governments publicly accept that a problem exists and announce that they will solve it, without first asking what the solution will cost, or what benefits it will bring. This may be a highly inefficient way to allocate scarce resources to protect the planet. Voters do not always get most excited about the things that do the most environmental damage.

Without putting a value on environmental gains, it is also impossible to know how far an environmental policy should go. Ought every scrap of pollution to be eliminated? Economists point out, incontrovertibly, that although the first steps in cleaning up are relatively cheap, each additional step produces smaller and smaller results. The costs of getting rid of a pollutant will rise steeply as it diminishes. Environmentalists, who tend to think in absolutes, often argue that no level of pollution is safe. Economists disagree. Some kinds of pollution, they admit, ought to be totally prevented: thus a nuclear power plant should never leave highly radioactive waste lying about, nor should factories dump cyanide in the local river. In general, though, economists think that it may be wiser to tolerate some pollution than to try to get rid of it all, whatever the cost.

Measuring the Threat

Economists use two basic approaches to set values on environmental assets. One is direct: they ask people questions. The other approach is indirect. Economists hunt for a real-world market in which to try to capture the value of environmental assets.

The questions asked in the direct approach are, at their simplest, along the lines of "What would you be willing to pay to stop the Grand Canyon from being shrouded in smog?" Some answers are shown in Table 2.1. Over time, such questions have become more and more refined in order, for instance, to try to stop people from naming huge sums on the sensible assumption that others will share the bill through higher taxes. Some surveys ask a set of questions once, then give interviewees a pep talk on the environmental issue at stake, and ask the questions again. Not surprisingly, such experiments prove the importance of environmental education in raising people's willingness to pay to prevent environmental damage. People name even larger values if they are given a day or two to reflect after the pep talk.

Surveys have some advantages over the second method of establishing environmental values. The use of indirect valuation captures only the market value of some environmental assets. That may not be the whole story. For example, what people spend to travel to a park gives a guide to the value they put on the experience. But travel costs say nothing about the values of

Table 2.1 A Value on Nature: Non-Use Values for Unique Natural Assets ($, mid-1980s)

Asset	Value per adult
Animal species	
Whooping crane	1
Emerald shiner	4
Bottlenose dolphin	6
Bighorn sheep	7
California sea otter	7
Northern elephant seal	7
Blue whale	8
Bald eagle	11
Grizzly bear	15
Natural amenities	
Water quality (S. Platte river basin)	4
Visibility (Grand Canyon)	22

Source: K. Samples, M. Gowen, and J. Dixon, "The Validity of the Contingent Valuation Method for Estimating Non-Use Components of Preservation Values for Unique Natural Resources," paper presented to the American Agricultural Economics Association, Reno, Nevada, July 1986.

those who might like to travel to a park the next year and would pay to keep that option open. Surveys capture more of the picture: what people say they would pay reflects, at least in theory, not only the market value of some environmental assets, for instance the higher price their house commands because it fronts onto an unpolluted river, but also the priceless enjoyment a person might get from fishing on that river, and the value that might be derived by another person, far away, from the comforting thought that the river was clean. Only surveys can hope to capture the most metaphysical of all the values that economists attach to the environment: those that reflect the benefit people draw from simply knowing that species or habitats continue to exist.

This kind of psychic value is important. One of the advantages of using surveys is that they are the only way to discover values put on some environmental assets by people who do not actually make use of them. People in industrial countries especially may put a value on a species or a habitat they may never see, even if they know they will never see it. They may be pleased to know that the oceans still contain whales and the Himalayas snow leopards. They may even attach value, however hazily, to the notion that these creatures will continue to exist long after they do. An indication of this is the size of voluntary contributions people are prepared to make to conservation bodies that hope to save wild species and places. The World Wildlife Fund (WWF), largest of all, receives nearly $100 million a year. Another is the effort that people in rich countries particularly will put into conservation campaigns.

Surveys have drawbacks, too. One is the large differences that regularly appear between the answer to the question "What would you be willing to pay for a 50% improvement in air quality?" and the apparently similar question "What would you accept as compensation for a 50% worsening in air quality?" When these questions were put to 2,000 people in Haifa, Israel, the answer to the first question was about $12 per household per year (1987 prices).[1] But the compensation the households wanted if air quality were to worsen was roughly four times as much. Sometimes surveys find that people simply say that nothing would be enough to compensate them for an environmental loss, implying that its value to them is infinite. Ask a "What would you pay" type question, and the numbers are always much more modest (see Table 2.2). One possible explanation is that people feel more strongly about losses imposed on them than about gains that they choose. The loss of something a person already "owns," like clean air, is valued more highly than the potential gain of something new, like even cleaner air. People feel that they are the owners of an endowment of environmental rights, which they are deeply unwilling to abandon.

This may be why companies trying to site a polluting plant seem to find it easier to give the local community a sense of control over the decision. But the differences between what economists dub "WTP" (willingness to pay) and "WTA" (willingness to accept) questions are interesting from another point of view. Normally, economists draw curves to show how people are

Table 2.2 Calculation Disparities of Models in Various Studies, Between WTP, "willingness to pay," and WTA, "willingness to accept" (year-of-study $)

Study	WTP	WTA
Hammack and Brown (1974)	247.00	1,044.00
Banford et al. (1977)	43.00	120.00
	22.00	93.00
Sinclair (1976)	35.00	100.00
Bishop and Heberlein (1979)	21.00	101.00
Brookshire et al. (1980)	43.64	68.52
	54.07	142.60
	32.00	207.07
Rowe et al. (1980)	4.75	24.47
	6.54	71.44
	3.53	46.63
	6.85	113.68
Hovis et al. (1983)	2.50	9.50
	2.75	4.50
Knetsch and Sinden (1983)	1.28	5.18

Source: Cummings et al. (1986), quoted in David Pearce and Kerry Turner, *Economics of Natural Resources and the Environment* (London: Harvester Wheatsheaf, 1990).

willing to trade, say, apples for oranges, or money for matches. They assume that people are willing to move smoothly—"indifferently"—along these curves, trading gradually increasing amounts of apples for rising numbers of oranges, or a few pennies less for a declining number of matchboxes. Some environmental economists argue that the answers to their valuation surveys suggest that this key assumption of conventional economics may be meaningless in the real world. Such curves may simply not exist. People's reactions may depend on whether they are paying to get more or being compensated to accept less.

Using the Market

The indirect approach to discovering environmental values involves trying to find a real market that offers some guidance. In developing countries, where the environment is literally what most people live off, such markets are often easy to find. In richer countries, the link between environmental damage and a real market may be more tenuous. Take the property market. If two identical houses on neighboring streets sell for widely differing amounts, and the less expensive one is on the street with the noisiest traffic, it is reasonable to assume that the price difference may at least partly reflect the value people put on quiet streets. In fact, it may be hard to disentangle environmental nuisance from many other factors. A study by economists at Salford University of 3,500 houses in Stockport, England, found that those in the areas most affected by noise from Manchester Airport were on average 6% less expensive than others; but most of this price difference could be explained by other characteristics of the neighborhood and the houses.[2] Even if they had not been under the flight path, the houses would still have been less expensive.

Sometimes environmental damage has measurable costs. When air pollution corrodes stone, the cost of repairs can be reckoned. That is one way to get at the value of cleaner air. When polluted water makes people ill, economists may try to put a value on the loss of health.

In third world countries, it is often much easier to use these indirect measurement techniques. Natural resources have values that can be readily estimated. The products of wild nature are harvested commercially. Examples range from animal skins, ivory, fish, and timber to resins, rattans, mushrooms, and game. The cash value of wild products is often the only way in which biological resources appear in national income accounts. In some countries their impact on the economy may be considerable. This is especially true for countries with forests: timber from wild forests has been Indonesia's second largest source of foreign exchange, and teak is now providing Burma with hard currency. Other kinds of forest products may also be important exports: two-thirds of India's forestry exports in the early 1980s came from products other than timber. That might be true for other forested countries, if statistics were available, but figures on the value of forest products other than timber are rarely collated.

Local people may use wild nature as an important source of food that may well pass through no market and so not appear in national accounts.[3] Without wild protein, firewood, medicines, and building materials, though, people would be poorer; and it is possible to calculate with some precision just how much poorer they would be. For example, one study by the New York Botanical Gardens of the net present value of fruit, latex, and timber from a patch of Amazon rain forest looked at the price of these products in local markets.[4] Using those values, it reckoned that a hectare of forest was worth $9,000 (but only $3,000 if destroyed and used for cow pasture). The timber alone was worth only 10% of the total, and if cutting down a tree for timber killed latex or fruit trees, the gain from logging was wiped out.

Forests are a source of food, fuel, and furniture for the world's 500 million forest dwellers. In many African countries, wild food is an important part of diet, especially for the poor. In Ghana, for example, three-quarters of the population depends largely on wild foods such as fish, caterpillars, maggots, and snails. In Zaire, three-quarters of the animal protein that people eat comes from wild sources.

Amazonia is not the only place where the value of products harvested from the wild exceeds the value of the same land when used for unfamiliar domesticated animals. In developed countries the value of wild food may be tiny compared with the value of the industries that grow up around hunting and fishing. The market value of the hooked salmon or shot pheasant is a fraction of the amount human predators frequently pay to catch them.

Robert Scott, a rancher from western Montana, dreams of turning the cattle off the Montana great plains, where they have grazed for not much more than a century, and replacing them with species that preceded them. He yearns to persuade the owners of 12 million acres, on which live 3,000 people and 350,000 cattle, to pool their land, which now brings in a net agricultural income of less than zero (offset by the government subsidies on which people live). Fences would fall, cattle would go, and in their place would be wandering bison, elk, antelope, bighorn sheep, and hunters. The revenue from hunting fees, guiding, accommodation, and butchering would bring in perhaps $60 million. Conservationists would have a wilderness, hunters a paradise, and landowners a genuine income.

Wildlife tourism is another way in which protected nature can earn a cash return. Tourism, mainly to see wild animals, is Kenya's biggest foreign-exchange earner. One estimate gives each lion in Amboseli National Park a value of $27,000 a year in visitor pulling-power. The park's net earnings, mainly from tourism, run at about $40 per hectare per year, a net profit 50 times as high as the most optimistic projection for agricultural use.

Some of the functions of wild nature have enormous value in making possible other kinds of economic activity, but are nonetheless hard to quantify. Wild trees may pollinate domestic ones; wild birds may keep down pests. If either go, the cost will be lost crops or money spent on developing man-made alternatives. One example is the brazil nut, which needs a particular species of bee to pollinate it, and a forest-dwelling rodent called the agouti to open its hard shell and allow the tree to seed itself. As the bee needs pollen from a forest orchid to mate, and the orchids need insects or hummingbirds to pollinate them in turn, the continued production of brazil nuts needs enough forest to accommodate bees, insects, hummingbirds, orchids, and agoutis. Other examples are marshes and wetlands, rich homes for wildlife, which often play an important role in purifying water supplies or preventing floods. One study estimated that retaining a swamp outside Boston, Massachusetts, saved $17 million in flood protection alone.[5] In other countries, coastal mangroves and coral reefs provide barriers against the fury of the sea and at the same time sustain valuable fisheries.

The functions performed by trees are even more profuse and valuable. Their roots stabilize soil and regulate the run-off of rainfall. Streams in forested areas continue to flow in dry weather and are less likely to flood when storms come. Their enormous value in preventing soil erosion has been recognized in Venezuela, where the government recently tripled the size of Canaima National Park, which safeguards a watershed that feeds some of the country's most important hydroelectric facilities. In Honduras the 7,500-hectare La Tigra National Park guards more than 40% of the water supply for Tegucigalpa, the country's capital. Rain forest has an even more important economic function, that of feeding rainfall as well as absorbing it. Cut down the trees and nearby regions suffer higher temperatures and more drought. The destruction of Africa's rain forests may well have caused the Sahara to advance, fatally impoverishing millions; destroy the Amazon, and large tracts of central and northern Brazil may suffer the same fate.

Most of the uses for wild nature accrue locally. A price can be put on them without too much ingenuity. But there are other, less quantifiable ways in which natural resources may have considerable value to the human race as a whole, but where it is difficult to turn that value into earnings for the country that has to preserve species.

Those would-be tourists who will never go to Amboseli reward television companies, not Kenyans, when they watch nature programs. Many medicines on the shelves of Western chemists have been developed from plants or (more rarely) animals and bugs. In the mid-1980s, the value of prescription and over-the-counter, plant-based drugs in OECD countries was put at about $43 billion. Tropical species are especially useful because they are often chock-a-block with poisons that scare off predators. Those poisons—like curare, used by Brazil's Yanomani Indians to tip their arrows, and by doctors as a muscle relaxant—may be the active ingredient in modern drugs. But drug companies have rarely put money into drug research in developing countries.

Wild species also play an essential role in restoring or replacing domesticated ones. The tiny group of domesticated species that account for most foods on supermarket shelves need to be able to draw on the gene pool of their wild relatives to maintain or increase yields. Ever since 1845, when potato blight wiped out the Irish potato crop, people have been aware that the genetic uniformity of cultivated plants makes them highly susceptible to disease and pests. Stripe rust in American wheat was defeated in the 1960s with germ plasma from a wild wheat found in Turkey.

Russ Mittermeier, a former official of the World Wildlife Fund in Washington, DC, used to thrill American audiences by pointing out that "Democracy in Latin America may depend on conservation in Madagascar. If rust hits the coffee crop, the continent could lose its main source of income. There are 50 species of wild coffee, many of them caffeine-free, in the rain forests of eastern Madagascar." His audiences particularly liked the bit about "caffeine-free." Some primitive farmers recognize the importance of genetic diversity for agriculture by planting several varieties of a crop in the same field. Modern farming uses plant breeding for the same effect. Most domesticated plants and animals come from countries other than those in which they are most used. In America, for example, at least nine out of ten commercially grown species are not native. They rely on wild relatives growing in other countries for periodic reinforcement. Only a small proportion of the wild relatives of many commercial crops have been collected and stored in seed banks (see Table 2.3).

Little-known plants, fish, and animals sometimes turn out to be valuable foods. In Panama and Costa Rica attempts are being made to domesticate the endangered but edible green iguana. Quinua, once a staple grain of the Incas, turns out to be one of the world's most productive sources of plant protein. Teosinte nearly became extinct. That is the name local people gave to a species of maize found in 1979 on a small hillside in Mexico that was being cleared. Unlike other known species of maize, it was a perennial, and is now being used to develop a perennial hybrid for commercial cultivation.

But however valuable teosinte may turn out to be for commercial agriculture (and one study hazarded a figure of nearly $7 billion), not a penny is likely to go back to the owner of the Mexican hillside. A recurrent problem with all these returns on biological diversity is the virtual impossibility of turning them into cash for the people who might see it as an incentive to continue conserving. In the past the royalties on medicines made from useful medicinal plants have accrued to drug companies, not the Yanomani. Several Western schools of botany—including the New York Botanical Gardens and the Royal Botanic Gardens at Kew—now insist, before they will undertake a research contract on medical applications of tropical plants, that the commissioning companies agree to pay a share of any royalties to support research by local scientists. That is a big advance. But

Table 2.3 Wild Species in the Bank

Crop	Wild species held in all seed banks as % total holdings	Estimated % wild species still to be collected
Cereals		
Rice	2	70
Wheat	10	20–25
Sorghum	0.5	9
Pearl millet	10	50
Barley	5	0–10
Corn (maize)	5	50
Minor millets	0.5	90
Root crops		
Potato	40	30
Cassava	2	80
Sweet potato	10	40
Legumes		
Beans	1.2	50
Chickpea	0.5	50
Cowpea	0.5	70
Groundnut	6.0	30
Pigeonpea	0.5	40

Source: International Board for Plant Genetic Resources, 1988 estimates.

drug companies are not likely to use for long a plant that must be collected from the wild. Supplies are likely to be too erratic. Instead, they usually either cultivate the plant nearer home (which means in the developed world) or synthesize it. Either way, the plant's native country loses income.

Of all the ways in which nature makes possible those economic activities that are more readily measurable, none is more important than its role in regulating the planet's life support system. Plants and plankton help recycle oxygen, absorb carbon dioxide, and regulate rainfall. Individual countries may make this possible by the way they preserve their natural resources; all humanity gains.

However refined the methods by which economists value the environment, politicians and businesses may take more notice of cash payments than the value people say they derive from this or that aspect of environmentalism. One of the great dilemmas of the coming years will be to find ways of rewarding poor countries for their contribution to the public good. There may be no mechanism that enables those who want to protect a resource to compensate those who want to destroy it.

A Premium for Insurance

One complication in setting environmental benefit against the costs of taking action is the difficulty of proving what will happen if nothing is done. Because environmental science is an uncertain art, most policy decisions involve a weighting for risk. If sulphur dioxide from coal-burning power stations were undoubtedly the cause of acid rain, then the decision to install scrubbers would be a (relatively) simple matter of balancing their cost against the value people place on forests. But there are probably several causes, including nitrogen oxides from car exhausts, and disentangling the main culprit will take time. In the meantime, governments have to decide whether to compel power stations to cut sulphur-dioxide output now or to wait for harder proof. If power stations are indeed the problem, then the sooner governments take action, the less it will cost; if they are not, then governments waste money by making electricity more expensive than gas.

The difficulty of making such decisions is compounded where the consequences of inactivity are likely to be irreversible. Clean the sewage out of a river and the fish will come back; stop homes from burning coal and air quality will improve. Many important environmental improvements of this very sort have occurred in the past few decades. But once the rhino is extinct, no earthly power can reinvent it; once the Amazon forest has gone, it probably can never be replanted; once the world has warmed up, we will have to wait for the next ice age to cool it again; and once genetically engineered organisms have escaped, they may never be recaptured. The problems that most preoccupy environmentalists are precisely the irreversible sort. The stakes are highest, and often the costs of correction are highest, too.

Politicians frequently turn to scientists to help them measure environmental damage. But scientists will not necessarily agree with one another—any more than economists. Establishing scientific proof of environmental damage is much harder than, say, finding a link between a falling apple and the force of gravity or even cigarette smoking and lung cancer. Environmental damage may occur far from the original cause. Acid rain in Norway may be caused by British coal-fired power stations or by German cars. It may take place long after the original event, too late for preventive action. Nitrates in the water supply may come from spreading nitrogen fertilizers today or from ploughing grassland 20 years ago. By the time we know for sure how the greenhouse effect will warm the earth, large amounts of warming gases will already have built up in the atmosphere. The only option for politicians who want to be environmentalists may be to pick their scientists and bet voters' money on the pet view.

To deal with the problems of risk and irreversibility, some governments have adopted the "precautionary principle," the precept that it may sometimes be wise to take action before scientific knowledge is sufficiently advanced to justify it. The British government tried to spell out what that meant in its environmental policy paper of September 1990. The paragraph proved the hardest one to draft in the entire lengthy document.

In the end, it set out a concept against which the government had previously fought tooth and nail:

> Where the state of our planet is at stake, the risks can be so high, and the costs of corrective action so great, that prevention is better and cheaper than cure. Where there are significant risks of damage to the environment, the government will be prepared to take precautionary action to limit the use of potentially dangerous pollutants, even where scientific knowledge is not conclusive, if the balance of likely costs and benefits justifies it.

Gauging Benefit

One reason for trying to set environmental benefits against the costs of taking action is to make sure the public realizes the price it is paying for a particular gain. Governments may often be tempted—or lobbied—to pursue policies that will bring little environmental benefit, at huge expense. This is particularly true of policies whose immediate costs fall on companies in industrial countries. Companies, after all, may lobby, but they do not vote.

One of the oddities of human behavior that has played a large part in determining environmental policy is an apparently irrational attitude toward risk. Although people in rich countries live longer than ever, they are more fearful than their ancestors were about the world about them. One reason may be nervousness about new technology. Another is mistrust of scientists, who have too often claimed that a process or substance is safe and then changed their minds. Familiar risks are less frightening than the unfamiliar; visible risks less scary than the invisible sort. People clearly feel more frightened by the remote risk of a large catastrophe than by the greater risk of an equivalent number of deaths spread out over a long period. Hence the greater fear of nuclear power stations than coal-mining fatalities, and of aircraft crashes than road accidents. People feel more frightened by risks over which they feel they have no control than by those they inflict on themselves. Hence the greater desire for regulation of pesticide use than of alcohol consumption. One study found people willing to accept risks from voluntary activities (such as skiing) roughly 1,000 times as great as those they would tolerate from involuntary hazards, such as food preservatives, that brought much the same level of benefit—as far as such different commodities could be compared.[6] Better measurement techniques bring no reassurance: on the contrary, it seems that many people find the idea of one part per billion more frightening than one part per million, on the innumerate grounds that a billion is a larger number.

Such quirks may not matter when they influence the behavior of an individual. It is a different matter when the quirks become votes and the votes become government policy, as has happened in some countries with environmental policy. Much environmental regulation, especially in the United States, is dominated by a view common in the early 1970s that the "environment" is responsible for 80% to 90% of all cancers. Since then, epidemiologists have generally become convinced that only a few human cancers are caused by exposure to contaminated air, water, or soil. Cigarettes are responsible for 30% of all avoidable cancer deaths (plus many deaths from heart disease and other causes); polluted drinking water, in developed countries, for well under 1%. The best estimates suggest that 2% to 3% of all cancers are associated with environmental pollution, and 3% to 6% with radiation. Research by the Environmental Protection Agency (EPA) suggests that up to half of all cancer deaths from environmental risks each year may be caused by one factor: exposure to indoor radon, a radioactive gas that seeps into houses through the soil. Just under a quarter may be caused by exposure to ultraviolet light as a result of the depletion of stratospheric ozone.

Research by Michael Gough of Resources for the Future suggests that, at the outside, regulation by the EPA might be able to prevent about 6,400 American cancer deaths a year.[7] If cancer risks are estimated by means of a method employed not by the EPA but by the Food and Drug Administration, the numbers are tinier still. On that basis, the entire expensive panoply of EPA regulations might prevent a mere 1,400 of America's 485,000 cancer deaths—or fewer than 1%.

Sometimes, environmental regulations expose people to greater, not lesser, risks. This view has been repeatedly set out by Bruce Ames, a leading American cancer specialist and director of the Environmental Health Sciences Center at Berkeley, California. Environmental regulation has been based heavily on tests carried out on rats and mice. But those tests may be misleading. Of 392 chemicals tested on both rats and mice, 226 were carcinogenic in at least one test, but 96 of them—almost half—were carcinogenic in mice but not in rats or vice versa. Common sense and Ames both suggest that if rats and mice, closely related species, react so differently to different substances, then the entirely different human species may react even more differently.

Ames also argues: "Our normal diet contains many rodent carcinogens, all perfectly natural or traditional (for example, from the cooking of food)."[8] Even if a food is natural, he points out, it may still be laced with naturally occurring chemicals that are toxic, as Table 2.4 shows. Most plants generate natural pesticides as part of their protective mechanism. Americans, he calculates, ingest at least 10,000 times more by weight of natural pesticides than of the man-made kind. Only a few of these chemicals have been tested on rodents, and many of those have turned out to be carcinogens.

Ames is concerned less with stopping people from sprinkling their food with black pepper or eating grilled chicken, both effective ways of eating large doses of rodent-killing chemicals, than with restoring a sense of proportion to environmental policy. "The total amount of browned and burnt material eaten in a typical day is at least several hundred times more than that inhaled from severe air pollution," he protests. Sometimes, banning a product may prevent some cancers but raise the risk of others. He cites the EPA's decision to ban EDB, the active component in the most commonly used grain fumigant in America, after a risk assessment, which concluded that, at worst, residues in grain might cause 1% of all American cancers. Yet peanut butter is a much more potent source of rodent tumors and remains unbanned. And EDB was banned without any attempt to decide whether the alternatives, such as food irradiation or more mold, might be more hazardous to humans.

Table 2.4 Natural Cancer-Causing Pesticides Found in Food

Food	Carcinogen[a]	Parts per m
Celery (stressed)	5-and 8-methoxypsoralen	25
Parsnip (cooked)	5-and 8-methoxypsoralen	32
Honey	benzyle acetate	15
Jasmine tea	benzyle acetate	230
Apple	caffeic acid	50–200
Carrot	caffeic acid	50–200
Coffee (roasted beans)	caffeic acid	1,800
Coffee (roasted beans)	catechol	100
Mushroom (commercial)	glutamyl-p-hydrazinobenzoate	42
Orange juice	limonene	31
Black pepper	limonene	8,000
Nutmeg	safrole	3,000
Mace	safrole	10,000
Cabbage	sinigrin (allyl isothiocyanate)	35–590
Brussels sprouts	sinigrin	110–1,560
Mustard (brown)	sinigrin	16,000–72,000

[a]Cancer-causing in rodents.
Source: Bruce Ames, quoted in *Financial Times*, October 9, 1990.

Because environmentalism is fashionable and scientific proof is hard to obtain, people may readily assume that pollution causes problems when the truth may be simpler but less welcome. A striking example of this is to be found in Eastern Europe, where many attempts have been made to link people's lower life expectancy with the high levels of pollution in those countries. Life expectancy is undoubtedly lower (67 years for a male Pole at birth, compared with 74 years for a man in nearby Sweden). It has been declining. Pollution is high and rising. Some links between pollution (especially air pollution) and health clearly exist. But consider the following: 81% of Polish men and 57% of

Polish women in their early thirties smoke cigarettes; cigarette smoking did not decline between the mid-1970s and mid-1980s; Polish cigarettes are probably more harmful than those smoked in the West; and cigarette smoking almost certainly compounds the respiratory harm done by air pollution. If you combine all these factors, many Poles could clearly enjoy a cheap shortcut to better health by stopping smoking.

When Costs Exceed Benefits

As industrial countries become cleaner, the benefit from additional pollution control will inevitably diminish. The amount of money that governments will need to spend to achieve further improvements will increase. A review of America's policies by the EPA estimated that the cost of complying with them was already higher as a proportion of GNP than in any other country (except, perhaps, West Germany), and would rise to at least 2.6% of GNP by the end of the century.[9] Already, such policies cost one-third of the nation's spending on medical care. The bigger the cost, the more it matters that it should not be wasted.

The Clean Air Act of 1990 will add about $4 billion to $5 billion annually to the costs of controlling emissions of sulphur dioxide from America's power stations. It is not clear that the environmental benefits from these measures will justify their cost. A ten-year study by the federal government, through the National Acid Precipitation Assessment Program, found that fewer lakes were acidified than had been feared; that acid rain had virtually no effect on agricultural output and that it damaged forests mainly on mountaintops in the northeastern United States; and that it was hard to calculate harm to buildings. All these findings reduce the benefits to be expected from curbing sulphur dioxide.

In a study of benefits and costs of the Clean Air Act, Paul Portney of Resources for the Future added in something for improved visibility and for a reduction in illnesses caused by air pollution.[10] Even then, he guesses at benefits totaling between $2 billion and $8 billion—in other words, maybe half or maybe double the cost of the controls. Measures for improving air quality through cleaning up car exhausts are included in his figures. These might, he thinks, add $19 billion to $22 billion to the annual cost of compliance by the year 2005. The main results might be better health and gains in farm output. Added together, the figures indicate that the overall environmental benefits might be $4 billion to $12 billion a year. Controls for reducing toxic air pollutants from industrial plants will cost from $6 billion to $12 billion a year. At the outside, such controls might prevent 500 cases of cancer a year.

Trying to put a value on a human life is always difficult. But if each of those 500 cases were to result in death, the best techniques for valuing life would suggest the total cost might come to $1.5 billion. Adding all three measures together, Portney concludes that the United States may be committing itself to spending an extra $29 billion to $39 billion a year (or $300 to $400 for every household) to gain benefits worth, perhaps, about $14 billion. Why are people willing to accept that? One possibility is that they simply do not realize what the costs are. One of the beauties of regulation, from a politician's point of view, is that its true costs are largely buried; this is even more the case if the regulation falls on companies in the first instance rather than on individuals. Another possible explanation is that people are prepared to pay an extraordinarily high price for each cancer death avoided.

William Reilly, the EPA administrator, has called for more public debate on environmental priorities. These are mainly imposed on him by Congress, which expects the EPA to devote more than a third of its budget to cleaning up hazardous waste dumps. Yet two scientific reports have told the EPA than such sites should have lower priority than other environmental problems, including threats to wildlife habitats, which voters seem to care less about.[11]

How to change public perceptions of environmental risk? Better education is essential. People have to understand that some environmental goals must come before others. Public education may help; better mathematics teaching certainly would. In the meantime, companies find it impossible to talk sensibly to the public about the concept of "acceptable risk": any cancer risk is unacceptable.

The people with the greatest power to reassure or to disturb are environmental lobbyists. They should think carefully about environmental costs and benefits before demanding regulatory change. Irrational the public may be, but only up to a point. If people discover that enormous costs have been imposed on them to achieve environmental goals that have little value, they may revolt against the pursuit of goals that really are worthwhile. To win on toxic waste and lose on global warming would be a hollow victory for environmentalism.

3

Where Governments Fail

Governments ideologically hostile to the idea of intervening in the marketplace sometimes see environmentalism as a left-wing plot to extend the role of the state. After all, one of the principal reasons for environmental damage is the failure of markets to provide the right signals. Because clean air is a public good—nobody can be excluded from using it—nobody has an incentive to pay to use it. Governments therefore have to step in and set standards. Because Antarctica undeveloped is not a commodity that can be bought or sold, only government fiat can ensure that it remains undeveloped.

Thoughtful right-wingers accept the premise that government has a stewardship role, which extends to the environment. Mrs. Thatcher brought herself to accept the need for government intervention by drawing an analogy with monetary policy: just as government has a duty to ensure the stability of the value of the currency, so it has an ethical responsibility to look after our planet and to hand it on in good order to future generations.

A more down-to-earth point is that although government may indeed often need to step in to make sure that polluters take full account of the costs of their actions, just as much environmental damage is done by government intervention as by the lack of it. In every country, governments deliberately subsidize the wasteful use of natural resources. This chapter looks at four examples of this—water, energy, agriculture, and forestry—drawing on a series of studies by the Washington-based World Resources Institute.[1] By removing environmentally harmful subsidies, governments would save their taxpayers money and reduce environmental damage. Two for the price of one. Ending such subsidies ought to be a matter of commonsense economics. But when do governments ever practice commonsense economics?

Such misdirected subsidies are most common wherever markets are most heavily administered. When government intervenes in an effort to set prices throughout an economy, it is usually tempted to set the lowest prices for the things that are seen as most basic. This explains why water, energy, and agriculture are most likely to be subsidized. In the centrally planned economies of the erstwhile Communist block, this natural tendency was further encouraged by the Stalinist emphasis on developing heavy industry. By channeling investment into heavy industry and energy production, the governments of the Communist countries hoped to stimulate the rest of the economy. What was stimulated was pollution. Third world countries make similar mistakes, although they tend to subsidize farming, especially by underpricing irrigation water and holding down the prices of fertilizers and pesticides. Western countries sin in rather different ways: they tend to use agricultural protection to subsidize agriculture and tax relief to hold down energy costs. The effect, though, is the same: an incentive to damage the environment at a cost to the taxpayer.

Mismanaged Water

Of all nature's resources, none is more likely to be consumed at less than it costs to deliver it than water. True, people are as likely to view air as a natural gift, but breathing the air requires no pipes or sewage treatment; water is rarely consumed without some intervening technology. And the full costs of installing and maintaining that technology, almost invariably provided mainly by the state, are rarely recouped from consumers.

This is particularly true of domestic consumers. No European country yet charges all its households for the amount of water they use, although France and the Netherlands are moving in that direction. Yet the amount of water people use is closely related to the amount they discharge. If water were metered, more people would continue to wash dishes by hand rather than buy dishwashers, or would buy washing machines with an economy cycle. But industrial customers are also frequently charged in a way that does not reflect the full costs of treating the sewage that their activities generate. In America the federal government began to pay subsidies in the mid-1950s to help meet the capital costs of building sewage facilities. In 1972, legislation set the level of subsidy at 75% of capital costs. This has since been reduced and is planned to be abolished by 1994. Not surprisingly, the effect of the subsidy was to encourage municipalities to build larger, more sophisticated sewage works rather than to press for better ways of reducing or recycling effluents.

An even more dramatic example of undercharging for water is found in irrigation, both in the United States and in many third world countries. As irrigated agriculture accounts for about 70% of the world's use of fresh water, it needs to be efficient. At the moment, only one-third of the world's irrigation water is used to grow crops. The rest is wasted, often because farmers are not made to pay a price that properly reflects its scarcity. Undercharging for irrigation not only puts an unjustifiable burden on taxpayers; it may mean that countries where water is scarce grow less food than they would if water were distributed in a more efficient manner. It is hard to see how the world's burgeoning population could have been fed without an enormous expansion of irrigation in the second half of this century. A third of the world's food comes from irrigated land, although barely one-fifth of cropland is under irrigation. That proportion has trebled since 1950, making possible the green revolution (two-thirds of all irrigated land lies in Asia). For the rest of this century, the proportion of food coming from irrigated fields will increase.

That is, if there is enough water to go around. Irrigation has absorbed vast quantities of investment. Since 1940 irrigation projects in Mexico have taken up 80% of all public investment in agriculture. Aid agencies pour money into developing water for farming: irrigation mopped up 28% of all World Bank agricultural lending during the 1980s. In current prices, calculations by the World Resources Institute suggest, $250 billion has already been spent to create irrigation capacity in the third world alone.

Yet public-sector irrigation projects perform badly. They frequently take longer than expected to build, have higher maintenance costs, and produce lower yields than those who plan them generally expect. Above all, they are a drain on government budgets. Virtually everywhere, the costs of installing, operating, and maintaining irrigation systems are carried largely by the taxpayer.

One study of six Asian countries—Sri Lanka, Indonesia, South Korea, Nepal, the Philippines, and Thailand—estimated that receipts from public irrigation projects covered on average less than 10% of the costs of the service (see Table 3.1).[2] In Pakistan, the corresponding figure was 13% in 1984; in Mexico, 11%; in China, even after a sixfold increase in water charges, farmers pay less than a quarter of the average supply costs.

Nor is this true only in the third world. In the western United States, failure to recover more than a fraction of the costs of irrigation projects administered by the Federal Bureau of Reclamation meant that in the 1980s farmers enjoyed an implied subsidy of $1 billion a year. In California's Central Valley, farmers pay less than 10% of the average supply cost of irrigation water. America's National Wildlife Federation, which has lobbied to abolish this subsidy, claims that approximately 40% of the subsidized water is used to irrigate crops that are already in surplus. Everywhere, the consequences of undercharging are, predictably enough, overuse. A 1981 study of irrigation in the western United States found that over 30% of the area irrigated with federal water was planted with low-value crops such as hay, alfalfa, and other pasture. Another study found that almost one-third of the water used for irrigation by the Bureau of Reclamation leaked and was wasted: not surprising, as a survey in the 1970s found that 85% of the bureau's 14,000 miles of canals were unlined.[3]

Everywhere, future supplies are jeopardized by using water extravagantly. In recent years the world's two main food producers, America and China, have both experienced unplanned declines in their irrigated cropland (of 7% in America and 2% in

Table 3.1 Cost Recovery Through Direct and Indirect Irrigation Charges Relative to Recurrent and Total Costs of Public Irrigation Systems

Country	1 Actual revenue from farmers $ per ha	2 Operation & maintenance costs	3 Moderate est.	4 Total capital & recurrent costs High est.
		as % of column 1		
Indonesia	25.90	128	735	1,490
South Korea	192.00	107	550	881
Nepal	9.10	181	1,388	2,270
Philippines	16.85	83	443	984
Thailand	8.31	362	1,818	3,276
Bangladesh: major surface systems	3.75	500	1,000	

Source: Robert Repetto, *Skimming the Water* (Washington, DC: World Resources Institute, 1986).

China). Overuse of irrigation water means that saturated land becomes waterlogged. The salts carried in irrigation water are deposited in the soil as the water evaporates, eventually leaving the land too saline to cultivate. The dams needed to increase supplies alter the flow of rivers and may harm fishing. Wetlands and bogs that may be rich in wild fowl are unnecessarily drained, or contaminated (as in a notorious case in California) by salts flushed from overirrigated land. Subsidizing irrigation penalizes future generations as well as existing taxpayers. In 1986, the U.S. Department of Agriculture reported that more than a quarter of the country's 21 million irrigated acres were being watered by pulling down the water table. Under parts of the north China Plain, around Beijing and Tianjin, the water table is dropping by 1 to 2 meters a year. In the Soviet Union, the area covered by the Aral Sea has shrunk by 40% since 1960, mostly because of irrigation from the rivers feeding it. World Bank projects for intensifying agriculture, especially in the Middle East, are being stymied by water shortages.

The WRI study found plenty of evidence in the third world that farmers use water less efficiently when they obtain it inexpensively from the government than when they pay an economical price to a private irrigation scheme. Often, charges are based on the area irrigated rather than the amount of water used: a farmer pays nothing extra to flood a field. Inevitably, when supply is not rationed by price, it is rationed by availability: farmers at the far end of a canal are starved of water while farmers at the near end have plenty. Rationing by availability empowers those who control the rationing—often local administrators or politicians. As farmers downstream would willingly pay more for water than they are officially charged, to ensure a steady supply, there is much room for corruption and every incentive to demand much more inexpensive irrigation.

In a dry land, a supply of cheap irrigation water is obviously an important part of the value of a farm. In the United States, for example, a 1985 study found that the subsidy enjoyed by farms irrigated by Bureau of Reclamation schemes was worth 56% of the average market value of the irrigated land. Not surprisingly, one kind of corruption found both in the United States and in the third world is a tendency for big farmers to do best out of subsidized irrigation. A survey by the U.S. Bureau of the Interior in 1981 found that the largest 5% of farmers creamed off half the value of the irrigation subsidy, while the smallest 60% of farmers were left with only 11%.[4] An attempt to cap the size of farm eligible for subsidized water has failed: a 20-square-mile ranch in California was split into 15 units, all operated as one farm with a single loan, but each received federal water worth a total of $500,000 more than they paid for it.

These wealthy farmers in America and in the third world make up a formidable lobby for the continuation of subsidized irrigation. In 1990, a congressional attempt to stop subsidized water from being used to grow crops already in surplus was toned down. The forces that may ultimately bring sense to irrigation subsidies are not environmental. In California, where the rice crop consumes as much water as three cities the size of Los Angeles, the water shortage is beginning to hold back industrial development. In third world countries the drain on the national budget has become unsustainable: several Asian countries have privatized public-sector schemes; other governments have begun to demand that irrigation agencies repay the cash they have borrowed to finance new projects. The Philippine government cut grants to its irrigation agency, forcing it to depend on fees collected from users. In China local goverments have been made responsible for financing irrigation development. Poverty may drive third world countries to pursue good economic sense even if it cannot influence the United States to do so.

Wasted Energy

Although subsidies for irrigation water probably enjoy the most solid political protection, underpricing energy follows close behind. Indeed, more countries probably underprice energy than any other natural resource. It is not only that current energy prices do not reflect the many environmental costs of energy consumption: global warming, acid rain, oil spills, smog, and so on. Frequently, energy is sold below world-market price or below its long-run marginal cost of production. The effect may not be a drain on the national budget, in the way that undercharging for irrigation schemes may be, but it may mean that imports of energy are higher and government revenue from energy taxes are lower than economic efficiency would imply.

A study of more than 30 countries conducted by the WRI in 1987 found that almost all countries intervened to influence energy prices through taxes, tariffs, subsidies, and price controls (see Figure 3.1).[5] Different countries tended to underprice different kinds of energy. Petroleum products, which account for two-thirds of the commercial energy needs of the third world (excluding China), were most persistently underpriced by third world oil exporters. China and India account for 70% of third world coal consumption; in both, it is heavily subsidized. Electricity prices are below long-run marginal costs in almost every country in the world. In the United States and a number of other countries, they are set to recover average costs plus a guaranteed rate of return, an approach that fails to reflect the cost of providing new generating capacity. One study reckoned that the reductions in economic subsidies that would accrue from proper electricity pricing in the United States are more than four times

Figure 3.1 Commercial Energy Efficiency and Energy Prices, 1983

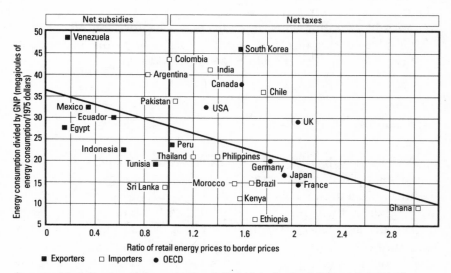

Source: Mark Kosmo, "Money to Burn? The High Costs of Energy Subsidies" (Washington, DC: World Resources Institute, 1987).

those that could be made in China and India together.[6] Prices do not even recover average costs in Brazil and India.

Some supposedly environmentally conscious European countries devote large sums of taxpayers' money to supporting coal industries, even though coal burning is a large source of atmospheric carbon dioxide, the primary man-made greenhouse gas. Before unification, West Germany pumped DM12 billion ($7 billion) a year into its coal industry by forcing power companies to buy coal from mining companies at prices well above market level and reimbursing them through the Kohlenpfennig, an 8.5% levy on consumers' electricity bills. Another enormous subsidy induces the electricity industry to buy expensive coke. Britain's government also effectively subsidizes coal by forcing the electricity industry to buy the expensive output of British Coal. Spain, France, and Belgium also subsidize their coal industries, thwarting the EC Commission's attempts to create a single market for energy and mocking the European Community's commitment to tackle global warming.

Energy subsidies do not always take the form simply of holding down prices by administrative fiat. In poor countries energy consumers rarely pay taxes but in rich countries, where most motorists do, governments often use the tax system to reduce prices to favored motorists. Thus America's Internal Revenue Service treats free parking for employees much more generously than company contributions to fares on public transportation. Germany gives tax relief to those who commute by car to work, and in 1989, the Dutch government fell as a result of its attempt to remove such a tax relief from its commuters. In Britain, drivers of company cars are taxed on the value of their cars at a rate that still makes it an attractive part of any pay package. Britain, alone among EC countries, charges no value-added tax (VAT) on domestic energy, although (as the Association for the Conservation of Energy, which represents Britain's energy conservation industry, frequently complains) building insulation does carry VAT. Sometimes the subsidy may take the form of limits to liability for damage (as with nuclear power programs, whose liability for accidental damage is usually restricted by national law) or of cheap access to capital. France's Electricité de France (EDF) has embarked on an enormous program of building nuclear power stations, assisted by borrowings that in 1990 amounted to one-fifth of the entire French national debt.

Underpricing has a number of predictable consequences. First, it means higher levels of energy intensity. Low energy prices tend to encourage people to use more energy. One study estimated that prices explained roughly half the difference in energy intensity between countries: the remainder could be put down to differences in climate, wealth, and industrial structure.[7] The most striking examples of these differences come from Eastern Europe. There, energy prices were held down in the mid-1970s as a deliberate act of policy. When oil prices rose in the West, Soviet prices were constrained. Communists regarded this as an advantage. In fact, development stultified. Consider just one example: inexpensive energy has meant that the open-hearth furnace, an energy-wasteful technology now largely abandoned in the West, still accounts for roughly half of Eastern Europe's steel production. As Figures 3.2 and 3.3 show, inexpensive energy and the preoccupation with heavy industry mean that Eastern European economies (including the former East Germany but not counting Albania or Yugoslavia) use more than twice as much primary energy per dollar of national income as even the more industrialized countries of Western Europe (and therefore cause more pollution). Poland, with—on some counts—a GDP smaller than Belgium's, uses nearly three times as much energy; Hungary, whose GDP is supposedly only a fifth of Spain's, uses more than a third as much energy. Yet these are countries where car ownership is still lower than it was in Western Europe in 1970. Almost all the energy is used to generate electricity, drive machinery, or heat homes.

A second effect of chronic underpricing is loss of government revenue and of foreign exchange. In China, energy subsidies equal 7% of GDP and 20% of export earnings. In Peru, petroleum subsidies equal nearly three-quarters of the country's oil-export revenues. In Egypt, where energy prices are a ludicrous 20% of the world average, petroleum subsidies cost the government even more: in 1985, as Table 3.2 shows, they totaled twice the value of the country's petroleum exports. Some 15% of Egypt's massively underpriced electricity (generated in part by the Aswan dam) goes to support an aluminum-smelting industry,

Figure 3.2 Energy Intensity, 1987 (gross energy consumption, kg of coal-equivalent per head)

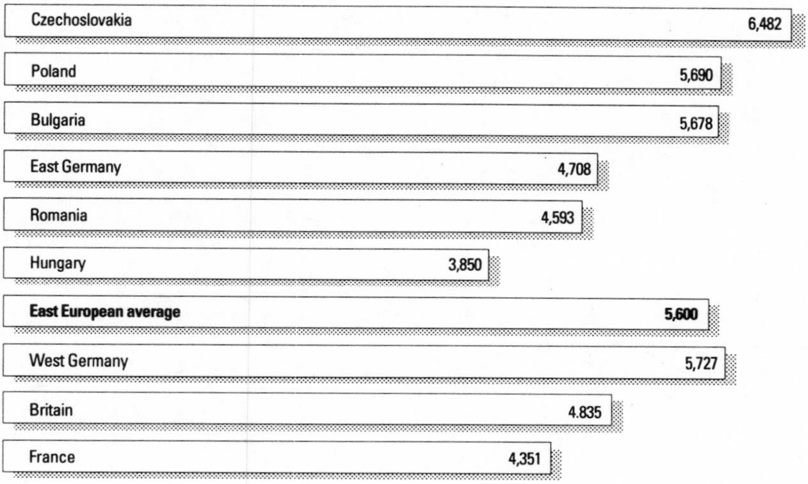

Czechoslovakia	6,482
Poland	5,690
Bulgaria	5,678
East Germany	4,708
Romania	4,593
Hungary	3,850
East European average	**5,600**
West Germany	5,727
Britain	4.835
France	4,351

Source: World Bank.

Figure 3.3 Sulphur-Dioxide Emissions per Head, 1984 (kg)

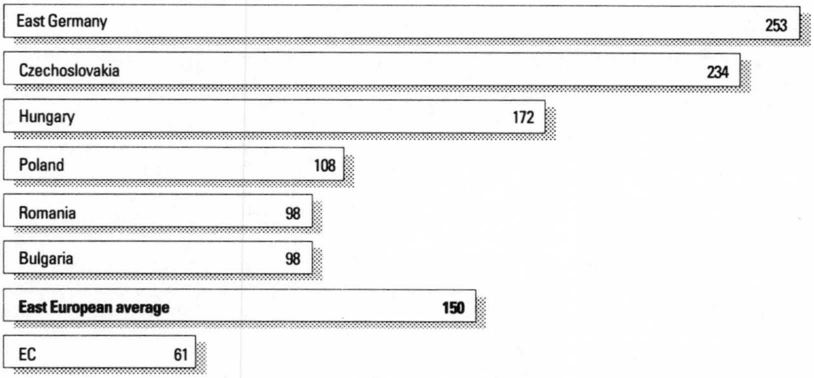

East Germany	253
Czechoslovakia	234
Hungary	172
Poland	108
Romania	98
Bulgaria	98
East European average	**150**
EC	61

Source: Zbigniew Bochniarz, University of Minnesota.

even though the country has no bauxite of its own. Energy subsidies have in the past mopped up 13% of the country's GNP, making even China look like a model of good sense. Prodded by the International Monetary Fund and the World Bank, Egypt now plans to raise its electricity prices to industrial consumers from 47% of the long-run marginal cost of power in 1990 to 70% in 1992.

A third consequence of underpricing is that cheap energy creates economic distortions. It encourages capital-intensive industries at the expense of labor-intensive ones: foolish for coun-

Table 3.2 Energy Subsidies and Energy Exports in Selected Oil-Exporting Developing Countries, 1985[a]

Country	Energy subsidies ($m)	Energy exports ($m)	Energy subsidies Energy exports (%)	Energy exports Total exports (%)	Energy subsidies Total exports (%)
Bolivia (1983)	224	329[b]	68	42	29
China	5,400[c]	6,600	82	24	20
Egypt	4,000	2,000	200	44	88
Ecuador	370	2,000	19	64	12
Indonesia	600	9,000	7	66	5
Mexico	5,000	15,000	33	70	23
Nigeria (1984)	3,000	13,000	23	90	21
Peru	301	410	73	20	15
Tunisia	70	690	10	41	4
Venezula	1,900	13,000	15	95	14

[a]Economic subsidies = (average border price − average retail price) × (total consumption of petroleum products). Average border and retail prices are based on a weighted average of the prices of gasoline, kerosene, diesel fuel, and heavy fuel oil.
[b]Primarily (99%) natural gas exports to Argentina.
[c]These are subsidies for fuel oil and crude oil only. Estimate excludes $10.4 billion in coal subsidies and $8.9 billion in electricity subsidies.
Source: Mark Kosmo, "Money to Burn? The High Cost of Energy Subsidies" (Washington, DC: World Resources Institute, 1987).

tries with large, poor populations. It also diverts investment into building new generating capacity rather than using existing supplies more efficiently. Amory Lovins, director of research at the Rocky Mountain Institute in Colorado and a passionate advocate of energy conservation, reckons that expanding American electricity-generating capacity costs $60 billion a year in private investment and federal subsidies. That is about the same as the total annual investment in all durable-goods manufacturing. If conservation could keep electricity demand constant, then the capital available for those industries (or others) would be doubled.

For third world countries, desperately short of investment capital, underpricing energy is especially dangerous: investing in new energy supplies leaves less cash to invest in other, more productive industries. In Colombia, for example, debt incurred by the power sector accounts for almost a third of all government-guaranteed debt. Yet petroleum products in Colombia sell at less than world-market prices. Multiplied on a world scale, potential savings from energy conservation are immense. A study for a meeting of the World Bank's Energy Sector Management Assistance Program (ESMAP) in 1989 reckoned that if 20% of commercial energy could be saved, total gross savings for developing countries would come to about $30 billion a year.[8] That would be about 60% of the net flow of resources out of developing countries for debt service in 1988, and about two-thirds of official aid from OECD and OPEC countries in 1987. These calculations take no account of the costs of making the savings, but ESMAP reckoned that about 10% of energy use in many developing countries could be saved in industry at no cost at all, and a further 10% to 15% by investments with a payback period of one to two years.

Finally, underpricing energy causes environmental damage. Eastern Europe's inexpensive power helps to explain why, as Figure 3.3 shows, Comecon countries' output per head of sulphur dioxide is more than double that of the EC. It is four times higher relative to GDP. (Another consideration is the prevalence of lignite, or soft coal, which accounts for high proportions of energy use—60% in Czechoslovakia—and which has the highest concentration of sulphur dioxide of any fuel in common use.)

Underpriced power in Brazil has played an important role in destroying large tracts of the Amazon area. Electrobras, the Brazilian government's power monopoly, plans to build 18 dams in the Amazon basin by 2010 to provide hydroelectric power. A further 62 dams are planned. All told, the 80 dams would flood roughly 100,000 square km in a region with one of the highest concentrations of indigenous people. Power tariffs in Brazil are, on average, much lower than the cost of energy production. This has inevitably helped build up a concentration of energy-intensive industries. Aluminum smelting, for example, is favored with a rate for electricity that is roughly one-third that charged to domestic consumers. The most lunatic electricity-generating project of all, the Balbina dam, has flooded 2,360 square km of tropical forest to generate an average of only 112.2 mw of electricity for the town of Manaus in the heart of the Amazon. "Were electricity sold at a rate reflecting its cost," argues Philip Fearnside of the National Institute for Research in the Amazon, "people and industries would probably leave Manaus, thus eliminating the need for additional generating capacity."[9] Instead, the power from Balbina will largely benefit international companies that have set up factories in Manaus, at the expense of Brazil's taxpayers.

Underpriced power does environmental damage on an even grander scale. Burning fossil fuels give off carbon dioxide, which builds up in the atmosphere, trapping the sun's returning rays and helping to warm the planet. If carbon-based fuels were priced to reflect the private opportunity cost of producing them (world prices in the case of traded fuels and long-run marginal cost in the case of electricity), then less carbon dioxide would be sent into the atmosphere. People would use fuel more sparingly.

How much more sparingly? In 1990, Joanne Burgess did some rough sums for 11 countries, primarily in the third world but including the United States, China, and India.[10] Looking only at the electricity industry, she found that the total annual reduction in carbon dioxide in those countries that would be achieved by pricing to reflect private opportunity cost would come to 145m tonnes, or just under 3% of the global total of carbon dioxide given off by burning fossil fuels each year. Such pricing would still be too low to reflect the costs imposed on the environment

by burning fossil fuels. But the figures suggest that energy pricing that makes sense economically also starts to make sense
environmentally.

Subsidized Farms

Once, farmers seemed the natural stewards of the land. That
romantic vision, fostered by childhood books about charming
farmyard animals and by television advertisements for country-
fresh eggs, has become increasingly at odds with farming in the
first world. The apparent harmony between caring for nature
and feeding the populace has made farm subsidies far harder to
eradicate than protection for nasty, dirty industry. Only slowly
have people in developed countries begun to feel that the urban
majority has rights to the countryside, too, and to realize that the
kind of countryside that taxpayers in towns want may be harmed
by the way in which farming is subsidized.

Governments subsidize farmers in many ways. In poor countries, they frequently receive cut-price credit, pesticides, and
fertilizers. In rich countries, they get grants or—harder to value
but often more valuable—trade protection. The way the state
gives cash to farmers influences the way they farm and therefore
the effect they have on the environment.

To squeeze more output from their soil, farmers in both rich
and poor countries have applied increasing quantities of pesticides and artificial fertilizers. The damage done by agricultural
chemicals to human health is easily exaggerated. Figures are
hard to come by, but deaths from pesticide poisoning seem to be
between 3,000 and 20,000 a year, almost all of them in developing
countries. Artificial pesticides and fertilizers between them have
saved from starvation many more lives than they have cost
through misuse. But farmers in first world countries worry increasingly about the contamination of rural wells. And other
kinds of environmental damage may occur if chemicals are
wrongly used. Thus excessive use of pesticides puts farmers on
a chemical treadmill: bugs and weeds become more resistant to
poisons and so next year's poisons must be more lethal. The use
of artificial fertilizers may make possible the growing of single

crops without allowing the ground to recover in traditional
ways, by rotating crops or allowing the land to lie fallow. Crops
grown in monoculture tend to be more susceptible to pests—and
thus to need more pesticides—than those grown in more old-
fashioned ways.

Failure to rotate crops may also may make soil erosion worse,
although in the United States, where soil erosion has been studied most carefully, the evidence is mixed. A study in 1982 found
that about one-fifth of cropland was losing topsoil at a rate likely
to cause a decline in productivity; a subsequent study, however,
by the Department of Agriculture in 1989, found that even in the
Northeast, the area most affected, soil erosion productivity had
reduced by only 7% in 100 years.[11] That could be replaced with
less than four years' normal growth of productivity. More important than the loss of soil productivity may be the effects of
erosion on streams and air, both of which are likely to be polluted
in ways that raise society's costs but not those of farmers.

The use of artificial fertilizers and pesticides in rich countries
and poor has been rising. A study by the OECD pointed out that
fertilizer use has trebled in the United States over the past quarter century, doubled in Denmark, and increased in the Netherlands by 150%.[12] The quantity of pesticides applied has risen too:
by 69% since 1975 in Denmark, for example, with a rise of 115%
in the frequency of application between 1981 and 1984. As Figure
3.4 shows, pesticides and fertilizers account for over half the cost
of American corn crops.

Recently, pesticide use has begun to level off or fall in developed countries, as chemicals with more precise effects have become available. America's pesticide consumption dropped 20%
between 1973 and 1983. But farmers still frequently spread more
chemicals than they need to on their crops. A study by America's
National Research Council (NRC), published in 1989, reckoned
that 25% to 70% of the nitrogen spread on crops was absorbed
by plants.[13] Much of the rest ends up in rivers and lakes. What
causes such waste? For waste is what much of it is. More than
half the nitrogenous fertilizers applied to crops in America's corn
belt are not needed to achieve maximum profits. A study by the
International Rice Research Institute of pesticide use by farmers
in the Philippines found that even moderate applications of

pesticides on pest-resistant varieties of rice frequently cost farmers more than they saved.[14] The answer lies primarily in the system of farm support. Pesticides are heavily subsidized in most developing countries. That kicks away any incentive to develop more labor-intensive ways of dealing with pests even though these may, in the long run, be more effective and may make better sense in the labor-rich countries of the third world. A study of nine developing countries by the WRI found that the median level of subsidy was 44% of the total retail cost.[15] In Senegal, where subsidies were highest, they accounted for an average of 89% of the full retail cost. Like water subsidies, such subsidies go mainly to bigger farmers. This is especially true in countries outside Asia, where pesticides are used mostly on cash crops, which tend to be grown on large estates. And of course, it is usually hired landless laborers who are poisoned. The cost of such subsidies falls on taxpayers. As low prices encourage farmers to use more pesticides, the burden on the taxpayer rises. In

Figure 3.4 Average American Cost of Pesticides and Fertilizers, Seed, and Fuel as % of Total Variable and of Total Variable and Fixed Costs by Crop, 1986

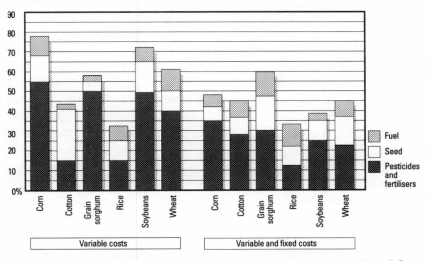

Source: National Research Council, *Alternative Agriculture,* Washington, DC, 1989.

Indonesia, where the WRI study estimated that subsidies for pesticides used on food and other annual crops accounted on average for 82% of their retail price, pesticide use trebled between 1978 and 1982. In 1985–1990, subsidies were expected to cost the government at least $1 billion.

Artificial fertilizers also tend to attract heavy subsidies, often from aid donors. In developed countries, the donor tends to be the agriculture department or—in the EC—the Common Agricultural Policy (CAP). It may be that farm support inevitably encourages monoculture, with its attendant rise in chemical use. Fear of fluctuating prices once led farmers to hedge their bets, keeping pigs in their orchards and cows on their stubble fields. Simply by providing farmers with the insurance against loss of income that once came only by raising many different crops, farm support removes some of the need for diversity. This in itself can be environmentally harmful.

Certainly, the pattern of farm support frequently rewards high yields per acre, regardless of the effect on the environment. By supporting the prices of agricultural products, governments do not ensure that farmers get higher incomes—or not for long. Subsidies and price supports are quickly capitalized into the value of agricultural land. Buying a farm becomes tantamount to buying the right to receive a subsidy. Farmers must squeeze every last drop of output from their land in order to earn back the large investment that they now have to make to buy the land. This may mean draining wetlands, destroying woodlands, cutting down hedgerows, or closing footpaths. Capital grants and tax reliefs encourage more capital investment—including farm buildings, which in Britain are not controlled by planning regulations—than would otherwise occur. Farming becomes more capital-intensive, less labor-intensive. By raising the value of farm land, price supports drive up the cost of not maximizing the cash return on it, that is, the crops it produces plus the subsidy it attracts. The cash crops from a farm in the shape of food and subsidies are frequently substitutes for what one might think of as environmental services: public access, woodlands, hedgerows, unsprayed corners of fields. As the return on the cash crops rises, so does the cost to a farmer of producing these noncash crops. The lost income is greater. Thus the more a government spends on price support, the less willing farmers are likely to be to farm in environmentally friendly ways.

More intensive farming has helped wipe out habitats and rare species. Almost all the dry chalk grasslands of Champagne in France have disappeared in the past 30 years; in Germany, grassland intensification threatens 45 species of butterflies; in Britain, 80% of chalk downland and half of all lowland bogs and marshes have vanished or been damaged since 1945. Most of these losses are caused by more intensive farming. Not surprisingly, the Council for the Protection of Rural England and the WWF have begun to attack the CAP. They point out that such environmental damage is expensive for taxpayers and shoppers alike. The costs of the policy to Britain, in government revenue and in inexpensive food forgone, are double the benefits, while for the EC as a whole costs exceed benefits by 30%.

Price supports also indirectly encourage the use of fertilizer. Agriculture in the developed world is one of the most energy-intensive and chemical-intensive industries, and any pressure to increase output is likely to raise the use of these crucial inputs. Fertilizer is, in a sense, a substitute for land: if farmers cannot raise output by buying extra fields, then applying more fertilizer is a partial alternative. High land prices, by raising the incentive to increase output, encourage the application of more fertilizer. One study estimates that a 1% rise in the price of land relative to the price of fertilizer increases fertilizer use by 1.4% in the United States and by 0.4% in Japan.[16]

The way agricultural support is administered in the United States has almost certainly aggravated soil erosion. As the National Research Council report pointed out, farm support has been based on the average acreage devoted to a particular crop over the previous five years. This is a powerful disincentive to rotating crops and avoiding erosion. Between 40% and 45% of the American corn crop is now grown in continuous monoculture, planted on the same tired land year after year. Not surprisingly, corn, together with wheat, accounts for half of all the nitrogen fertilizer used in the United States. By paying farmers for higher yields, agricultural support effectively tips the balance in favor of farming today and against farming tomorrow. It makes it more attractive for farmers to use up soil fertility now, rather than farming conservatively. Indeed, it would be entirely rational for a farmer who had watched negotiations to curb spending under the CAP, or under the GATT (General Agreements on Tariffs and Trade) Uruguay round, to farm even more unsustainably on the grounds that the present rate of farm support will probably not last. Better make hay while the sun shines and grab as much support as possible today. Thus do agricultural ministers exacerbate the environmentally unfriendly workings of high discount rates. As Alan Winters put it, in an article in OECD's *Economic Studies,* "By far the easiest way of reducing pressure on the soil would be to reduce the incentive for intensive, and especially capital-intensive, farming methods. Moreover, this should be done quickly, for it is anticipated price falls that most encourage over-exploitation."[17]

In time, farm support may play another part in the environmental debate. One of the most potent greenhouse gases is methane, which is given off by coal mines, garbage dumps, and leaky gas pipes—and also by stewing rice paddies. Cattle account for three-quarters of the methane given off by domestic livestock. This is partly because they eat more, but also because more of what they eat is converted into methane: up to 9% of their gross energy intake, compared with an average of 1.3% for pigs. One study argued that a 50% cut in beef consumption in the first world and a corresponding rise in consumption of pork would allow a 40% cut in methane production from the developed world's farms.[18] It urges a climate tax on beef consumption. After the collapse of the GATT Uruguay round in late 1990 and the opening of negotiations on a treaty to deal with greenhouse gases, American climate negotiators talked darkly about cuts in EC agricultural support as part of a package of measures to reduce Europe's output of greenhouse gas.

Governments in Europe have begun to try to counteract the most damaging influence of farm support on the countryside by providing another group of subsidies, this time attached to environmentally friendly behavior. The greater the damaging influence of the first set of subsidies, the larger the second set has to be in order to have any impact. The EC now allows, at the behest of the British, payments for farmers in areas designated as "environmentally sensitive" if they reduce stocking rates, repair old stone walls, and so on. Another subsidy goes to farmers in areas where heavy plowing of grassland and the use of fertilizers have helped pollute streams with nitrates. This subsidy bribes farmers to use techniques that release less nitrogen into the soil.

Although such policies may sound crazy, it may be easier for governments to use them than to take the sensible course of reducing agricultural protection. Cuts in farm support mean, inevitably, a reduction in the prosperity of farmers. Like doctors, farmers are skilled at tugging at the public heartstrings. The first whisper of reform fills newspapers with sad stories of (in America) westerners fighting to make a living on a plot their grandfather settled or (in Britain) upland sheep farmers struggling to survive. Subsidies become rights—rights to pollute, perhaps, but rights nonetheless. A government that threatens such rights runs straight into powerful, articulate, and well-organized lobbies; the beneficiaries of reform are invariably many, but their benefits are more thinly spread and less easily discerned than the losses of those who lobby.

Destruction in the Rain Forest

The destruction of the rain forests, so important for conserving species and carbon dioxide alike, has taken place partly at the expense of taxpayers in the countries that have lost them. Governments have lost money not just by paying for unneeded hydroelectric projects in forests, but by subsidizing forest clearance and by grossly undercharging for logging rights. Subsidies have encouraged deforestation in Brazil, home to 30% of the world's tropical rain forest. A study for the World Bank in April 1989 suggested three routes.[19] First, agricultural income is virtually exempted from income tax, making farming a tax shelter (although income from nonfarm activities could not be offset against gains from farming). That encourages urban investors and companies to buy up land. Where land happens to carry forest, it is cleared to qualify. Because taxes are so low on farm investments, farmers have an incentive to undertake projects with a lower rate of return than they would otherwise contemplate. And because tax relief stimulates a demand for land and thus pushes up its price, it becomes harder for the poor (who pay no tax and so get no relief) to buy a holding. This in turn gives them a greater incentive to settle and clear frontier lands.

Second, subsidized credit for farmers also helps reduce the rate of return that cleared land needs to earn, and drives up the value of land (just like those Californian water subsidies and EC farm price guarantees). Third and most damaging, SUDAM, the government agency charged with development in the Amazon region, and other government lenders have in the past offered special tax credits for corporations. A large share of those credits, which cost more than $1 billion in 1975–1986, was used to encourage forest to be cleared and stocked with cattle. These ranches have produced no more than 16% of their expected output. Many cleared the land, took the tax credit, but never raised a single joint of beef. As a second World Bank report put it, "More than two decades of experience have shown that livestock projects have been responsible for much environmental damage and yield little in the way of production or employment . . . most of the benefits have accrued to a small group of wealthy investors who have used these resources to appropriate large tracts of land on the agricultural frontier."[20]

Some of these damaging policies were subsequently temporarily dropped. In 1989, new tax credits were suspended, although projects already begun continued to be subsidized. Inexpensive loans have been scaled down. And the rules that made land title conditional on forest clearance have been repealed. At the same time, Brazil's financial difficulties have virtually stopped new road building in the Amazon. As a result, the rate of deforestation dropped dramatically: from 80,000 square km in 1987 to an estimated 20,000 square km in 1990.

Another study for the World Bank argues that subsidies destroy the Amazon in a rather different way. An unpublished paper points out that small cattle herds grew much faster in the years 1970 to 1985 than larger ones. Herds with under 50 animals grew by 70%; those with over 500, by 17%. Subsidies and tax breaks tend to go to large farmers first, small farmers last. More probably two other forces were at work. The value of land in southern Brazil, relative to that in the north, rose by a factor of ten over that 15-year period, greatly increasing the incentive to sell out and move north. This may have been partly a reflection of tax breaks for farmers, which encouraged the growth of large, capital-intensive soya farms in the south at the expense of smaller, more labor-intensive cocoa plantations. Second, a big increase in urban populations in the north preceded the growth of cattle herds. Because of the long transport distances from south to north, cattle farming may have increased in the Amazon region to feed the new cities.

If this latter paper is right, that suggests that the impact of state transfers of cash on the Amazon may be more complex than had previously been thought. The principle of regional aid for the north is embedded in Brazil's constitution. But that aid, by fostering the growth of towns such as Belem and Manaus, and by encouraging road building, may subtly lead to greater deforestation. Meanwhile, farm subsidies in the south may drive people from the land, into Brazil's overcrowded cities and its fragile north.

Although more deforestation has been caused by farming than by logging in Brazil, the reverse is true in Asia and in parts of Africa. There, the problem is different: loggers have no incentive to replace the trees they chop down. Some economists have argued that governments undercharge for logging licenses, discouraging loggers from putting a proper value on the trees they chop down. Loggers therefore tend to cut more trees than they otherwise would, and have little incentive to spend money on replanting or on taking care of surrounding forest when they take out trees.

More convincingly, a study by two economists at the Asian Development Bank argues that higher charges may encourage more logging, not less, by creaming off revenue that might otherwise be invested in forest management. "Only the certainty of property rights to future harvests can promote responsible and careful logging," they claim.[21] They suggest instead that logging rights to a defined area of land should be given for a specified period of time in exchange for a forestry guarantee bond. This would be deposited for the period of the lease, and forfeited to the government if the leaseholder broke the conditions of the lease, which would include an obligation to protect parts of the forest from damage by others. The proposal emphasizes a particular issue for third world countries: the need to find policy instruments that do not require sophisticated policing but are largely self-regulating.

Third world countries say, with some justification, that first world countries have made most of the mistakes for which they now blame the poor. That is certainly true of forests. The Brazilian provision that clearing land established title to it had its equivalent a century ago in the laws that helped clear North America's forests. Even now, America subsidizes the harvesting of timber in its national forests. For many years the Wilderness Society has been campaigning to end the subsidies that the American Forest Service pays to logging contractors. The environmental damage enrages American environmentalists. The most heavily subsidized logging is on land too arid and cold to reforest. That often means taking the trees from mountain ridges, which are visible from miles away. Worse, subsidies are encouraging logging in America's last great temperate rain forest, the Tongass in Alaska.

In Britain, government forestry subsidies have had the opposite effect—to encourage tree planting—but led to the same reaction: vehement environmental opposition. Forestry in Britain has long been a tax shelter, as farming is in Brazil (except that in Britain, unlike Brazil, income from activities other than forestry could effectively be set off against losses in forestry). Rich individuals bought inexpensive hill land, setting off the costs of the purchase and of planting it against their income taxes. When the trees matured, a quirk of financial law allowed the landowner to sell the land to a financial institution, paying capital gains tax on the land but not on its crop of growing trees. Taxable income could thus be converted into untaxed capital. By the late 1980s, the cost to the British Treasury in lost income-tax revenue amounted to £10 million to £15 million a year. Because the tax relief was determined by the cost of planting, it provided an incentive to buy land as inexpensively as possible. That meant buying moorlands, whose previous use had been for sheep grazing. But moorlands, like America's forested ridges, tend to be conspicuous; they also tend to have more than their fair share of rare wildlife. Planting them with subsidized trees destroyed those habitats.

Because tax relief was automatic, neither central government nor local authorities could control where planting took place (although foresters who wanted an additional grant had to abide by rules laid down by the Forestry Commission). And because the relief was simply attached to tree planting, regardless of the kind of tree, many foresters planted the trees that gave the quickest returns: primarily imported species of sitka spruce and lodgepole pine. An industry of subsidized tree farming grew up, with the same tendency to monoculture and overuse of chemical fertilizers and pesticides of other kinds of subsidized farming. In the 1988 budget the government abolished the special tax treatment of forestry and replaced it with grants. Forestry is still subsidized, but in a way that gives the government more control over where the subsidies (and the forests) go. The environmentalists are still worried: applications to plant, which had diminished for a while, began to increase again in 1990.

Reassessing Government Intervention

Realizing that environmental damage typically resulted from market failure, environmentalists have traditionally seen the cure as government intervention. This ignores the fact that intervention has costs of its own, justified only if the costs of market failure exceed the costs that may come from badly directed actions by the state. The example of British forestry is telling: in theory, subsidizing forestry ought to be a thoroughly environmentally friendly thing to do. In practice, the policy has done great harm. Governments that see tree planting as the easiest way to reduce the effects of global warming may find that their policies, unless designed with extreme care, backfire. Government subsidies sometimes do environmental good. But environmentalists and economists alike would be wise to approach such claims with caution. Many environmental lobbyists, for example, would like to see more state money spent on public transport. This, they argue, would wean people away from their cars and reduce all their nasty environmental side effects such as congestion and smog. Sadly, there is little evidence that subsidized public transport is an efficient way of discouraging car travel.

Raising the price of gasoline is more effective, especially once car drivers have had time to adjust. In the long term, a 10% rise in the price of fuel may lead to a 5% fall in its consumption.[22]

The cure for market failure, in short, is not necessarily state intervention. The cure may be to make the market work better. One interesting example has been privatization. The industries that governments have transferred to private ownership in the 1980s (primarily in Britain but in other countries as well) have often been those that are most environmentally sensitive: transport, energy, and water. Privatization alone will not necessarily improve (or worsen) the impact of a given industry on the environment. It will put greater weight on profit and less on output as an industry goal.[23] To the extent that more output means more pollution, a greater emphasis on profit may reduce the harm the privatized industry does to the environment.

The distancing of regulation from ownership may be more important. Before the British water industry was privatized, ministers argued in private that the strongest reason for selling it off was the extreme difficulty of persuading the Treasury to allow enough spending on environmental improvements. That argument clearly could not be used in public. Now that the government is answerable for water quality but not responsible for the industry's finances, ministers may find it easier to raise standards. The industry's shareholders and customers may squeal; but the Treasury, infinitely more powerful, will keep quiet.

Governments do not necessarily need to undertake sophisticated calculations about the costs of environmental damage or to devise ingenious pollution taxes (discussed in the next chapter) in order to combine an improvement in their environmental policies with a gain in revenue and in economic efficiency. This is one of those rare occasions in public life when politicians can enjoy two gains for the price of one. They will need to stand up to the lobbyists who have enjoyed government protection in the past and have come to regard it as their right. Those lobbies may be immensely strong, which is why governments so rarely stand up to them. But good green governments now have a new ally: environmental pressure from their citizens. They have a wonderful chance to spend their taxpayers' cash more sensibly and to improve the way in which their citizens use water, energy, and soil—all in a single swoop.

4

Making Polluters Pay

Governments almost always tackle environmental damage by telling companies or individuals to stop it. They pass laws, set standards, promulgate bans, enforce regulations. Such policies present a paradox: although they are popular, they are rarely the most cost-effective way to clean up. Other policies—for example, taxes and tradable permits—deliver more environmental improvement at lower cost. Governments have begun to look at these market-based instruments.

Why do governments need to intervene at all? The answer is that in environmental affairs, the invisible hand of the market fails to align the interests of the individual or the individual company with those of society at large. Individuals may drive their cars to work rather than take a bus; companies may use CFCs to insulate and cool refrigerators. In both cases, the costs to the environment and thus to society at large exceed any private cost to individual or company. That is inefficient. Governments need to step in to align private costs with social costs.

This concept is embodied in the "polluter-pays principle." The industrial members of the OECD adopted this as a guide to proper environmental policies in 1972. The principle, it was argued, would ensure that polluters carried the full costs of their actions. It would thus improve economic efficiency. In practice, the principle is frequently broken by, for example, policies that subsidize polluters to clean up. In the real world, and particularly (see below) in international agreements, victims of pollution seem to be as likely to foot the bill for reducing it as the perpetrators. As earlier chapters have argued, environmental policies may cost dearly in terms of the loss of conventionally measured national income. It is therefore extremely important to design policies that achieve their goal as cost-effectively as possible. The policies that politicians find easiest to sell to the voters may well not be the ones that deliver the greatest environmental benefit with the least loss of economic growth.

Standards

The way in which governments have traditionally aligned private and social costs is by setting standards. Most pollution controls, in most countries, work through standard setting. Companies agree to drain wastewater into rivers only when it can be diluted to a prescribed amount, or to build cars that meet set targets for fuel efficiency or exhaust emissions. Standards have important advantages, especially in the eyes of industry and politicians; but they also have drawbacks, some of which have become more apparent as the nature of pollution problems has changed.

Polluters often prefer standards: they know where they stand, and they know that every other polluter will have to meet the same target. That seems fair. In reality, it may not be fair at all, for some polluters will inevitably find it less expensive to apply a given standard than others. The usual goal is best available technology. Taken literally, that implies that if a better technology exists, companies should use it, however expensive it may be. For some polluters, compliances will be far more expensive than for others. A factory with two-year-old machines may not want to scrap them; one with a ten-year-old plant may be about to replace it anyway. So regulators generally have to compromise. In 1987, 12 years after the standards for air quality set in America's 1970 Clean Air Act were meant to take effect, more than 100 million people lived in areas that failed to meet those standards. Standards that cannot be fairly enforced may suffer a lack of credibility with the public, and impose higher costs or those who comply than on those who bargain their way into mitigation.

In Britain, where pollution regulation has traditionally been a cozier affair, new regulations introduced in 1991 tried to make standards more flexible by building in the concept of BATNEEC—"best available techniques not entailing excessive cost." Pollution inspectors and companies will have room to haggle over what involves "excessive cost" and what amounts to "best available techniques." BATNEEC is an attempt to tailor the cut in pollution each firm delivers to its particular cost structure. It will inevitably be labor-intensive. To judge whether costs are excessive may involve pollution inspectors in wrangling with company finance departments as well as with engineers.

Similar problems of hidden inequity arise when standards are applied to individuals. It is usually inexpensive for owners of new cars to have them converted to run on unleaded gas. For owners of elderly jalopies, though, it is far more expensive. If, when it belatedly realized the need to promote unleaded gasoline, the British government had simply passed a law insisting that all cars be converted within a certain time, it would have inflicted huge costs on owners of older vehicles. Instead, it chose a sensible economic instrument: a higher rate of duty on leaded than unleaded gasoline. This has allowed owners of some oldish cars to weigh the benefit of cheaper gas against the cost of converting their cars.

Those who find standards expensive to meet do not do so, but those who find them relatively inexpensive have no incentive to go beyond what the law requires. In fact, companies often do go further than environmental regulations insist, but only because other incentives, created by the market and the courts, encourage them to do so.

Because meeting standards is often possible only when a company or an individual makes a new investment—builds a new office, for instance, or buys a new car—standards tend to operate disproportionately on new equipment. Yet by driving up the cost of such equipment, they tend to encourage polluters to postpone the very investments that pollution control requires. This "new-source bias" is a deterrent to innovation, just as, in America, tough controls on new drugs relative to old ones have reduced the number of new drugs brought onto the market compared with other countries. In 1977, the American Congress insisted on a less polluting design for new coal-fired power stations. Sulphur dioxide was to be scrubbed from exhaust gases until they were as clean as those produced by stations that burned low-sulphur coal. Because such scrubbers added up to 20% to the capital cost of a new plant, and old generators can last for 40 years or more, replacement of old equipment inevitably slowed down.

Sometimes, standards may be used deliberately to protect dirty old industries rather than to encourage new clean ones. Robert Crandall, of the Brookings Institution in Washington, DC, has collected examples. Electrical utilities are one, metal-smelting another. In both cases, tighter emissions limits have been set for new entrants, mainly in southern and western states, but not for older, dirtier enterprises in the Midwest. This dirty protectionism, he argues, is partly a reflection of America's political system, which gives two senate seats to old industrial states that have lost population as well as to the fast-growing new ones. States where industrial jobs are being lost frequently back high new standards because they know they will apply mainly to newer industries in rival states.

By discouraging replacement purchases, raising standards on consumer goods may depress sales. Thus each time emission standards on American cars have been tightened, car prices rise and the average age of the car fleet creeps up. In the mid-1950s, the average American car was six years old; in the late 1960s, 5.5 years; by 1987, 7.6 years. This may in part reflect a slower rise in incomes, encouraging people to replace their cars less often. It may also mean that cars have become more durable, so that they need replacement less often. But it probably also reflects tighter emission standards. For part proof, compare the smaller rise in the average age of American trucks, whose emissions are less heavily regulated: the fleet was 7.7 years old in the late 1960s and eight years old at the end of the 1980s. Higher emission standards mean not only that cars become smaller and lighter and have lower performance. They also make cars more expensive. By the mid-1980s, reckons Crandall, higher environmental and safety standards accounted for almost 20% of the cost of a new car in gadgetry and in extra fuel consumption over its lifetime. Safety standards represented only one-fifth of that figure.

Finally, standards may be easier to apply to large polluters, such as companies, than to individuals. An inspector may be able to bargain with a hundred companies but not with a thousand households. Yet the least tractable pollution problems, at least in the first world, are increasingly those caused by individual behavior for which setting standards, if not combined with other measures that affect prices, may also have perverse effects. For instance, if governments try to reduce energy consumption solely by insisting on more fuel-efficient cars, people may find driving so much cheaper that they will make more journeys at higher speed. Or if governments insist on better-insulated buildings but the price of electricity does not change, people may use their savings to turn up the thermostat even more. As environmental standards tighten, diminishing environmental returns set in. As the clean air legislation wound its way through Congress in the summer of 1990, General Motors was vociferously arguing that yet tougher controls were a daft way to cut emissions. Why spend millions developing more fuel-efficient engines when the cost per mile of fuel had halved in the 1980s in real terms and stood, on the eve of the Gulf crisis, at 2 cents, its lowest level ever? A carbon tax would be better. What conceivable interest could a car manufacturer have in pushing for a carbon tax? Easy. It would not only be the most cost-effective way to reduce emissions; it would also shift most of the cost from purchasers of new cars to the users of existing vehicles. Indeed, it might provide a positive incentive for drivers of old, smoky cars to trade them in for a newer, more economical model.

Market-Based Instruments

Introduce the market, and many of these difficulties diminish. Most economic instruments for tackling pollution work by creating incentives to become cleaner. When properly designed, they should impose on a polluter the costs that would otherwise be dumped on the environment. Economic instruments, as Figure 4.1 shows, have been embraced with varying enthusiasm in different countries. They have two primary advantages over standards. In the short term, they will generally provide a given level of environmental improvement at a lower cost to society than will regulations. This is because, in theory at least, polluters will have an incentive to reduce the amount of muck they produce for as long as it is less expensive to do so than to pay more environmental charges, using the technology they judge to be most efficient. Regulations, by contrast, take account of the costs of cleaning up only in a rough and ready way.

Second, in the long run, economic instruments offer companies and individuals a continual argument for going further than a standard would demand. If companies pay a higher rate for every pound of toxic rubbish they dump, they have an incentive to use as little toxic material as possible and to look for new processes that use none at all. If gas taxes are high, individuals have to drive frugally all the time and to replace their car with one that uses less fuel, whatever the standards say. The difference in cost to the community between typical regulation and well-designed economic instruments may be as much as five or ten

Figure 4.1 Number of Environmental Economic Measures, 1987

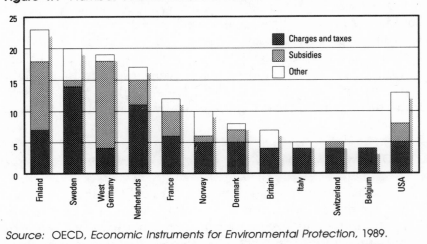

Source: OECD, *Economic Instruments for Environmental Protection*, 1989.

times, according to some American studies.[1] In reality, the savings are usually much smaller but still important.

Economic instruments have several other strengths. For example, they can affect the behavior of millions of people—think of those gas taxes again—in a way that may be impossible with standards. That effect will become more important, the more governments realize that pollution is the result of millions of decisions by many individuals and small businesses, rather than by a few large and easily regulated companies. To levy taxes, governments require much less information about the costs of curbing pollution. A higher tax on leaded gas will ensure that people whose cars can be inexpensively converted will do so; the rest will not. The fact that economic instruments do not require detailed information about the costs facing individual polluters in order to work (any more than a value-added tax requires a knowledge of all the taxpayer's circumstances) has another advantage: it means that they are less vulnerable to cozy deals between regulators and regulated.

Economic instruments also provide a positive incentive to buy less polluting technologies instead of (as with standards) an incentive to postpone change. Such technologies, as the second half of this book argues, play an important role in taking the pain out of greenery; they are also the primary way countries can hope to grow richer by growing greener.

Green Taxes

The oldest and most familiar of all economic instruments are green taxes. Although governments began to show a lively interest in them at the end of the 1980s, the idea has been around for some time. In 1920, the Cambridge University economist Arthur Pigou proposed the idea of a tax as a way to bridge the gap between private and social cost which is at the root of environmental damage. But old as the concept of green taxation may be, remarkably few countries have put Pigou's insight into practice. Taxes or charges on polluters have in the past usually been intended to raise the revenue to pay for regulation rather than to deter polluters. They have been levied, principally in European countries, mostly on dirty water, although occasionally on aircraft noise. They have rarely been used to discourage air pollution or waste dumping. They have almost always been set at levels too low to affect polluters' behavior.

Then at the end of the 1980s, some northern European governments began to discuss taxes to be levied on the amount of carbon dioxide given off by burning fossil fuels, as part of an attempt to reduce output of greenhouse gases. Sweden and Finland actually introduced such carbon taxes. The EC Commission also became enthusiastic, primarily because a carbon tax seemed to offer a new source of environmental revenue to spend on good deeds such as supporting tropical forestry. More modest taxes were also introduced. Italy brought in a tax of 100 lire on plastic bags, which caused an initial fall of 40% in their use. Several American states have considered imposing taxes on packaging, but hesitated because of the complexity and the difficulty of raising them to a level high enough to have an impact on corporate behavior. Denmark put a charge on pesticides sold in small containers, since such containers and their toxic contents usually ended up in household rubbish bins. Finland introduced a tax on single-hulled tankers bringing oil into the country, since the tankers were often more likely to spill their contents if they ran aground. The United States and Norway both taxed CFCs.

Other green taxes are being discussed. Italy would like to increase substantially its landing charges for noisy aircraft and to tax farmers who keep more than 200 pigs but have no waste-treatment facilities. Germany has plans to change the basis of its car tax from engine size to exhaust fumes and noise. Denmark plans a tenfold increase in the taxation of raw materials and a tripling of the existing tax on rubbish, both measures intended to economize on scarce landfill. Singapore and Oslo both impose tolls on cars entering the city center. Other cities are thinking hard about road pricing, arguing that it is a more efficient way of sharing out scarce road space than forcing everybody to sit in traffic jams. A study of congestion in California came up with an ingenious variation.[2] It suggested a charge for rush-hour trips. Drivers would have a free monthly allowance, which a meter would debit electronically every time a car entered or left the freeway. At the end of the month, motorists would discover their balance and sell any spare units. This would benefit frugal motorists and penalize extravagant ones.

Green taxes have caused tussles between environment ministries and finance departments. Environment ministers often see green taxes as a way of raising revenue to spend on other green causes. They like the idea of using some of the yield from road pricing to pay for public transport, for instance, or of reinvesting the takings from effluent charges in building sewage works. Finance ministers, on the other hand, dislike having a source of revenue tied to a particular item of state spending. They have two objections. They argue that it is unlikely that the tax will yield exactly the right amount that ought to be spent on whatever good green cause is involved. A carbon tax that reduced carbon output by just the right amount will only by utter fluke yield the sum that should, in an ideal world, be devoted to tropical forestry. It is far more likely to yield more—or less.

Finance ministries also see green taxes as a new revenue source. In this, there is a paradox. If a tax successfully reduces the polluting behavior on which it is levied, its yield will diminish. Just as governments that tax cigarettes are suspected of wanting to keep many people puffing, so a pollution tax might give government a vested interest in dirt. That, of course, is only partly true. Although there is no point at which the benefits of cigarette smoking, either to the individual or to society, exceed the costs of the habit, it is possible to reach a point where further reductions in some kinds of pollution would cost more than the value of the benefits that would result. A few gallons a day of raw sewage in the Thames or the Hudson matter not one jot: a few million gallons matter a great deal. A wise government could live happily off the proceeds of taxes that kept pollution at the point where the costs of prevention threatened to exceed the benefits of greenery. Because such taxes might often be levied on basic materials—water or energy consumption, for instance—they could yield a good deal of revenue before they reached the point at which people changed their behavior. To raise more revenue from such taxes, and less from taxing income and capital, would be a farsighted thing for a government to do. Most taxes are levied on things that are good for an economy. Governments obtain revenue at the expense of some economic welfare.

Because income is taxed, people may work a bit less hard than they otherwise might; because capital is taxed, they have an incentive to save and to invest less than they otherwise might. The WRI calculates that these distorting effects of the tax system cost America 4% to 7% of GNP each year. Rather than taxing good things, why not tax bad ones, such as pollution? If taxes make people work less or save less, that is bad; if taxes make people pollute less, that is good.

Indeed, it will become more important to switch taxes away from income in the years ahead. Most of the industrial countries are entering a period when their labor forces will stop expanding. It will be foolish to tax the resource whose supply is most static. Yet that is exactly what the rich countries may be tempted to do. Because capital is mobile and goods can be moved easily across frontiers, taxes on savings and on spending may well decline. People move less freely than do money or goods. So income will be easy to tax. Easy, but ultimately expensive.

Green taxes do have some disadvantages, some of which explain why they have not been more widely adopted. Occasionally, green taxes are simply not appropriate. They work best when the market works best. Where one dirty company has a monopoly—of electricity generation, say—it may be better to regulate than to tax it: if taxed, it will simply pass the whole bill on to the consumer and remain dirty. Green taxes may also be less helpful than regulation when what matters is the concentration of filth: a river can tolerate a given concentration of effluent through the day, say, but not a sudden flood jammed into a brief half hour. A tax per unit of muck would not discourage sudden discharges. Where what matters most is the capacity of the environment to absorb pollution, regulation may be the wisest course.

There is a bigger problem. The revenue that green taxes raise represents an increase in costs to the polluter. Splendid, say greens. That is the way taxes give even cleanish companies a continuing incentive to become cleaner. Politicians may be more doubtful. For companies, the counterpart of that extra revenue is an increase in their costs, which inevitably makes them less competitive against companies (in other countries for example) that bear no such burden. For individuals, the counterpart is also a rise in costs, which is another reason why politicians fret about the inflationary impact of green taxes. Moreover, since such taxes would generally be flat rate (a couple of pennies on a gallon of water, for instance) they would, like all indirect taxes, tend to hurt the poor proportionately more than the rich. They would be regressive, though in countries where the poor—often women or old people—rarely drive cars, gas taxes would be a partial exception.

Two points soften this harsh picture. First, standards carry costs, too. From society's point of view, the costs imposed by standards are always higher, although they are better hidden. Who knows how much national income is lost by raising the standards for building insulation or for the fuel efficiency of cars? For the company or the individual, though, standards will be a less expensive way to clean up, because taxes will be levied on all the pollution an individual or a company causes, even if it is as clean as an alternative standard might require. To illustrate the point, imagine that a country sets a standard for fuel efficiency for cars. Three-quarters of the cars in the country meet the standard. Then the government decides to replace the standard with a gas tax, set at a level designed to keep the same average level of fuel efficiency. The owners of cars that have already met the standard will find that the cost of driving is higher. This is precisely why they will have an incentive to buy cars that are even more efficient. But it is also why people dislike green taxes.

Second, the revenue that causes these hardships can always be redistributed. The government could use the proceeds of the gas tax to raise old-age pensions or to cut income taxes. The yield from a tax that hurts corporate competitiveness could be used to cut the corporation tax. Such measures do not necessarily hand the gains from green taxation back to the losers: the dirtiest companies would still experience higher costs, but the cleanest would be better off. An alternative—although this drives a coach and horses through the "polluter-pays" principle—is to use the revenue to pay a sort of negative pollution tax. Companies or individuals that improve on a benchmark level of pollution control might get money back, on a sliding scale; for example, those whose cars were of above-average efficiency might receive a fuel-tax credit each year. Governments would apply a stick to the dirty and offer a carrot to the clean.

Tradable Permits

Green taxes have another drawback, even in the eyes of green economists. It is almost impossible to set them at the "right" level. That magic point, at which the costs of pollution prevention catch up with the benefits, is hard enough to discover even on paper. To hit it by setting taxes at precisely the right level is even more difficult. Keeping taxes at that right level, year after year, is probably impossible. Nothing annoys politicians more than the idea that they may have to change a tax simply because it was set at the wrong level in the first place. Yet nothing is more certain than that most green taxes are set too low to meet their goal.

American economists have developed an economic instrument that avoids this problem. Instead of setting a pollution target in terms of price, as a tax does, it sets the target in terms of quantity. Such instruments have been known in the past as "marketable pollution rights" or "tradable permits"; American green lobbyists were furious at the thought that anyone might acquire a right to pollute, and so tactful economists now speak of "emission reduction credits." That carries comforting overtones of rewards for good behavior rather than profits from bad.

Under these schemes, governments set a standard in terms of, say, tons of sulphur dioxide a year. That total is then shared out among companies or power stations, giving each polluter a quota of gas that it can emit. If the polluter introduces new, cleaner technology so that its emissions fall below its permitted level, it can sell its unneeded share to other polluters or to new companies that may want to enter the business. Companies for whom cleaning up is relatively inexpensive thus have an incentive to be as clean as possible. But the dirty can also stay in business, though carrying the extra cost of buying more pollution credits. One company may also lease its credits to another if it does not need them but thinks that it may do so in the future.

Companies can choose which course is more cost-effective: to clean up and sell or to stay dirty and buy. Because both high- and low-cost polluters do better if they trade, there is an incentive to do so. Because high-cost polluters save money by buying extra permits rather than cleaning up, pollution will be concentrated among those companies for whom prevention is most expensive. Yet the environment as a whole will be cleaner, because there is a finite limit on allowable pollution.

These schemes are attractive. They combine the certainty of regulation with the flexibility of the market. They allow governments to stand back and say, "We are simply setting an overall pollution target. It's up to you how you share it out. We are not raising prices: if prices go up, that is the fault of polluters, not us." They even make it possible for those who care about the environment to do something constructive: buy up permits and freeze them. Green lobbyists, who want to see power-station emissions decrease more quickly, could raise the cash to buy up permits and sit on them. Companies get the cash; lobbyists get cleaner air.

An important aspect of these permits is the way they are distributed in the first place. One option is to hand them out on the basis of existing patterns of pollution. A dirty company will get many; a clean company, fewer. In America, such a process is called "grandfathering." It is a way of recognizing that existing polluters have a de facto right to pollute; if they are deprived of the right, they will feel that they have been robbed and make sure every politician knows it. The drawback, of course, is that grandfathering is unfair to those who are already cleaner. Because permits will be traded for hard cash, a dirty company will receive a larger endowment than a clean one.

Another option is to auction off the permits. That way, government can ignore the rights that polluters may feel they have to pollute. Moreover, while grandfathering does not raise revenue, auctioning does. In that sense, an auction is similar to a pollution tax. If the government holds an auction, then the counterpart of the revenue it raises will be a loss of income to polluters, as with a tax; although government can use that revenue to soften the social impacts of its policies, it cannot claim that its hands are clean.

Although economists love the idea of tradable permits as a device for curbing pollution, they have rarely been tried. (The concept has been frequently applied in other contexts: EC milk quotas in Britain, fishing catches in New Zealand, and quotas for textile exports to the United States have all been traded.) There are circumstances in which they are clearly not appropriate. It would be hard to apply them to the control of toxic gas emissions by companies, for instance: local people would not want to let companies decide whether to meet a minimum safety standard at one plant but not at another. But even when permits seem the appropriate mechanism, they cannot always be made to work in practice as neatly as they do in economic literature.

Easily the most successful experiment with permits was carried out by the Environmental Protection Agency in 1985 when it gave oil refineries two years in which to cut the allowable lead content of gas. Refineries received quotas of lead, which they could trade with each other. The effect was to let them phase in the cut in lead at their own pace. Half of all the refineries took part in trading. The lead scheme had three special features that helped make it work. The amount of lead in gas was easily monitored with existing regulatory machinery; the number of firms involved was quite small; and the environmental goals of the program were clear and widely accepted. The EPA's attempts since 1974 to allow companies to trade air-pollution permits have been less successful. Many cities failed to meet the standards laid down in the 1970 Clear Air Act. Rather than stop companies from moving to such places, the EPA allowed them to buy the right to pollute from established firms that had cut their own emissions, adding other refinements.

Trade in air-pollution permits has undoubtedly kept down the costs of compliance. The effect has been to cut the capital cost of pollution-control in the United States cumulatively by an estimated $10 billion, although it has been done primarily by letting companies offset increased emissions from one outlet against smaller emissions from another outlet within the same plant. But the amount of trading, particularly between companies rather than within a single firm, has greatly disappointed enthusiasts. One reason has been the complexity of trading rules. Another has been that America's litigious green lobby resented the idea that companies should have a right to pollute, let alone make money by selling permits to another firm. They saw the tradable permits scheme as a way to postpone meeting the goals of the Clean Air Act, rather than a way of achieving them more cost-effectively. Moreover, to work well, emissions trading needs better records of emissions than most American states possess. Otherwise, companies see no reason to pay for what others are illegally taking for nothing.

In 1990, America decided to try again. Congress passed a new Clean Air Act based on ideas developed by the Environmental Defense Fund (EDF), one of the few environmental groups dominated by economists rather than by lawyers, and by Project 88, a highly influential study of economic answers to environmental problems.[3] Once again, an important feature of the legislation was tradable permits but this time in a more workable package. The act sets a cap on the output of sulphur dioxide and nitrogen oxides from electricity-generating plants. The output of sulphur dioxide must be cut by 10 million tons, and of nitrogen oxides by 2 million to 4 million tons, over the next decade. The final legislation allowed trading only in sulphur dioxide.

Whereas environmentalists saw the old trading scheme as a way to prop up a law that had failed, the new cap is intended to be a guarantee that, whatever else happens, emissions will fall for good. The cap was also designed to prevent politicians from arguing about overall emission totals. Instead, they were able to argue over how that total should be shared out. Dan Dudek of the EDF says gleefully that the cap ensures that politicians would concentrate on the task they were best at: "that of passing out the pork." The process will be devalued if some polluters cheat. So draconian penalties are a second vital feature. By 1993, power stations must fit pollution-monitoring equipment on all chimneys. Plants that emit more than their allowance are fined, at a rising rate and with no appeal, and must then cut by enough to compensate for past excess.

A constant worry about tradable permits is that a proper market may not develop. Only if polluters trade permits will pollution be reduced in the most cost-effective way. If they simply sit on them, trading will be no better than old-fashioned regulation. Indeed, if those that have been allocated permits buy up more to make sure that new entrants cannot enter the market and compete, the net effect may be even worse than that of standards.

In practice, American experience of tradable permits for air pollution has been that trading is thin. The staunchest advocates of permits blame this on restrictions on trading and on the opposition permit schemes have met from green lobbyists in the courts. But large polluters have sometimes refused to trade, thus effectively keeping out new firms.

Permit markets are most likely to thrive, like all markets, when there are plenty of traders. They work best, as do green taxes, where firms cannot simply pass on to consumers the entire cost of permits. In Eastern Europe, ingenious proposals to curb air pollution by introducing tradable permits run the risk of being thwarted if companies simply up the price of their power or products. In Britain, where two giant generators dominate the newly privatized electricity industry, it is equally hard to be sure that a proper market in permits could evolve.

To stop existing polluters from cornering the market in permits, the American clean air legislation insists that the government retain up to 5% of the permits and auction them off. That approach has another advantage: it will provide a public reference price. If a utility asks its regulator for permission to raise prices to pay for the installation of scrubbers, the regulator will be able to see at once whether that will cost the utility more than buying extra emission permits. Anyone in the business of installing pollution-control technology will be able to see how inexpensive that technology needs to be if it is to be worth installing rather than buying extra permits.

As governments have become increasingly interested in green taxes (although politicians find the idea harder to grasp), so they are starting to look at other uses for tradable permits. A few American schemes have tried to apply the concept to river pollution. Dutch economists have suggested trying to tackle the Netherlands' appalling difficulties in disposing of manure by setting up a manure bank: only farmers would be charged for their deposits rather than rewarded for them. Farmers would be able to trade the right to a heap of a certain size with each other. Britain has been considering a permit-trading scheme to solve the problem of overcapacity in its fishing fleet. Fishermen would be assigned a quota of fish, which they could sell to each other if they wanted to raise capital and leave fishing. Such schemes in Canada, Iceland, and New Zealand seem to have given fishermen more incentives to conserve stocks.

If tradable permits introduced under America's clean air legislation are a success, a whole new industry may grow up around them. They are already encouraging a new kind of trader. Under the older, less satisfactory bit of clean air legislation, most permit trades were put together one at a time by attorneys. After the new clean air bill came before Congress in 1990, other firms became interested. Successful pollution-permit trading will require unusual combinations of skills among brokers. John Palmisano, a former EPA official whose company AER*X was the only specialized broker dealing in permits under the original clean air legislation, employs engineers who have worked in regulatory agencies. Other companies are now putting together brokering skills, engineering expertise, and an understanding of environmental regulations, in the hope of benefiting from the new legislation. They will then approach companies, offering to cut their emissions and pay for it by selling their spare emission rights. "My best client is the finance manager," says Palmisano. "Not the pollution-control manager, who is probably an engineer with a strong not-invented-here attitude." He emphasizes the importance of making sure that no cheating takes place, for cheating devalues the permits. "I make sure that everything that goes through here is completely kosher," he says.

International Permit Trading

America is eager to extend the idea of tradable permits into a completely new field: that of international environmental agreements. In particular, it wants an international trading system for greenhouse gases as part of a deal to tackle global warming. Although they may be hard to apply internationally, tradable permits might be an ideal way of sharing environmental obligations among a limited number of countries. One obvious use might be in the EC. The community has set targets for air quality, including maximum allowable concentrations of particulates (gritty dust) and sulphur dioxide, that must be met by 1993. Pollution in Britain, and in many other parts of the EC, exceeds these levels. It is not easy to see how Britain can reach these targets, especially for sulphur dioxide, without restricting growth in the offending areas.

One option might be to introduce a system of permit trading, either within Britain or (better, because the market would be larger) among EC countries. Such a scheme, suggested by Scott Barrett of the London Business School, would allow new firms moving into an area to buy permits from existing firms. Because their technology was newer, they would produce more output from fewer permits. Expansion, instead of being thwarted by pollution controls, would become a mechanism for cleaning up.[4] Britain has already taken a modest step in this direction, by allowing electricity generators to offset reductions made in emissions from one plant against increases from another, to meet the EC directive for large combustion plants. But one generator cannot trade with another.

Within the EC such schemes have many other uses. They might be used to allow the community to meet the goals of the Large Combustion Plant Directive, adopted in November 1988. It insists on large cuts in sulphur dioxide and nitrogen oxides emitted by large combustion plants. Or they could allow the Community to phase out ozone-gobbling CFCs more cost-effectively (as America phased out lead in gas).

Deposit Refunds

A third kind of economic incentive to clean up may turn out to be the most popular of all, although—or perhaps because—it raises no revenue for governments. Deposit-refund schemes were originally introduced by companies as a way of retrieving drink bottles or other containers. As containers became cheaper and labor more expensive, companies abandoned the programs. Now governments, increasingly worried about the high costs of trash disposal, are exploring deposit schemes with new interest. Easily the most common use of deposit-refund schemes is to ensure the return of bottles. But deposit refunds have been used with a wide range of products. Thus since 1978, Norway has charged buyers a deposit on new cars. When the car reaches the end of its life, the deposit and something extra is refunded if the car is brought to an approved site. Over 90% of cars are properly disposed of.

Such schemes make good economic sense only if the costs they entail are less than the costs of disposing of waste in other ways that are equally environmentally friendly. The deposits that have to be charged to ensure adequate rates of return may be so large, or the costs of collection may be so high, that other methods of disposal are often more efficient.

Besides, even if consumers scrupulously return every container or used tire, the waste product does not vanish. It still has to be disposed of. A theme of the second half of this book is that waste will be easy to dispose of in environmentally friendly ways only if thought is given at the start of a product's life to its final destination.

The Limits to Markets

Different kinds of pollution require different solutions. It will be easiest to apply economic incentives where the causes of pollution are easy to pinpoint: a factory sewage outlet, for instance, rather than a culvert for rainwater from oily roads. It is easy to charge one factory for its muck; harder to devise a solution that discourages muck from accumulating on roads. It will be easier to use economic measures where a narrow range of readily measurable pollutants is involved. Factories may not mind paying a single charge to cover everything that leaves their chimneys; they will make more fuss if the charge rises steeply as a particular pollutant increases in concentration. The administrative nuisance of measuring the pollutant, hour by hour, may mean that the cost of such finely tuned measures exceeds their benefit.

Devising economic instruments will be hard where what matters is the ability of the environment to absorb a pollutant rather than the absolute amount emitted. It makes sense to discourage a factory from belching smoke over a crowded city; less sense to discourage one sited downwind or miles from habitation. This is a special problem with regard to water pollution: the total amount of dirt discharged into a river rarely matters as much as the extent to which it is diluted. In general a company can safely discharge more muck at high water than when a river is low and sluggish.

Most of these difficulties have to be solved whether pollution is dealt with by "command-and-control" or by cozier systems of regulation, or whether economic instruments are used. Regulations impose costs; they have distributional effects (poor people may not be able to buy a car if higher fuel-efficiency standards make cars more expensive); they harm competitiveness.

The greater flexibility sometimes claimed for regulations may be illusory: polluters may insist that all their competitors are treated equally. As the process of setting regulations becomes more open and more public, the more inflexible it is likely to become. This particularly applies in Britain, where there has traditionally been great resistance to setting quantitative standards for environmental quality, and where pollution control has tended to be a matter for quiet negotiating between companies and the pollution inspectorate. That will be changed, partly by the environmental protection legislation of 1990, which aims for a more distant relationship between inspectors and polluted; partly by that act's insistence on more public access to the way standards are set; and partly by the more quantitative approach of the EC Commission. As standards become more rigid, the arguments for economic incentives may appear more attractive.

Any set of standards will only be as good as its enforcement. Use of the market, through taxes, charges, or tradable permits, will work only if the market works. Eastern European countries, the dirtiest in Europe, have elaborate arrangements for regulating and penalizing polluters; yet the fines are uncollected. In Poland, a 1987 survey of pollution fees paid by 1,400 manufacturers found that, on average, they amounted to 0.6% of production costs.[5] Czechoslovakia, Hungary, and Poland also have effluent charges for water pollution, and in Poland, serious thought has been given to the use of tradable permits to reduce the country's appalling air pollution. Such schemes need a free market in order to work. It makes no sense to fine a firm when it cannot buy good antipollution equipment because that can only be imported and imports are restricted. Nor does it make much sense to charge an enterprise for pollution when it is a monopoly and can simply pass on the entire increase in costs to its customers. Countries with highly controlled markets will find it harder to use market-based incentives to tackle pollution.

In general, regulations and economic instruments are likely to be employed together, one reinforcing the other. This approach will be most justifiable where markets function worst. A prime example of the need to combine standard setting with economic instruments is energy efficiency, the subject of the next chapter.

5

Energy Efficiency

Using energy probably causes more environmental damage, one way or another, than any other peaceful human activity (except perhaps reproduction). Nuclear waste, acid rain, ground-level ozone are all ultimately environmental costs incurred in the course of using energy. Most dramatic and irreversible of all, global warming is likely to be the result of the buildup of carbon dioxide, methane, and nitrous oxide—all gases released when energy is used—in the atmosphere.

No commercially available form of energy comes free of environmental problems. Even hydroelectric schemes, while not releasing carbon dioxide, blight rivers, and were the first source of additional electricity to be banned in austere Sweden. Tidal power, endlessly renewable, mostly clean, involves destroying estuaries. Proposals for tidal barriers in Britain breed fury among bird lovers. So people have to decide which environmental threat is most dangerous and switch to forms of energy least likely to cause it. In the case of global warming, which heads the list for most environmentalists, the decision would mean switching from burning high-carbon fossil fuels to lower-carbon kinds: from coal to oil, and from oil to natural gas. Or it would mean shifting toward "renewables": hydropower, solar power, and, inevitably, nuclear power.

Of course, sources of energy that cause fewer environmental problems may well be developed commercially in future. Nuclear power stations may become smaller and safer. Burning hydrogen produces only air and water (and the potential for extremely unpredictable explosions). For the moment, however, the primary alternative to using lower-carbon fuels and "renewables" is to use less energy. In practice, all these courses are likely to be necessary. Most projections of world demand for energy forecast a sharp increase, largely in the developing countries, where energy use is still tiny by Western standards and where most of the expected doubling of world population will take place. By the end of the next century, people in today's poor countries may use twice (or maybe almost three times) more energy per person than they do today. How much more energy will depend on how much effort has been made to conserve energy.

The scale of savings urged by climatologists is immense. Simply to stop the concentration of carbon dioxide in the atmosphere from increasing further—never mind reducing it—means making enormous reductions in the present use of fossil fuels. Calculations by William Emanuel of Oak Ridge National Laboratory in the United States suggest that today's output of 6 billion tons of carbon dioxide a year (or its equivalent from other greenhouse gases) would have to fall to about 1 billion tons a year, and stay there, to stabilize the quantity of atmospheric greenhouse gases.[1]

How can energy conservation best be encouraged? First, technology advances usually bring conservation in their wake. As economies develop, their demand for energy, relative to GNP, tends to rise rapidly and then to peak, as the basic infrastructure is completed. Basic industries, which convert raw materials into semimanufactures, are the largest energy guzzlers: as an economy gobbles less steel, cement, bricks, and so on, it comes to need less energy to produce the same volume of new wealth. It shifts from bulk to bites. An aluminum smelter spends $1.20 on energy for every dollar spent on wages and capital; a computer manufacturer, only 1.5 cents.[2] As Figure 5.1 shows, the ratio of energy demand to real GDP has been falling in Britain since 1880 and since the early years of this century in most other industrial countries. Between 1973 and the end of the 1980s, the amount of energy used in the OECD countries to produce a unit of output fell by a fifth.

The continuing savings in industrial countries came from two sources. First, there were changes in the industrial structure: for example, steel plants closed down, partly because the domestic growth of steel demand declined and partly because other, poorer countries built up steel industries of their own. Second and more important, new and more energy-efficient technologies developed. Making steel by the open-hearth method used roughly twice as much energy as the basic oxygen conversion process that began to replace it in the 1960s; the fuel consumption of the average German car has dropped by a quarter since the mid-1970s. As almost all technological innovation comes from the OECD countries, such changes gradually influence global energy consumption.

More energy efficiency is clearly possible. One study, by the International Energy Agency in 1987, reckoned that known technologies could economically cut energy demand by at least a quarter by the end of the century, compared with the demand

Figure 5.1 Primary Energy Consumption Relative to Real GDP (tons of oil equivalent per $000)

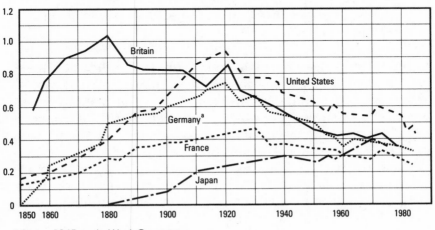

[a] Since 1945, only West Germany
Source: Jean-Maria Martin. *Revue de L'Energie.* No. 415, November 1989.

that present levels of efficiency implied.[3] Some are even more optimistic. Amory Lovins thinks that cost-effective savings of 75% could be achieved in the United States by the complete adoption of the most advanced technologies, including insulating all houses, and by near-perfect maintenance. Improbable: but a study by the WRI suggested that OECD energy consumption could be halved over the course of 30 years.[4] If equally advanced technologies were employed in developing countries, their use of energy might be restrained enough for them to achieve the living standards of present-day Western Europe, while global energy use increased by only 10% above current levels.

Energy conservation makes economic sense as well as environmental sense. At the margin, it is almost always cheaper to save an additional kilowatt than to generate one. No country uses energy in the most efficient way. Investing in conservation almost invariably yields a higher rate of return than building new power stations. Some studies have driven home this point, including one carried out in Canada using 1984 prices, when oil was $22 a barrel. The Canadian study found that it would cost only $13 to save the equivalent of a barrel of oil by cutting average domestic energy use by 30%. To make the same sort of savings by increasing the efficiency of gas furnaces would cost $8 to $10. To bring on stream the least expensive source of new energy, offshore oil, would cost $30 a barrel. Clearly a new gas furnace would be a better buy than a nuclear power plant ($60 for the equivalent of a barrel of oil).

Conservation may also make sense from other points of view. It can be undertaken in small chunks, unlike building additional generating capacity. The technology is often relatively simple— as simple as mending leaks in gas mains or insulating houses. No tiresome planning permission is needed, no furious residents demonstrate. And the technology is, generally speaking, safe. Conserving energy never caused a Chernobyl.

The most powerful argument, however, is that of improving economic efficiency. In some countries the evidence of inefficiency is glaring. Capital going into energy production might more fruitfully be steered into other parts of the economy. Thus Lovins points out that if the United States could reach Japanese levels of energy efficiency, which would imply halving the amount of energy it uses to produce each unit of GNP, it would save roughly $300 billion a year, or roughly the equivalent of the 1990 military budget. If the investment used to expand the supply could be shifted from electricity to other industries, what might it not do for America's competitive advantage?

Inefficiency is most striking in the third world and in the countries of Eastern Europe, the Soviet Union, and China. A study for the World Bank points out that "It is not unusual to find from one-quarter to one-third of public resources available for investment going solely to electric power. And it is still inadequate."[5] China, easily the largest energy consumer (and producer) in the third world, also wastes more energy than any other country. In 1982, China used twice as much energy to produce a unit of GNP as the Soviet Union, and four times as much as Japan.[6] Chinese steel mills use up to twice as much electricity to make a ton of steel as do mills in the OECD countries.

China's energy intensity has been exacerbated by a long-term policy of pegging energy prices well below world market levels. That policy sprang from an emphasis on developing heavy industry. By 1980, industry accounted for almost two-thirds of all energy use. The same policies, pursued in the Soviet Union and Eastern Europe, have produced similar results. The erstwhile Soviet Union is (after the United States) the world's second largest energy consumer—but uses that energy to produce far less wealth. In Hungary, 70% of energy is used to process raw materials that provide only 15% of GDP.[7] In Poland, which until the start of 1990 priced electricity at a quarter of the world market level, coal production imposes heavy burdens on the economy. It swallows one-fifth of all the steel used in the country for structural supports and almost a tenth of electricity output. A study by the World Bank pointed out that Poland could turn a prospective coal deficit in 1995 into a surplus by achieving modern European standards of energy efficiency and still enjoy moderate economic growth.[8]

Saving energy would leave all these countries better off, certainly compared with investing in new supplies and at times in absolute terms. Why are not such investments made? Part of the answer lies in energy prices: if they are low, investments in conservation may look better than investments in bringing new

energy supplies on stream, but they may look unattractive compared with other demands on capital. Another part of the answer
lies in the inadequate way the energy market works. Many
barriers, some institutional, some organizational, discourage
countries from investing in energy conservation.

One reason that energy is used inefficiently is that it is underpriced. If energy is inexpensive, people are more likely to waste
it than if its price reflects its true cost—to the economy as well
as to the environment. True, a change in energy prices takes time
to influence behavior. This is not surprising. If people can switch
from one activity to a similar one, prices are likely to have a rapid
and important influence. One strong argument for a carbon tax,
which would tax energy on its carbon content, is that it would
encourage a gradual shift along the spectrum from coal to oil,
and oil to natural gas, and natural gas to renewables. Where
energy prices are raised in unison, no such adaptation can take
place. Because there is no close substitute for energy, change will
be slower and more modest.

This is a common dilemma in environmental policy. When
people can, say, switch from leaded to unleaded gas, pricing
policy will work well. Often, though, what is at stake is encouraging people to find ways of economizing on a scarce environmental resource: using less water or throwing away less rubbish.
When substitutes are hard to find, people will change their
behavior more reluctantly and with more difficulty. The change
will be least painful if it is phased in slowly—if people are
warned that prices will rise and governments stick to their guns.

Raising energy prices quite clearly hastens investment in efficiency. Consider two bits of evidence. First, a study of the impact
of energy subsidies by Mark Kosmo found close links between
energy prices and the rate of change in commercial energy efci-
ency.[9] The relative energy efficiency of American and European
industry bears this out. Figures from the International Energy
Agency show that energy consumption per dollar of value-
added in the United States in 1985 was almost three times as
high as in Japan and almost twice as high as in Germany. Energy
prices in Japan and Germany have long been well above those
paid by American firms. Sometimes, such differences show up
in an industry's technology: American cement production is

about twice as energy-intensive per ton as German production, because the "wet kilning" process typically used in America (but not Germany) involves lavish use of power.

Second, look at the way energy demand in industrial countries responded to the price rises of the mid-1970s. Kosmo draws particular attention to the contrast between the OECD countries and Eastern Europe in the years 1973 to 1981. In the OECD, real energy prices increased by 82%, while in Eastern Europe they remained virtually constant. As a result, energy efficiency improved in the OECD: in the United States, energy efficiency, which had remained almost constant from 1952 to 1972, improved by 32% over the following decade. In Eastern Europe, it hardly altered.

When the oil price collapsed in 1986, investment in energy efficiency declined as well. By the time Saddam Hussein marched into Kuwait in August 1990, real energy prices (see Figure 5.2) in some countries were at their lowest level ever. Not surprisingly, conservation was no longer a priority either for companies or for individuals. A plateau had been reached. A review of the efficiency of domestic appliances in the main industrial countries by a team from the Lawrence Berkeley Laboratory in California has found that conservation stagnated in the mid-1980s. Consumers no longer worried about the fuel efficiency of cars or refrigerators (see Figure 5.3). Most manufacturers had already built in all the simpler (i.e., cheaper) energy-saving devices. More sophisticated technology would take longer to pay for itself. Indeed, in Japan, where the strong yen caused oil prices to fall particularly dramatically, there was a marked trend toward less efficient cars. In 1988, the average new car in the Japanese fleet did only 27.3 miles per gallon, compared with 30.5 in 1982. New Japanese cars were actually less fuel-efficient than new American cars, which, thanks to tough fuel-efficiency standards, managed 28 miles to the gallon in 1990.

To kick-start investment in energy efficiency means higher real energy prices. That means, first, stripping out the many ways in which governments subsidize energy consumption. As I have argued, energy is one of the natural resources most likely to be deliberately underpriced. At the least, each extra unit of energy sold fully reflects the cost of producing it. The industrial coun-

Figure 5.2

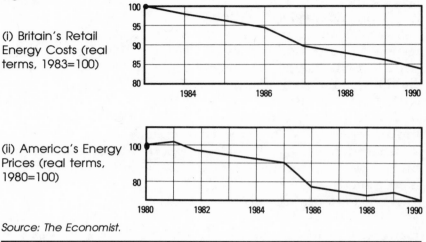

(i) Britain's Retail Energy Costs (real terms, 1983=100)

(ii) America's Energy Prices (real terms, 1980=100)

Source: The Economist.

Figure 5.3 Energy Intensity^a and Fuel Consumption

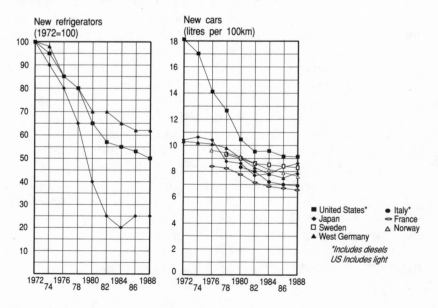

^{a}Energy consumption divided by volume of refrigerator
Source: International Energy Studies.

tries might ask themselves whether that cost ought properly to include a chunk of the defense budget. The troops in Saudi Arabia in 1990–1991 were sent (in the nice phrase of Bill Robinson, erstwhile director of the London Institute for Fiscal Studies) to retrieve "an oil well dressed up as a nation."

Tax Energy

The arguments for taxing energy more heavily are formidable. Sheer self-interest may help to push governments in that direction. Voters are already used to being taxed on their energy consumption. Now they may be persuaded that energy taxes are a virtuous way for governments to make money. Besides, energy offers an immense tax base. A tax adding a mere 1% to the price of coal would raise about $350 million a year for the EC, or $2.5 billion if levied globally. Yet its impact on prices would be minute: smaller, indeed, than the variations in spot coal prices from week to week.[10] In the United States, where taxes on energy use are tiny in comparison with other industrial countries, a tax on the carbon content of coal, oil, and gas would raise enough revenue to wipe out much of the budget deficit and simultaneously restrain energy consumption. Calculations by the Council of Economic Advisers early in 1990 suggested that a tax of roughly $28 per ton of carbon might raise $163 billion over five years and stabilize America's output of greenhouse gases in the 1990s. Others have argued that this goal would require even higher taxes—and thus yield even more revenue.

Why are governments reluctant to tax energy more? Most of the arguments rehearsed earlier apply. Energy taxes are seen as inflationary; they are thought to harm the poor more than the rich; they are regarded as harmful to a country's competitive position abroad, especially if they are adopted by one country in isolation. These arguments assume that an energy tax is not seen as a substitute for some other tax—on spending, payrolls, or corporate profits—whose effects would be even more harmful. The impact of energy taxes will depend essentially on how the revenue is used. The inflationary impact can be offset by using the revenue to reduce other taxes on spending. It can also be reduced if governments announce, well in advance, plans to make sure that real energy prices go up and stay up. If investors confidently expect real energy prices to be permanently increased, they will bring forward investments to reduce energy bills. To protect the poor, whose energy bills tend to be lowest in absolute terms but highest in relation to their incomes, some of the yield from energy taxes can be steered into welfare benefits or into a flat-rate energy allowance. And the impact on competition, which in any case will be concentrated on the most energy-intensive industries, can be partly offset if higher government revenues allow lower interest rates or reductions in other corporate taxes.

What of the impact of higher energy taxes on economic growth? Policymakers who recall the 1970s remember not just the improvement in energy efficiency, but the dire recession that followed the oil price rise. Did increased energy prices curb economic activity? Not necessarily. For one thing, it was the oil exporters, not importing governments, that drove up the oil price. The result was a transfer of income from oil consumers in importing countries to oil producers. But, although oil consumers tended to spend all but a small fraction of their incomes, oil exporters, on the whole, did not. The undeveloped countries of the Middle East, from where most oil exports came, simply put most of their vast additional wealth in the bank. In time, they found ways to spend it. At first, however, world savings shot up—and a recession ensued.

Moreover, sudden change is always likely to disrupt economic activity. If the oil price rise of the mid-1970s had been announced in advance and phased in over two decades, both consumers and producers would have had time to adapt. The impact on growth would have been negligible. It might even have been positive.

For if it is true that energy is wasted, then policies that encourage it to be properly priced will make economies more efficient. Higher energy taxes would, in time, leave America with more cash to invest in other industries; cut the state borrowing programs of most third world countries; and encourage the countries of the old Communist block to move out of unprofitable heavy industries and into more promising light manufacturing and services. If higher energy taxes encourage people to invest in technologies that save resources, they will make an economy work more efficiently. Properly designed and carefully applied, they could often have that effect.

Barriers to Conservation

If low energy prices were the whole of the problem, the solution would clearly have lain in energy taxes. They aren't, and it doesn't. Several barriers seem to prevent the market from making the rational decision to invest more in conserving energy than in developing new supplies. Such barriers are not a reason to avoid imposed increases in energy prices. But the more they can be knocked down, the smaller will be the price increases needed to achieve a given level of energy saving.

Energy users seem to need to earn much higher rates of return to induce them to make investments in conservation than do producers of energy to encourage them to invest in supply. If the market worked perfectly, both would seek the same return. Companies would step in and look for ways to arbitrage between them until their rates of return moved into line. If a country's energy-producing capacity were fully used, then users would gain as much from cutting their demands as producers would gain from increasing supply. But this does not happen.

Large investments in new energy supplies—opening a mine, for instance, or building a power station—typically need to show a real return of 5% to 10%. By contrast, companies tend to look for paybacks on energy-saving investments of one to three years, implying a much higher 30% internal rate of return. Work at Britain's Science Policy Research Unit found that in the early 1980s, companies grappling with recession sought payback periods that were even shorter. Obsessed with rapid returns, many companies are reluctant to make even obvious investments. Under a British scheme to coax firms to save energy in the early 1980s, the average age of boilers replaced was 41 years. Several were more than 70 years old. When the scheme began, the average payback period was expected to be 3.7 years. Rising fuel prices cut the actual payback to two years. By any standard, that was a remarkably good return. Private individuals also apply high discount rates to investment in energy efficiency. One American review of the market for space and water heaters, refrigerators, and freezers found that people were willing to pay more for energy efficiency only if the extra cost were covered by savings within less than three years. Some expected paybacks within a few months, implying a nonsensical discount rate of up to 800%.

Consumers are not wholly irrational. The true costs of investing in energy efficiency, for both companies and individuals, may be higher than they seem. Simply finding out how best to save energy is a cost in its own right, and often a high one. It may be difficult (impossible in Britain, where labeling is sparse) to find out which domestic appliance is most energy efficient, or what is the likely return on insulating a loft or replacing a boiler. In the case of transport and domestic uses of energy, a few basic solutions, widely applied, are sufficient to improve efficiency. The solutions for industry may need to be developed case by case. This uses up scarce managerial time. When fuel bills are a relatively small part of total costs, managers may simply not bother. They may prefer to concentrate on developing new markets and products, rather than retrenching in such a complicated and demanding way.

Companies and individuals alike may hesitate to replace old equipment with new simply because the new will save energy. The new equipment may have lower running costs over its lifetime than the old, but its initial cost may be higher (though, maddeningly for energy conservation, much less than the cost of providing new power supplies). An individual may regard the replacement of a boiler or air-conditioning system in a similar light. The individuals who stand to gain most from energy conservation are often the poorest. They are precisely the people least able to afford the capital cost of a new refrigerator or better insulation. A study by Jerry Hausman in 1979 found that Americans with incomes of $6,000 a year had implied discount rates of 89% on purchases of energy-efficient durable goods, while those whose incomes were $50,000 a year had discount rates of only 5%.[11]

Many other barriers may skew the market. For instance, insulating a commercial building is a cost that falls on the landlord; the returns, in the form of a lower electricity bill, accrue to the tenant. The landlord may find it hard to recoup the cost of the investment by raising the rent. Not surprisingly, private individuals are more likely to pay for energy efficiency if they own their own homes than if they rent them. Although the tenant may enjoy a lower fuel bill, some of the value of insulation will eventually go to the landlord. Within the public sector, cuts in spending on current budget which a school or hospital achieves by cutting its fuel bills will have counterparts in an increase in its capital spending. But although spending more on capital account may force it to cut back on other investments, the benefit to the current account may be taken by the government.

Tariff structures may also hide the gains from energy saving, from producers as well as consumers. Companies may be charged less, the more power they buy. Individuals may pay a standing charge and a variable tariff to cover operating costs. If they reduce consumption, they still pay the same standing charge, even if the effect is to reduce peak demand, and so the need for extra investment in power supplies. For example, Britain's regional electricity companies, privatized in 1991, make their primary profits from selling extra units of electricity; this gives them no incentive whatever to reduce customers' consumption. Worse, the cost of building new power stations, to supply the extra demand they generate, will fall first on the separately privatized generating companies.

Finally, the business of supplying power is normally carried out by entities that are state-owned or at least state-supported. Their investments may therefore appear to be risk-free. In any case, they are likely to have access to much less expensive capital than consumers of power. This will artificially raise the rate of return they can earn by building new power stations, relative to the return that the consumer can expect on investments in energy efficiency.

Proposed Solutions

Making the energy market work better means finding ways to remove as many of these barriers as possible. Probably the easiest to dismantle is the information barrier. Information is inexpensive and easy for governments to provide; but it may be difficult for the ordinary company and its busy managers to acquire without specialist help. Thanks to green consumerism, the manufacturers of insulating materials and energy-efficient domestic appliances may see it as in their interest to provide better information voluntarily. In America and Britain, some home builders are taking part in schemes to certify that a new house meets a certain minimum level of energy efficiency. This gives an incentive to buyers to purchase, and to builders to construct, more energy-efficient homes.

The imperfections of the market are also often taken as a reason for going further and setting standards: for the fuel efficiency of cars, for the insulation of new buildings, for the energy consumption of domestic appliances. Some California cities have recently tackled the problem of applying higher standards to existing products by insisting that rental dwellings and commercial buildings must be insulated to certain minimum standards before the title can be transferred. The weakness of standards has been discussed: they may, by raising the price of new products, actually discourage investment in new and more efficient technologies; and they may dictate solutions instead of encouraging companies to develop them.

One way to make standards work more flexibly, suggested by the Environmental Defense Fund, might be to give companies tradable efficiency credits. A manufacturer whose average refrigerator was more energy-efficient than an official benchmark, set in terms of energy use over the lifetime of an average machine, would get credits, while a manufacturer whose average was below the benchmark would have to buy them. That would leave an individual manufacturer free to make some refrigerators of below-average efficiency and others of a higher standard.

Michael Grubb suggested another ingenious option: to tax less energy-efficient products and use the revenue to pay a subsidy on more efficient ones.[12] The size of the transfer between less efficient and more efficient products would be calculated partly to reflect the difference in the payback requirements of energy producers and consumers. The effect of the plan would be to cut the price of products that were expensive to buy and inexpensive to run, and to increase the prices of those that were inexpensive to buy but used lots of energy.

Some proposals also draw on the idea of penalizing the energy-extravagant to benefit the energy-efficient. A scheme proposed in (but not passed by) the Massachusetts legislature in 1990 would have set revenue-neutral "feebates" for commercial buildings of 50,000 square feet or more. Buildings designed to use less electricity than average would get a rebate; those that tended to use more than average would pay a stiff fee for their electricity connection. Such a proposal could potentially make an enormous profit for builders of efficient buildings.

Other schemes, adopted primarily in the United States, try to bridge the gap between the payback periods demanded by consumers and producers by influencing the behavior of energy producers. The 1979 Public Utilities Regulation and Pricing Act (PURPA) declared that utilities could not automatically pass on the costs of building new power plants. They had to demonstrate to the local regulatory commission that new plants were the "least-cost" option for meeting peak demand. Some regulators have decided that options for reducing peak electricity demand must be considered side by side with options for increasing supply.

The effects of PURPA have been reinforced by the difficulties of building new power stations in the United States. When a utility is operating at full capacity, it may indeed make more sense to look for ways to shave the peak off demand, rather than go to the trouble and expense of building a new plant. As a result, American utilities have become interested in finding ways to persuade their customers to use less electricity. More than 60 utilities, serving almost half of all Americans, now have programs to encourage sales of devices for saving electricity such as energy-efficient light bulbs. Most pay rebates to buyers, but some give a subsidy to dealers, to encourage sales.

To be truly attractive, such schemes need to find ways to pay utilities more the more they reduce demand for their product. That perverse idea can be achieved only by increasing the rate paid by those customers who do not invest in energy conservation, another example of taxing the polluters to subsidize the virtuous. To make it possible, state regulators have had to allow the profits of utilities to be uncoupled from their sales. That enabled utilities to be compensated for the revenue they would otherwise get from selling electricity, and also to keep part of the savings enjoyed by their customers.

Thanks to one such program, the New England Electric System plans, over the 20 years to 2010, to cut the demand for its product by one-third below the level it would otherwise reach, by investing in a variety of conservation measures on its customers' premises. In the mid-1980s, the company carried out energy audits of customers' buildings but left it to the customer to decide whether to carry out the work. It now offers to pay part or all of the cost of insulating buildings or installing high-efficiency light bulbs or cooling systems. What has brought it into the energy-conservation business in a big way is a change in the way state regulators allow it to calculate its prices. A first step was to allow the company to pass on some of the costs of cutting customers' electricity bills to its customers at large. That was moderately helpful but provided no incentive to do the work. In 1990, the rules changed. Not only can it pass on, through higher electricity prices for all customers, the cost of making such investments; its rates also guarantee it a proportion of the savings made by its customers. The concept of "shared savings" has made it more profitable for the company to invest in energy conservation by its customers than to build new generating plant. "We add the cost of conservation into the rates in the year we spend the money," says New England's chief executive John Rowe. The principle is that today's electricity prices should reflect future environmental costs. The practical consequence has been to offset marginally the depressing effect on energy conservation of the fall in real energy prices in the late 1980s.

The size of the energy-conservation program is still quite small: the company spends 4% of its $65 million revenues on it, which is large in proportionate terms but small compared with what some utilities in California spend. But by the end of 1991, New England Electric expected to have saved over 300 megawatts in five years through energy conservation. Apart from shared savings, the company benefits in two other ways: from a good press, vital in conservationist New England, and from avoiding the burden of building new plant. That burden is not just one of debt; building a new plant means fighting with green community groups who do not want a power station in their back yards and fighting with regulators for a rate increase to cover the costs. New England Electric has not built a new plant since the early 1970s; by the late 1980s capacity was becoming tight. Shared savings, coupled with buying power from outside suppliers, have relieved the pressure.

America's utilities are far more regulated than most industries. The creation of financial incentives for utilities like New England Electric to invest in energy conservation is entirely dependent on the regulators. In other American states, regulators are finding similar ways of giving utilities an interest in energy conservation. In 1990, California and New York were considering shared savings. Wisconsin was the first state to give utilities a way to capitalize investments in conservation in their rate base, earning 2% more on investment in conservation than in new supply.

As such conservation programs blossom, utilities may see energy saving as a marketable concept, as marketable as electricity or gas. This is the ideal of Lovins, who has invented the concept of the "negawatt," meaning electricity savings. "One can think of a 14-watt replacement for a 75-watt lamp, for example, as a 61-negawatt power plant."[13] Lovins views with excitement the emergence of a market in negawatts. In at least eight American states, utilities that want a certain number of negawatts put them out for bid and see what customers are willing to provide or save at what price.

One man who has turned this approach into a business is Angus King. In 1988, he worked for a firm building small generating stations and selling electricity to utilities. Declining power prices made the business increasingly unprofitable. "For 9 cents a kilowatt hour, you can build a hydro-station," he discovered. "For 5 cents you can't build much of anything, but you can change light fixtures." So in 1989, his company, Northeast Energy Management, sold 48 million kilowatt hours of electricity to the Central Maine Power company, about a third of the growth in that utility's industrial and commercial load for the year. But King did so by contracting to get the power company's customers to cut their electricity use, rather than by building new power stations. His company offered to pay an industrial user about two-thirds of the cost of installing more efficient equipment. The user met the rest of the cost, and kept all the resulting savings on its electricity bill. For the user, the payback period on energy-saving investments was thus cut from about five years to 18 months. In 1989, King was being paid by the power company the same rate per kilowatt that he would have been paid for generating new electricity.

The pressure on power companies to find ways of conserving energy will increase as the costs and difficulties of building new power stations increase. Third world countries will find it harder to borrow the money as international aid organizations worry about the environmental effects of ever-greater energy supplies. First world utilities will be faced with increasing hostility to building new plants. Local people, anxious not to have a potential polluter as a neighbor, will join the greens to insist that there are less expensive ways of meeting demands for power. Already, that lobby has helped to mothball Britain's program for building nuclear power stations. For governments, and for many in the power industry, the shift of attitude will be painful. It has been easy to think of energy consumption, like GNP, as a mark of wealth, a measure of development. Third world countries need only look at Poland to see where that philosophy leads. It will be important to think in terms of producing energy services, rather than raw energy: warmed homes, working machinery, and mobile cars. Watts and gallons give no indication of warmth or mileage, but it is the latter that matters to consumers.

Conservation is more complicated than supplying new power. It involves many small investments rather than a few giant ones. That is why it is ultimately important to find ways of releasing the force of the market. Higher prices alone will not achieve that, although low prices will make sure the market stays asleep. Promoting energy conservation, however, is essentially an organizational problem. It needs organizational ingenuity to give people like King a useful role. More can be done to encourage conservation in the design of a utility's tariff structure than in the design of car engines or boilers.

6

Conservation

Extinction is a chilling word. It is the ultimate in irreversible environmental damage. Technological ingenuity may clean dirty rivers; with changes in human behavior, global warming may even be reversed. But the elephant or the whale, once gone, will be gone forever. No miracle of genetic engineering is likely to recreate them, any more than the pterodactyl or the dodo. After years of arguing for conservation for its own sake, some environmentalists have changed their tune. They realize that the prospects for conserving species and wild lands are better if people can be persuaded that conservation can pay. However hard economists struggle to ascribe option, bequest, or other values to nature, people are more likely to take conservation seriously if they see that failure to do so will cost them real money and that success will bring real rewards. In particular, local people will support conservation only if they can see that it will increase their incomes to do so.

This change has been prompted by desperation born of the realization that species are vanishing at an unprecedented and accelerating rate. Calculating the pace of extinction is complicated by the difficulty of working out how much there is to be lost in the first place. Informed guesses at the number of species on earth, from monkeys to mosquitoes and from mackerel to mosses, range from 5 million to 30 million. Of these, only 1.4 million have even been named and described. Many of those that are vanishing have not yet been discovered by man. A survey of 19 trees of the same species in a forest in Panama found 950 species of beetles, more than three-quarters of which had never met a scientist before. That rather confirms the view of J.B.S. Haldane, the distinguished biologist who, when a theologian asked him what his studies revealed about the nature of God, replied that He appeared to have an inordinate fondness for beetles.

This biological wealth is now disappearing faster than ever before. Some reckon that 5% to 15% of all species will go between 1990 and 2020. Indeed, the number may be larger still if the destruction of tropical rain forests continues at the breakneck speed of the late 1980s. In tropical rain forests live at least half—perhaps three-quarters—of all the species that creep or run, swim or fly, including 90% of the earth's insects. The Amazon forest alone contains one-fifth of all the bird species in the world, and in its rivers swim at least eight times as many fish as in the Mississippi and its tributaries. A small area of Malaysian jungle may contain more than 800 species of woody plants, about as many as live in the whole of North America. That is why saving the remaining tropical rain forests has become the top priority of many conservationists.

Earth's diversity of life increases enormously from the poles to the equator, with the result that nature is most varied in the very countries where human numbers are growing fastest and the pressure on land is greatest. The causes of extinction have altered as the human population has swollen. In the past, the introduction of new species and excessive exploitation were as important a cause of extinction as the loss of habitat. When people settle new places, they bring with them cats and rats, which catch creatures unused to predators; they bring pigs and goats, which eat plants previously ungrazed. Hunters des-patched the dodo and almost killed off the sea otter. Animal and human predators are still great exterminators: one-fifth of all vertebrate species are currently threatened by new arrivals; one-third by overexploitation.[1]

But loss of habitat has now become far and away the biggest threat. One sign is the way species are now being extinguished on mainlands. Three-quarters of the extinctions of birds and mammals between 1600 and 1950 were of island-dwelling species. Islands, where creatures can evolve and diversify in isolation, are especially rich in species not found elsewhere. Now, however, two-thirds of species known to be at risk are found on mainlands, especially in tropical forests.[2] The great danger is to creatures that need a large range: big cats, bears, and some tropical trees. Species that are found only in small areas or that are highly choosy about where they live are also at risk when their territory disappears. Often the survival of one species depends on that of several others. As a result, conservationists have shifted their attention from preserving individual species (such as the panda) to trying to save entire "eco-systems," with their intricate networks of insects, plants, birds, and animals.

But why save species in the first place? We might miss the panda, but it has no obvious economic function. Nor do the beetles that vanish when trees disappear. Lots of people sympathize with Ogden Nash's bewilderment:

> God in his wisdom made the fly
> And then forgot to tell us why.

Why, to take another example, would a scientist want to bring back the dodo? Like many wild creatures and plants, its value to mankind might be only as a curiosity. Humanity is no poorer, in harsh financial terms, for its passing. In fact, even the dodo had its value. Most of the Calvaria trees of Mauritius were at least 300 years old and seemed sure to die out. How to rescue the species? An ingenious botanist guessed that the trees' large, tough seeds had to pass through the gizzard of a big bird to germinate. Force-fed turkeys filled the dodo's ancient role and saved the trees. Thus does the fate of one species often determine the fate of many others, linked in barely perceptible ways and complex eco-systems.

Conservationists turned economists argue that losses of biological diversity are economic losses, sometimes in a rather vague sense but sometimes measurable in real or potential reductions in people's cash incomes. Arguments like that tend to carry more weight with governments in poverty-stricken but species-rich countries than ethical exhortations to conserve for the sake of conservation.

In many ways, nature's benefits are valuable not only to present generations but also to those as yet unborn. Extinction shuts doors. Plants that might have contained valuable drugs vanish unexamined; animals that might have been domesticated will never appear on the menu. The dodo, fat and flightless, might have made a better Christmas lunch than the turkey. In losing the dodo, we lost forever the option to discover.

The Economics of Extinction

In the days of the dinosaur, extinction was an act of God. Now, it is generally an act of mankind. Understanding the economic forces that cause the loss of species is an essential first step in deciding what to do about it. Hunting or fishing a species need not necessarily drive it out of existence. Although extinction can be caused by overharvesting, nature's renewable resources can be increased as well as decreased. However, no species (not even human beings) can increase to levels greater than the carrying capacity of the forest or ocean in which it lives. Human beings can harvest species because they can increase, and can continue to harvest them indefinitely. As long, that is, as human beings do not become too greedy. A plantation of trees or a herd of deer reaches a point at which the harvest it yields is the largest that can be sustainably produced. That will not necessarily be the point at which the owner of the plantation or the herd harvests it: that will depend also on the costs of culling. For trees of a commonplace variety growing a great distance from the nearest road, those costs might be so high that the plantation would be left to grow beyond the point at which the yield was the largest that could be sustainably reaped; for deer commanding a high market price and grazing next to an abattoir, culling rates might be higher than the maximum sustainable yield—though not necessarily high enough to wipe out the herd. The yield, in other words, might still be sustainable, even if it were not the maximum.

Such logic is fine for natural resources that have a single owner whose rights of ownership are clearly defined and easy to enforce. But cut a hole in the fence surrounding those deer, or graze them on common land, and all the problems of easy access and common ownership start to emerge. Just as a product that makes a high profit attracts new entrants eager for a bit of the market, so a valuable natural resource can attract poachers. Once that happens, the danger of extinction increases enormously. It does not become a certainty. That will happen only if harvesting is costless—conversely, if the poachers risk going to prison, the deer are more likely to survive—or if harvesting is persistently above the natural rate of regeneration.

The second condition is more likely to exist if a resource takes a long time to be replenished. If the trees in the plantation were not lodgepole pine but slow-growing mahogany, the owner would be moved by all the unenvironmental logic of discount rates. The way to maximize profits might well be to chop down the whole lot and replace them with fast-growing eucalyptus. How do these conditions apply to vanishing species? Many can be "harvested" extremely inexpensively.

The elephant is a good example. Before most countries agreed to ban imports of ivory in 1989, four-fifths of the world's traded ivory came from poaching. Moreover, poachers have extremely high discount rates: they have little desire to curb their killing to stop a species from being wiped out. This is even more likely to be true if the poachers are poor and their quarry is valuable. Sometimes a species may become extinct not because it is so valuable but because it appears to have no value at all (like rain forest beetles). Then, a habitat may be destroyed because it is worth something in its own right (as when a forest is cleared); if the forest contained something worth harvesting, it might stand a better chance of protection. With its habitat gone, the species goes too.

The threat of extinction may be greatest for places or crops that have no clear owner. Elephants in the wild belong to no one; nor do whales. The ownership of tropical rain forests, where species extinction is fastest, is unclear. Where ownership is vested in the government, the effect may be to speed up destruction: no individual or group of people has clear responsibility for conservation. When ownership rights are weakly enforced, those who are able to pay most are those who exploit the resource, not those who value it most. That is why conservation, like so many environmental issues, has strong undertones of social justice. Conservationists need to keep such points in mind when trying to slow down extinction. Conservation is a sort of investment: and like all investments, it carries costs as well as benefits.

Conservation, for those who actually undertake it, is a matter of setting benefits against costs. If the benefits, as perceived by those who do the conserving, are smaller than the costs, then species will continue to vanish. In theory, the benefits may look promising: the countries with the greatest natural wealth are frequently the poorest, their people struggling to survive on subsistence agriculture. Surely it should be possible to live off all those valuable natural resources? In reality, the problems are often immense.

Some of the problems are created by governments. Many countries offer subsidies, set prices, or give tax relief in ways that positively encourage the destruction of a country's natural heritage. But even without perverse government intervention, it is often hard to devise effective incentives for conservation. One of the most important things that has dawned on conservationists in recent years is that although governments have enormous powers to encourage the destruction of natural resources, the cooperation of local people is usually essential to conserve them. As Jeffrey McNeely's excellent study *Economics and Biological Diversity* points out:

> Biological resources are often under threat because the responsibility for their management has been removed from the people who live closest to them, and instead transferred to government agencies located in distant capitals. But the costs of conservation still typically fall on the relatively few rural people who otherwise might have benefited most directly from exploiting these re-

sources. Worse, the rural people who live closest to the areas with greatest biological diversity are often among the most economically disadvantaged—the poorest of the poor.[3]

Sustainable Use

Schemes for encouraging conservation increasingly try to find sustainable uses that will bring in revenue for local people and give them a sense of ownership of the resource. When national parks are established, people may be driven off land that they have traditionally harvested, while park revenues go to the far-away government. In Zimbabwe's Matobo National Park, for instance, villagers are crammed on overgrazed lands around the park boundaries. Some villagers lived on the park lands until the mid-1950s, and their descendants still regard the land as theirs. Thatch is Zimbabwe's primary roofing material, but overgrazing has damaged supplies. In the park, thatching grass grows so well that managers periodically burn it off to prevent a dangerous fire. In 1962, the park authorities agreed to let local villagers cut an annual quota of thatch in the park in exchange for agreeing not to poach wildlife or graze cattle illegally. One bundle in ten goes to the park authorities (on the principle that people tend to undervalue "free" goods) and is used by them to thatch park buildings. A valuable crop of thatch has been cut by local people each year. Trespassing by cattle herders has been reduced and poaching minimized.

A more recent Zimbabwean experiment, in the dirt-poor northern district of Nyaminyami, began in 1988. Central government handed over to local people the right to manage the region's wildlife—and to keep the profits. In 1989, the district council hoped to make some Z$500,000 ($220,000) from sales of surplus game and licenses for safari hunting. Within five years, it is hoped that sum will double. Meat from culling impala is sold cheaply to villagers or used to rear crocodiles, whose skins are exported lucratively to France and whose tails are served in local restaurants.

There have also been attempts to bribe people more directly. The Wolong nature reserve in China is an important habitat of the giant panda. To reduce human pressure on the area, the government provided some $770,000 worth of food rations to 3,400 local people. In return, the people patrolled the reserve to feed starving pandas, built new free houses to resettle families from the most important parts of the reserve, and planted abandoned farmland with varieties of bamboo that pandas favor.

Returns from the African Elephant

Can the concept of sustainable use, rather than conservation, save two of the world's most endangered and precious natural resources, the large mammals and the tropical rain forests? Perhaps, though old-fashioned conservationists are skeptical. Take the example of the African elephant, whose numbers have been halved by poaching, falling from about 1.2 million in 1981 to just over 600,000 by 1989. In some countries (see Table 6.1) the decline has been even more appalling: Kenya's elephant population fell by two-thirds between 1981 and 1989, Zambia's and Tanzania's by almost three-quarters. The beasts have been killed primarily for their ivory. In the hope of stemming the slaughter, a decision was taken in October 1989 to ban trade in ivory. The richest of the final consumers of ivory—the United States, the EC, and Japan—all banned its import. Splendid, said conservationists. In the wake of the ban, the price of ivory plummeted and poaching fell sharply. The elephant, it seemed, might possibly have been saved. Since trade in the skins of wild cats, including leopards, was banned, their numbers have greatly revived. On the other hand, the black rhino was given the same protection in 1975, yet its numbers dropped from 500,000 to fewer than 40,000 by 1991.

Which fate awaits the elephant? The most convincing answer comes from a group of economists at the London Environmental Economics Centre (LEEC) in a study they carried out in 1988–1989 as part of the groundwork for the conference that eventually banned the ivory trade.[4] They argue powerfully that a ban may eventually speed up the disappearance of the elephant from the wild, because it destroys one of the main ways in which governments could, if they chose, earn back the costs they incur in conserving the species. They suggest that the ivory trade did not cause the elephant's decline. The key factor was the failure of African governments to use the world ivory market to their best advantage. A ban on the trade will not help, for two reasons. First, the initial effect will be to cause a sharp drop in ivory prices. That will encourage a new demand for ivory among potential importers previously priced out of the market such as South Korea, Taiwan, and African countries themselves. This trade will be unmonitored, because the new importers have not subscribed to the international convention that governs trade in endangered species.

Second, a ban destroys a possible incentive to preserve elephants. If elephants are to survive, they must be seen in Africa as an immensely valuable source of foreign exchange. The problem for the elephant is not that it lacks value but that it is too valuable, and that it is, in effect, available to anybody who wants to risk killing it.

Table 6.1 Estimated Elephant Numbers: Regions and Selected Countries

	1981	1989
Zaire	376,000	112,000
Central African Republic	31,000	23,000
Congo	10,800	42,000
Gabon	13,400	74,000
Central Africa total	**436,200**	**277,000**
Kenya	65,000	16,000
Tanzania	203,900	61,000
Sudan	133,700	22,000
East Africa total	**429,500**	**110,000**
Botswana	20,000	88,000
South Africa	8,000	7,800
Zambia	160,000	32,000
Zimbabwe	47,000	52,000
Southern Africa total	**309,000**	**204,000**
West Africa total	**17,600**	**19,000**
Africa total	**1,192,300**	**609,000**

Source: African Elephant and Rhino Specialist Group, Ivory Trade Review Group.

But conserving elephants is expensive. Even if the ivory trade were indeed to be stopped by the ban, elephants might continue to vanish. "If they are not killed for their ivory, they will be killed for the land they occupy," argue the LEEC economists. Conserving elephants not only means forgoing the use of the land on which they forage, but also spending hugely to prevent poachers. Zimbabwe reckons that it costs $200 per square km to protect wild elephants from illegal hunting. For Africa as a whole, an effective war against poachers might well cost $80 million to $100 million a year.

With a ban in place, only a few countries have an incentive to conserve, and they are the ones whose tourist trade has been built on showing wildlife to visitors. Elephants are one of the mainstays of the Kenyan tourist trade. Properly exploited, they might bring in even more than they do. A back-of-an-envelope survey of tourists in Kenya, by Gardner Brown of the University of Washington in Seattle, found that the average tourist was happy to pay a $100 surcharge to protect the elephant. Even allowing for exaggeration, that suggests Kenya's 1 million game-park tourists could bring in an extra $20 million a year in revenues, one-third as much as all Africa gets from killing the beasts.

The elephant's best hope of survival in other countries still lies mainly in its tusks. The aim should be to cull elephants at a sustainable rate and use the revenue to help pay for conservation. One intriguing study (see Table 6.2) in Botswana compared the value of managing elephant herds just for the enjoyment of tourists with the value if tourism is combined with elephant cropping. The cropping reduces yields from tourism by about 10% but leads to other gains, such as tanning elephant hides, ivory carving, and producing meat for crocodile farming. The extra benefits almost double the total economic value of a herd.

Even larger revenues may be raised by selling to hunters from rich countries the right to kill their own big game. The value of an elephant to a party of German sportsmen exceeds by a large margin its value to an ivory poacher. Zimbabwe has long found big-game hunting a lucrative use for its elephants. A group of European or American hunters stalking one of the 100 to 200 elephants a year that are allowed to be killed this way can easily spend $15,000 all told, some of it going to local people who work as guides and bearers. That is perhaps five times as much as those same people could make by poaching an elephant themselves. Some hunters argue that their very presence, armed to the teeth with guns and field glasses, is a deterrent to poachers. They are probably right.

Above all, local people need to see the elephant as a source of income. As the LEEC economists argue:

> The history of wildlife conservation efforts in Africa has been dominated by a universal approach of divorcing local communities from any control or rights of exploitation of their wildlife. Wildlife utilisation, except perhaps for tourism and limited safari hunting, has been discouraged, and any safari and tourist revenues have gone to the state, not to local communities.

Table 6.2 Economic Benefits of Different Elephant Management Options, Botswana ($1 = 1.8 pula)

Option	Net present value @ 6% (m pula, 1989)		
	after 5 years	after 10 years	after 15 years
1. Game viewing with no consumptive uses	34.7	98.1	160.6
2. Game viewing with elephant cropping	91.2	198.4	288.9
Difference (2-1)	56.5	100.3	128.3
Net benefits from consumptive uses[a]	60.0	110.1	144.4

[a]The difference between options 1 and 2 is only an approximate indicator of the net benefits from consumptive uses, as the introduction of elephant cropping reduces the benefits from game-viewing tourism by 10%. By allowing for this reduction, the net benefits from consumptive uses can be calculated.
Source: John Barnes, Department of Wildlife and Natural Parks, Botswana; quoted in Edward Barbier, Joanne Burgess, Timothy Swanson, David Pearce, *Elephants, Economics and Ivory* (London: Earthscan Publications, 1990).

The state's objective is to manage elephants and other wildlife for the benefit of the whole nation, whereas the local communities are denied access to protected areas and even to the right to hunt in areas neighbouring them. The incentives for the local population to engage in or assist in poaching increase, while their incentives to co-operate in reducing poaching or aiding conservation efforts decrease.

The best hope for conservation is to try to make sure that more of the gains from conservation go to local people. To achieve that, it is important to try to create clear ownership rights over elephants, preferably giving a big share in them to local communities. Until now, conservation efforts have cut links between local people and the wildlife they once hunted; restore some of those links, and hunting may return to sustainable levels. If local people are promised hard currency from the tusks of some of their elephants in the future, they have less incentive to kill them before they reach maturity and breed. Better still, if governments can turn potential poachers into effective gamekeepers, they save some of the cost of gamekeeping.

Because the African elephant is being driven to extinction by an international trade, its conservation needs an international solution. But with elephants, as with other wildlife valued by foreigners, there arises the question of sovereignty. If the world regards elephants as something whose preservation is important to the whole human race, then a conflict may arise between individual African countries and the world at large. Richer countries may say, in effect: "If elephants are a public good, we will help meet the costs of conserving them. If they are only your elephants, you cannot expect us to help."

Something like this emerged in the discussions over the ban on the ivory trade. Those countries that were most successful in conserving their herds—South Africa, Botswana, Malawi, and Zimbabwe—opposed a ban. They argued that their herds were not declining, and that one reason was that they were able to pay for conservation partly from the revenue they earned from exporting ivory and elephant hides from periodic culls. (Although conservationists argue that Zimbabwe makes most money from organizing hunts for rich tourists. The ban on the ivory trade does not stop the hunters from taking their trophies home.)

The LEEC economists vigorously support these countries that have made a large investment in conservation, and now see the return on it threatened. To raise the yield from elephants further requires not the banning of the ivory trade, but its control. African countries are lucky enough to have a product for which demand in some rich countries is highly inelastic: in other words, even if the price rises, people will continue to buy enthusiastically. Exporting countries could easily increase their take even without selling more ivory.

It would make sense for African governments to form a sort of ivory OPEC, a cartel that would closely control the offtake of ivory. They would gain a number of advantages. They could drive up the price, taking advantage of the inelastic demand. They could eliminate middlemen, who now take a large share of the profits of illegally exported ivory. They would have a new source of cash to help pay for conservation. And they would ensure that the elephant survived, to earn money for future generations. Such a cartel might stand a better chance than OPEC of surviving, because it is not in the long-term interest of the consumer of ivory to exterminate the elephant. On the contrary, consumers may be happy to ensure the survival of the elephant by helping to make controls on the ivory trade watertight if they receive a constant but restricted flow of ivory in exchange. Only those who carve ivory, who make more money the more tusks they handle, have little interest in making constraints work.

With the ban, however, the elephant's future is uncertain. Temporarily, the collapse of demand in the rich industrial countries will discourage poaching. The price of ivory within Africa has fallen dramatically. Large new dollops of aid from the West are helping to improve the pay and equipment of park guards. The danger is that poaching will revive. New markets will be developed. Some people who in the past bought ivory legally will now buy it illegally. That will drive up the black market price, raising the profitability of poaching and increasing the risks that poachers are willing to take.

Returns from the Rain Forest

The logic that applies to Africa's elephants is also being turned to try to save the world's vanishing rain forests. The core of the problem is similar. Rain forests have no clear owners; they are slow-growing and expensive to guard; once gone, they appear to be irreplaceable; their trees, left standing, may yield long-term benefits to local people and to the countries in which they stand, but chopped down they yield quick profits to a lucky or ruthless few.

Forests are more valuable than elephants. A single species may be an essential link in a biological chain, as the dodo was for the Calvaria tree. But a habitat is home to a whole group of species. Rain forests have all the values that elephants enjoy; they are valuable as a source of timber, for other forest products such as fruit and resins, and as a way to earn tourist revenue. They also have grander functions. They are home to many species of creatures and plants, as well as to indigenous people who frequently know far more about the use of species than do professional botanists. They protect watersheds by anchoring the soil. They store carbon dioxide, the main greenhouse gas (and release it when they burn). And they may influence rainfall in the surrounding lands.

Forests have been vanishing almost as alarmingly as elephants (see Table 6.3). Precise figures are hard to come by: just as counting elephants is often a hazy matter of checking piles of dung or of patchy airplane sightings, so deciding the precise extent of a rain forest and pronouncing the moment when degraded jungle becomes deforestation is a fine judgment. One set of guesses puts the annual rate at the end of the 1980s at 14 million to 17 million hectares a year, out of a remaining 8 million square km.

But why are forests burned or chopped down? To manage them in a sustainable way for their timber is likely to be generally less profitable than clearing them and growing trees for pulp in their place. Pulp trees simply grow faster and are easier to harvest. Timber alone, though, is not the only cash crop of a forest. As the study by the New York Botanical Gardens showed, nontimber products may be even more valuable. Some botanists hope that by adding together the value of sustainably managed timber and nontimber products, they can show governments that rain forests standing are worth more than rain forests destroyed.

One of the most energetic proponents of this view, Ghillean Prance, is director of the Royal Botanic Gardens at Kew, in west London. Professor Prance has worked hard to help the Body Shop, a British cosmetics chain with branches in the United States, find forest products to sell. In one project, the University of Belem, at the mouth of the Amazon, is searching for seeds and plants for potpourris and aromatic oils; in another, an Indian tribe is being asked to harvest brazil nuts. But processing the nuts and bringing them out of the forest is costly. It will take at least five years for the Body Shop to make a profit on either venture.

Table 6.3 Rates of Tropical Deforestation (m ha per year), 1980s (closed forest only)

	Late 1970s[a]	Mid-1980s[b]	Late 1980s[c]
S. America	2.67	9.65[d]	6.65
C. America	1.01	1.07	1.03
Africa	1.02	1.06	1.58
Asia	1.82	3.10	4.25
Oceania	0.02	0.02	0.35
Total losses	6.54	14.90	13.86

[a]Late 1970s data for the 34 countries covered in Myers (see below) from FAO, *Tropical Forest Resources,* Rome, 1981.
[b]Various years to 1986, taken from World Resources Institute, *World Resources 1990–1991.* Oxford University Press, Oxford, 1990. Table 19.1. In turn, the estimates are based on FAO sources, including an update for some countries of the 1981 estimates, and some individual sources. Note that the estimates cover closed forests only. Closed forests refer to dense forests in which grass cover is small or non-existent due to low light penetration through the forest canopy.
[c]N. Myers, *Deforestation Rates in Tropical Forests and Their Climatic Implications.* Friends of the Earth, London, December 1989. Myers's estimates cover 34 countries accounting for 97.3% of the extent of tropical forest in 1989.
[d]Myers estimates 5 m ha per year loss for Brazil in 1989: the WRI figure for mid-1980s is some 8 m ha per year for closed forest loss.
Source: David Pearce, "An Economic Approach to Saving the Tropical Forests" in Dieter Helm, ed., *Economic Policy Towards the Environment* (Oxford: Basil Blackwell, 1991).

Another enthusiast is Jason Clay, research director of a Massachusetts-based charity called Cultural Survival, which has set up a company to buy and market rain-forest products. Clay has found one eager customer in the Body Shop and another in Ben & Jerry's, a Vermont ice cream manufacturer, which has launched "rain-forest crunch" made with rain-forest brazil nuts and cashews from nearby cashew plantations. Clay has opened a small nut-processing plant in Xapuri, which is in the heart of Chico Mendes's rubber-tapping country. He hopes other products will follow. At present, not one factory in the Amazon area processes local fruit for export. He wants the processing and distribution to be owned and run by those who gather forest products.

In this way the concept of extractive reserves has gathered strength: tracts of forest set aside for sustainable activities such as rubber tapping, gathering fruit and nuts, and hunting. Such ideas have their critics, who point out that the reserves will not preserve the full diversity of plants and creatures that exists in untouched forest. And while they may provide livelihoods for the families who still make their living from traditional forest activities, they do nothing for the more numerous families who scratch a living from unsustainable agriculture on cleared land. Rather than confusing conservation and capitalism, say these critics, better to go back to the idea of national parks, aimed simply at conservation, and to look for less damaging and more lucrative things for peasant farmers to do.

Even more risky, but also more lucrative, is to develop "ecotourism." In 1986, Costa Rica, for example, earned $138 million from what was primarily nature-based tourism. The number of tourists arriving in Manaus, the largest city in the central Amazon, increased from 12,000 in 1983 to 70,000 in 1988. In the 1990s, tourism is expected to become the largest single source of income in Amazonas state.[5] Clearly not every country is likely to be attractive to visitors (most would probably prefer to visit Costa Rica than Zaire). But most rain-forest countries have hardly begun to think of their trees as tourist earners.

It may be possible to harness market forces to save large tracts of rain forest. That is far more likely to happen, though, if governments do not give incentives to cut them down. As already explained, governments have long encouraged deforestation in a number of ways: by giving tax credits, which allow land speculators to offset the costs of clearing forest land for cattle ranching against their income tax; by providing subsidized credit for crops and livestock; and by building roads. Underpriced electricity encourages countries to build dams to provide hydroelectric power. Mechanization of agriculture, sometimes paid for by foreign aid and often supported by government grants, drives people from the land: in Brazil soya farming displaces 11 people for every job it creates. Some of the jobless head north to the Amazon, seeking cheap land. Poorly defined ownership adds to the pressures for clearance. Establishing legal title to land is often cumbersome. A Brazilian law (now rescinded) long allowed a farmer who cleared an acre of land to claim title to two acres. When Brazil first threatened to repeal this provision (and tax credits for cleared land, too) in 1987, the result was a surge of deforestation as farmers rushed to fell trees and grab extra land while they could. When agricultural colonists can win tenure this way, it is hardly surprising that they tend to win legal battles (and the more physical kind) against indigenous people. Some other, farsighted governments are trying to give native forest people firm title to the lands on which they live, reckoning that this will encourage conservation. In 1989, Colombia bravely added some 23,000 square miles to the 46,000 square miles already in Indian hands. The title to half the country's rain forest is now legally owned by indigenous Indians. Colombia's reasons are not purely altruistic: the indigenous lands are sparsely settled, inaccessible territories, primarily bordering Brazil. One foreign observer has described it as a strategy to "sandbag the border with Indians."

Transferring to forested countries the cash value that the rest of the world puts on their trees might be the biggest incentive for conservation. A study by Pearce tries to estimate some of these values.[6] He explores the possibility of paying a "carbon credit" to forested countries, to represent the value of protecting the earth from global warming by allowing growing trees to lock up carbon from the atmosphere. Attempts to estimate the damage, mostly by sea-level rise, that global warming is likely to do come up with a figure of $13 per ton of carbon. Tropical forests appear to sequester 100 tons of carbon per hectare per year. That could be the basis for paying a carbon credit of $1,300 per hectare a year to countries in which trees were left standing. But it seems that people in rich countries may be willing to pay something just to keep them standing. Pearce reckons that the appropriate amount might be about $8 per adult per year, at least among the world's richest 400 million adults in Western Europe, North America, and Australasia. If that money were paid into an Amazon Conservation Fund, the resulting $3.2 billion would be a quarter of the entire GNP of the Amazonia region.

Paying to Preserve

These calculations may yet form the basis of policy. National governments will start to look for ways to pay exploiters to become preservers. In Britain, the Country Landowners' Association has proposed an ingenious scheme under which governments are invited to pay landowners for their contribution to conservation. The British government has introduced a more modest scheme, under which farmers in areas designated as environmentally sensitive are paid to conserve stone walls, bogs, and other uneconomic but ecologically benign aspects of their land.

The idea behind such schemes is that the countryside is a consumer good; consumers are the majority of taxpayers who live in towns; some of the prettiest countryside, which is what these consumers want, is created by uneconomic farming. So farmers can justifiably claim to be rewarded by taxpayers for preserving it. The snag, of course, is that schemes are complicated to administer (in the British government's scheme, officials hunt through meadows for rare wildflowers before deciding whether to award a grant) and are likely to bring counterclaims from other conservationists. Those who fail to knock down their medieval cottage may wonder whether they too ought to receive a reward from the taxpayer each year for their forbearance.

Such national preoccupations may eventually become international ones. People have begun to think about a bio-diversity convention, an international treaty that would, in some yet unspecified way, confer obligations on countries to preserve nature's wealth of biological diversity. Such a treaty would inevitably involve payments from rich countries to poorer ones to reward them for failing to destroy their natural bounty. But poor countries might find such payments led to a change in the way their natural treasures were regarded. No longer would the Brazilian government be able to insist that the Amazon was its national heritage, to plunder or preserve as it chose. The counterpart of receiving international aid would be the recognition that the Amazon is an international treasure. Brazil held out until 1991 against offers by first world conservation organizations to swap its debt for money to be spent on saving forests. Such "eco-colonialism" is the counterpart of being on the receiving end of the metaphysical values that the citizens of other countries put on your natural resources. Developing countries may in time find it lucrative; they will not necessarily find it comfortable.

7

International Environmental Management

At one time, environment officials stayed at home and worried about dirty rivers and smoky air. No longer. These days they jet from city to city, haggling far into the night over clauses and subclauses, just like defense experts or trade ministers. The environment has become a matter for international diplomacy, as important and intractable as disarmament or tariff barriers.

What has changed? Environmental policy is not new. Every government now accepts that it has a responsibility for the environment of the country it rules, even if some take the obligation lightly. But the issues that increasingly dominate environmental policy are not national but international. The most difficult questions involve environmental damage inflicted by one country, or by a group of countries, on other countries or on the planet.

The reason these problems are so difficult to resolve is that they require the flimsy machinery of international agreement to assume the role that national governments perform at home. If a company is tipping sewage into a river, imposing on other users of the river costs that it incurs but does not pay, government can oblige the company to shoulder those costs by cleaning up its effluent. Without a world government or the prospect of one, no institution exists to ensure that countries do not inflict on the planet environmental costs that they are not willing to carry. No organization can compel Brazil to stop destroying the rain forest or force Chinese power stations to stop spewing sulphur dioxide or punish the United States if it refuses to curb its output of carbon dioxide.

The international aspects of environmental policy are the ones to which the most interesting new thoughts are being given by economists and political scientists. There is also a rising number of international agreements. In the past, countries made agreements to prevent a valuable species from being hunted or fished to extinction. Between 1930 and 1959, the United States put into force only a handful of such treaties, mainly on whaling. In the 1960s and 1970s, the number rose to five per decade, as marine pollution and endangered species became prominent issues. In the 1980s, the total was 11, of which four dealt with air and three with marine pollution (see Table 7.1).

International environmental problems take many forms.[1] Sometimes one or two countries do something that they may see as in their interest but that may harm other countries: for exam-

Table 7.1 Multilateral Environmental Treaties Entering into Force in US

Category	1930–39	1940–49	1950–59	1960–69	1970–79	1980–89
1. Fur and feathers	1	—	—	—	3	1
2. Whaling	1	1	1	—	—	—
3. Fishing	—	—	—	2	—	2
4. Marine pollution	—	—	—	1	2	3
5. Air pollution	—	—	—	—	—	4
6. Miscellaneous	—	—	—	2	—	1
Totals	2	1	1	5	5	11

Source: Robert Hahn and Kenneth Richards, "The Internationalisation of Environmental Regulation," Carnegie-Mellon University, February 1989.

ple, Brazil's destruction of the Amazon rain forest, or Britain's reluctance in the early 1980s to do anything to stop the sulphur dioxide emitted by its coal-fired power stations from falling as acid rain on the Scandinavian countries downwind of it. Such examples are the international equivalent of the timber company that logs out a hillside, making a large profit but inflicting floods on the farmers living downstream.

Sometimes those who cause environmental damage and those who suffer from it are the same countries. The extent to which countries cause and suffer damage may differ, but all or most share the problem. Consider global warming. Every country burns the fossil fuels that fill the atmosphere with world-warming carbon dioxide; every country will suffer if the world's climate changes dramatically. Another example is the hole in the ozone layer caused by CFCs. These instances are more akin at a national level to the congestion of urban roads: almost all drivers help to cause traffic jams, and all fume in them.

A national government could ban the timber company and tax the traffic. But how can sovereign governments be persuaded to accept self-restraint? Countries will rarely look beyond their own self-interest. With international agreements on wise environmental policies, countries are likely to do better than if each pursues such policies alone. One country bribing Brazil not to destroy the rain forest will have far less effect than if all countries did so together. Norway could, for instance, spend a large chunk of its smallish GNP writing off Brazil's debts and get little in exchange. But if every country handed over a smaller chunk of national wealth to a fund giving Brazil green aid in exchange for conservation, then Brazil might indeed be persuaded to keep its forest intact. The gains from cooperation are greater, relative to the costs, than the returns from going it alone.

Conversely, if most countries sign such an agreement, an individual country can generally do even better by dropping out of the pact. It can thus enjoy the rewards of what economists call, in a vividly expressive phrase, "free-riding." If bus passengers pay their fares on the honor system, they will do better if everyone is honorable than if only one or two pay up. But the few passengers who cheat do best of all. In the same way, if every country but one contributed to a fund to conserve the Amazon, that one country would still enjoy all the benefits that accrued to the rest.

This is the central paradox of world environmental agreements. All countries do better if the nations of the world cooperate than if they do not; and yet individual countries have a strong incentive not to cooperate.

Countries, like people, are more likely to free-ride, the greater the benefits of doing so relative to the cost. This is partly a function of numbers. If three countries bordering one lake reach an agreement to stop discharging sewage into it, all are more likely to stick to the bargain than they would if 20 countries were involved. The gains each enjoys as a result of an unpolluted lake will be much larger than if the lake is only two-thirds clean. The incentive is smaller if the choice is between a clean lake and an almost clean one.

People who cheat on buses run the risk of a large fine if an inspector comes aboard. Countries that welch on international agreements face no such risks. The ways that countries can impose their will on each other are limited and uncertain. Take, for evidence, Iraq's invasion of Kuwait in 1990. The only threats available to the world's countries, unusually united and determined, were trade sanctions and military attack. It is hard to imagine the destruction of rain forests or the ozone layer or even global warming leading to military action against the villains (though a dispute over fishing in the North Sea between Britain and Iceland in the first half of the 1970s activated the British navy), much less convincing global trade sanctions. It is highly likely that there will be an increase in the use of environmental trade restrictions of one sort or another; but they are unlikely to persuade a country to change its policies unless it is small and poor or the costs of change are insignificant.

The only threat of much use now in bolstering international environmental agreements is that of public opinion. Countries dislike being pariahs. Brazil bitterly resented the international abuse heaped on it at the height of the Amazon fires in 1988–1989, but it did react: it reduced the tax incentives to cattle ranchers and tried to attach tougher green conditions to new electricity proposals. Britain finally accepted the need to reduce sulphur-dioxide output from power stations and to stop dumping sewage sludge in the North Sea, primarily because of the political costs of being dubbed "the dirty man of Europe."

Countries may also agree to environmental policies that are not obviously in their interest in the hope of cementing relations with other countries. America in 1973 spent a large sum cleaning up the Colorado River in response to Mexican complaints that the water had become increasingly saline. Why? Probably because it wanted to appear friendlier with its Latin American neighbors, especially with Mexico.

The deal on the Colorado River and Britain's decision to stop dumping sludge are examples of the polluter-pays principle at work. Such examples will probably become rarer in the future. International agreements will increasingly embody what has been dubbed (by Göran-Mäler) the "victim-pays" principle.

Countries will often see the benefits of bribing those who pollute to stop. That will be particularly true when one country harms another, or many others, but is itself little damaged. It is also more likely to be the case with poor polluters, for whom bribes will be worth more and the costs of taking action more of a burden. A good example of this situation is in Eastern Europe, where there will probably not be much investment in preventing water and air pollution when there are other, even more pressing calls on scarce capital. The countries of Western Europe, which suffer from heavy metals dumped in the Baltic and waves of sulphur dioxide wafting into their forests, can buy more pollution control by spending money in Eastern Europe than by devoting yet more resources to their own sewage treatment and factory chimneys. Sweden helps Poland with technology to curb acid rain. For every $5 western Germany spends on cleaning acid from its atmosphere, it can achieve the same effect by spending $1 in eastern Germany. In 1982, when Germany was still divided, West Germany agreed to pay East Germany the equivalent of $36 million to help build a water treatment plant on the Spree River, which flows from East Germany into West Berlin.[2]

If third world countries are clever, they will see the victim-pays principle as a way to trade on the green consciences of first world countries. Debt-for-nature agreements, under which first world green organizations or governments redeem third world debt to channel cash into conservation, are a sort of victim payment; so is the $5 million America pledged to elephant conservation under the African Elephant Conservation Act. From another perspective, of course, such payments reflect the value that the rest of the world puts on conserving species.

By accepting green aid, developing countries strike a bargain. To complain about eco-colonialism is to miss the point. When a third world country accepts green aid, it accepts the fact that the rest of the world has an interest in what it does with its wildlife or its forests. Those who make such bargains accept some restriction of sovereignty as part of the deal.

Regional Agreements

Until recently, most international environmental agreements covered countries in a single region: for example, the 1976 Barcelona Convention for the protection of the Mediterranean or the 1975 Geneva Convention on long-range transboundary air pollution. Rivers such as the Rhine, or enclosed seas such as the Baltic or Caribbean, have been the most fruitful objects of conventions on water pollution. Recently, neighboring countries have increasingly signed agreements on air pollution. The countries of Europe, huddled together on a small continent, have not surprisingly been the most frequent instigators of such agreements, for good reasons: a fairly common set of greenish values (more common than, say, those of Indonesia and Australia) and, in the EC Commission, a body to which a dozen of them have transferred some supranational authority.

Under these agreements, the balance of costs and benefits to each country often differs. Rivers flow in one direction; winds tend to blow more from one quarter than another. The agreements quite often reflect this by setting different targets for different countries. For instance, under the 1976 Bonn Convention to protect the Rhine from chloride pollution, the four countries that share its banks—the Netherlands, Germany, France, and Switzerland—agreed to split the costs of abatement in the ratio of 34:30:30:6.[3] The EC's 1988 directive to limit emissions from large combustion plants sets target cuts in sulphur dioxide output of 70% by 2003 for Belgium, the Netherlands, and Germany; of 67% for Denmark; 63% for Italy; and 60% for Luxembourg and Britain. Greece, Ireland, and Portugal are temporarily allowed to increase their output of sulphur dioxide as they develop their poorer economies.

International Agreements

The world has begun to move from regional agreements toward global ones. The damage caused to the ozone layer by CFCs and the threat to the climate from global warming have led to attempts to reach agreements that are without precedent. Every country releases some CFCs into the atmosphere; every country is threatened by the hole in the ozone layer. An increase in the amount of ultraviolet radiation reaching the earth's surface could cause more skin cancer and cataracts in human beings as well as other biological damage. With global warming, it is even more true that every country bears some share of the blame, and every country's climate is at risk. Every country on earth therefore has an interest in seeing that an agreement is reached about both kinds of pollution; similarly, every country needs to make costly adjustments if an agreement is to be completely effective.

In the second half of the 1980s, most of the world's countries reached two agreements to curb the use of CFCs: first, the 1985 Vienna Convention, a broad and unspecific treaty, pledging governments to think more about the issue and discuss future action; and then the Montreal Protocol, a specific agreement attached to the convention in September 1987, committing signatories to reduce by half their consumption of five CFC compounds by 1998. In June 1990, the Montreal Protocol was extended to include more chemicals and tightened to pledge an end to CFC use by the end of the century.

This agreement, which had 67 signatories by early 1991, was a spectacular and unprecedented achievement. Many politicians hope that it points the way to a convention on global climate change, on which talks began in Washington, DC, in February 1991. In fact, there are important differences between the Montreal negotiations and those on global warming, which will make the latter infinitely more difficult. But some lessons can be drawn from past experience in designing treaties and environmental policies which might lead to a better treaty on global warming.

Like the negotiations over CFCs, talks on climate change begin with a large measure of scientific uncertainty about the scope of the problem. When negotiations on the Vienna Convention began, scientists believed that CFCs were harming the ozone layer, and indeed the United States had banned the nonessential use of CFCs as aerosol propellants in 1978. Canada, Sweden, Norway, and Denmark followed suit. But it was the discovery in 1984–1985 by a team of British scientists of the hole in the ozone layer over Antarctica that gave negotiations the fillip they needed. In the following years, more scientific observations of depletion helped to refine understanding. In 1986, Swiss scientists found an ozone hole over the Arctic.

Once the damage done by CFCs was no longer scientific speculation but visible on satellite photographs, it became easier to give negotiations a sense of urgency. A common characteristic of international environmental agreements is that they often require countries to accept economic costs on the basis of a fair amount of scientific uncertainty. Reducing uncertainty makes agreement easier. For years, West Germany held out against cuts in emissions of sulphur dioxide from its power stations. Only in 1982, when its forests began to die, did West Germany change its stance.

The uncertainties are greater about global warming than they were about CFCs. The theory is sound enough: few scientists argue that the accumulation of carbon dioxide, methane, nitrous oxide, and CFCs in the atmosphere is increasing. Beyond that, however, lie great areas of uncertainty. Scientists are unsure how far the greenhouse effect may be offset. As more water evaporates, the sky may be cloudier, and clouds will shelter the earth from some sunshine. The increase in carbon dioxide may cause plants to grow more vigorously, taking up carbon dioxide as they do. On the other hand, the greenhouse effect may be reinforced: warmer seas may absorb less carbon dioxide than they currently bury, and melting polar ice may release great bubbles of trapped methane.

As a result, although most scientists agree that the world will warm, they are unsure about the speed with which warming will occur. Yet speed is a crucial factor. The faster the warming takes place, the less time species will have to adapt to higher temperatures and the more creatures and plants are likely to become extinct as a result. Nor are scientists sure what the effect of warming will be on the planet. Expanding oceans and, perhaps, melting polar ice will increase the sea level, although it is just possible that increased evaporation may reduce it. Probably, storms will become more frequent. Perhaps the increased heat will cause deserts to spread; although if rainfall rises and plants thrive on their richer diet of carbon dioxide, perhaps deserts will shrink and crops will flourish. Scientists find it impossible to predict which regions will gain and which will lose. Some think there will be no winners; others are less pessimistic.

It would help the negotiations if there were clear evidence that global warming is taking place. The six warmest years on record fell in the 1980s, although 1990 topped them all. The 1988 drought in midwestern America was what finally turned global warming into an important political issue in the United States. But most scientists are not yet confident that this is incontrovertible evidence that global warming is under way. For the moment, and probably until at least the early years of the next century, the evidence for global warming will continue to rest on what computer-based models of the climate suggest, and on indications of carbon-dioxide bubbles trapped in Arctic ice.

Not only is the evidence for global warming still speculative; it is not clear where all greenhouse gases come from. CFCs are greenhouse gases as well as ozone destroyers; they are entirely man-made, and so easy to track down. Carbon dioxide comes partly from deforestation, which accounts for 10% to 30% of mankind's annual output of that gas. Most of the rest comes from burning fossil fuels: coal, oil, and gas. Two other greenhouse gases, methane and nitrogen oxide, are harder to trace, although both, molecule for molecule, are much more effective trappers of reflected heat than carbon dioxide. Methane comes from rotting waste, flatulent animals, leaking natural-gas pipelines, fermenting rice paddies; nitrogen oxide, partly from the engines of cars and the chimneys of coal-fired power stations but also from fertilizers and land clearing. Both gases are likely to be far harder to curb, for both technical and economic reasons, than emissions of carbon dioxide.

One reason for the successful negotiation of the Montreal agreement was the evidence that ozone depletion was dangerous to health. Global warming does not yet enjoy this perverse advantage. It may, if crops more frequently fail, and their failure results in more starvation; it may, if the sea level rises, make homeless the one-third or so of mankind that lives within 40 miles of the sea. But CFCs had a greater advantage in terms of scare value. In 1986, the American National Aeronautics and Space Administration estimated that a 3% annual increase in CFC emissions could deplete the ozone layer by 10% by the middle of the next century, and the Environmental Protection Agency predicted that a 10% depletion could cause nearly 2 million extra cases of nonmelanoma skin cancers in the United States alone. If scientists could establish a link between the greenhouse effect and the American cancer rate, a successful climate convention would be virtually guaranteed.

Perhaps the most important difference of all between negotiations on CFCs and those on climate change is one of technology. In the case of CFCs, a relatively simple group of products is involved, made by few companies in few countries (Du Pont alone accounts for a quarter of world output). For the biggest uses of CFCs—as refrigerants, aerosol propellants, and bubbles in insulating foam—there are possible substitutes. Du Pont reckons that by 2000, substitutes of various kinds might replace 70% of current CFC use, with two new families of chemicals, HFCs and HCFCs, collectively known as hydrofluoroalkanes (HFAs), accounting for some 40% of that total; a final 30% of current use could be met (see Figure 7.1) through conservation.

None of this is true of fossil fuels. Their use touches almost every aspect of human life. They are produced not by a handful of large companies, but by a great many countries, some of which rely on exports of fossil fuels for most of their foreign-exchange earnings. Above all, there are no convenient substitutes. The choices that face the world with present technology are stark: it can switch from carbon-rich to carbon-poor fossil fuels, it can build more nuclear power stations, or it can invest far more in energy conservation. In practice, all will be needed, but each is much more complicated than, for instance, substituting one chemical for another in the air-conditioner of a car.

The biggest manufacturers of CFCs are the very companies that have taken the lead in developing these substitutes. As Scott Barrett has pointed out, manufacturers played an essential part in achieving a ban.[4] A year after the Montreal Protocol set a target of cutting CFC consumption by half, Du Pont announced that it would support a ban on production by the year 2000. This preceded and greatly encouraged the decision by the United States and the EC to phase out all CFC use by the end of the century. Part of the reason for Du Pont's decision may have been its strong sense of environmental responsibility. Part may have been a fear of being sued at a future date by people with skin cancer. A third factor was probably the immense sum ($1 billion in the 1990s) that Du Pont intended to invest in developing and producing CFC substitutes. The world market for CFCs is worth only $4 billion to $5 billion a year. So a government-supported ban was essential to protect the market for substitutes.

In the case of fossil fuels, no similar alliance is likely to emerge. The only two groups with a powerful interest in a climate convention are the nuclear power industry and the manufacturers of equipment for energy conservation. Britain's Association for

Figure 7.1 How CFCs Might Be Replaced by the Year 2000

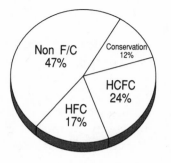

Source: Du Pont.

the Conservation of Energy, the trade body representing the latter group, has lobbied hard for a tough approach to energy use. But the nuclear power lobby is an awkward ally for environmentalists, and the energy-conservation industry is highly fragmented. The oil companies, by contrast, are enormous and are highly skilled political operators.

International agreements on the environment are, as Barrett has shrewdly observed, rather like producer cartels. Countries or companies join cartels because the gains from acting together are greater than those from going it alone. But if cooperation from time to time demands large sacrifices, some will cheat and the cartel will eventually collapse. OPEC pushed up the oil price on the back of strong demand; once demand fell and big production cuts became necessary to prop up prices, some producers preferred to free-ride. The gains to countries from cooperating on CFCs were clearly greater than those from acting alone. And the benefits of avoiding ozone depletion are both reasonably well defined and well distributed: no one country or group of countries stands to gain much more than others. Nor are the costs of cutting CFCs enormous: witness the many countries that had acted on their own even before the Montreal Protocol, and the large number that had signed it by the end of 1990.

Few of these points hold true for global warming. If the doomsters are right, the gains from international action would indeed be immense, far larger than any one country could achieve on its own. But they are uncertain and far off. As scientists become clearer about the effects of global warming on different countries, the balance of costs and benefits to each country will become clearer. This may not make an agreement easier. While Bangladesh or little Kiribatu may vanish under the sea, some of the biggest emitters of carbon dioxide (America or some parts of the former Soviet Union, for instance) may find that they can grow grain where grain never grew before.

If governments wait until they are sure of these costs before deciding whether to try to cut output of greenhouse gases, that output will certainly have increased. Reducing it then will be more painful and more expensive. Besides, during the delay, more greenhouse gases will have built up in the atmosphere.

Because they will linger there for years, the world will be locked into yet more warming. But it will be vastly expensive to reduce the world's output of greenhouse gases to a point at which future warming is not likely to be faster than the planet can bear. Governments therefore face an immensely difficult decision: take some action now, and risk wasting money; or delay, and risk more environmental damage.

Those who write about climate change are usually more interested in how to set about stopping it than in whether it is worth trying to do so. Most studies of global warming begin by asking what pace of climatic change the world can tolerate. The answer has two parts. Species can tolerate only very slow change: beyond about 0.1° Celsius a decade, some would not be able to shift or adapt and would become extinct. Human beings can tolerate much faster change: their ability to cope will be determined mainly by what happens to world food production and to sea-level rise. To some extent, they may be able to adapt to both. Food output may be sustained either by growing different crops or by growing crops in different places. Walls can be built against rising sea levels. Both adjustments carry costs, which will be greater for some countries than for others.

A study conducted by a team of climatologists and energy experts for the Dutch Ministry of Environment concluded that the absolute maximum warming the planet could tolerate would be 2° Celsius above current levels.[5] An international agreement to protect the climate could therefore establish a global budget setting out how much carbon dioxide can be spewed into the atmosphere by 2100. The study reckoned that the world could afford 55 more years of carbon-dioxide releases at current rates between 1985 and 2100, and that the central issue was to find fair ways of distributing that limit.

The scientific assessment undertaken by the International Panel on Climate Change in 1990 took a similar line. This body was set up to prepare the ground for negotiations on a climate convention. Its scientific study concluded that the output of long-lived gases building up in the earth's atmosphere—carbon dioxide, nitrous oxide, and CFCs—would have to be reduced by more than 60% at once in order to stabilize concentrations at today's levels. If no action is taken, global mean temperature will rise by about 0.3° a decade, and by a total of perhaps 3° by the end of the next century.

What the planet can tolerate may be less than what humanity will willingly pay. With greenhouse gases, as with other kinds of pollution, there will be a point at which the benefits of preventing an extra ounce of carbon dioxide from escaping into the atmosphere are overtaken by the costs. At that point humanity would be wiser to spend its scarce capital on preventing other kinds of environmental damage.

But what is that magic point? Economists have mainly added up the costs of curbs. A few, notably William Nordhaus of Yale University, have tried to attach numbers to the benefits. Trying to quantify the costs is controversial enough. It is hampered by scientific uncertainty (about how fast the world will warm and where the warming will occur) and by economic uncertainty (about what will happen to world energy demand, economic growth, and population over the next century). One attempt, by Alan Manne of Stanford University and Richard Richels of the Electric Power Research Institute, argued that the cost to the United States of stabilizing carbon-dioxide output at its 1990 level by the end of this century and then cutting it by one-fifth would be roughly 3% of annual GDP by 2030.[6] The costs would be lower for other OECD countries, with more nuclear power and greater reserves of oil and gas (both fuels give off less carbon dioxide than coal when they burn). For developing countries, China for example, even limiting carbon-dioxide output to double its 1990 level would cost 5% to 10% of their GDP.

Such immense numbers have to be treated gingerly. A tiny change in the assumptions behind a projection that runs a century into the future can have an enormous cumulative effect. Robert Williams of the Center for Energy and Environmental Studies at Princeton University has drawn attention to how much the study by Manne and Richels depends on getting the right number for the underlying trend toward great energy efficiency.[7] This trend has led to a steady decline in the ratio of energy demand to GDP in most developed countries for most of this century (in Britain, since 1880). It seems reasonable to assume that the trend will continue during the next century. But if Manne and Richels have underestimated the future pace of that trend by a single percentage point a year, energy demand by the end of the twenty-first century would be only one-third of the amount they assume. If so, the cost of curbing carbon-dioxide output may also be much lower.

Manne and Richels also assume that there is no underlying trend toward energy efficiency in developing countries. That may be true today, but not for long. The sheer impossibility of financing new power supplies fast enough to match economic growth will increasingly force developing countries to pay more attention to energy efficiency. At least one Indian utility has begun to explore the concept of least-cost supplies. Calculations of the costs of curbing carbon dioxide may be difficult, but they are easy compared with estimating the benefits. Here language can be muddling: a benefit of curbing greenhouse gases may take the form of avoiding some of the costs of adapting to a hotter world. Thus, while building sea walls is a cost of adapting to the rise in sea levels that global warming may bring, avoiding the need for the expense of building walls appears in the arithmetic as a benefit.

Estimating benefits calls for wild leaps of imagination. Nordhaus has leapt in a series of papers (including an essay in *The Economist* of July 7, 1990), and believes that the measurable gains may be small.[8] Only 13% of America's national output, he points out, comes from parts of the economy even mildly sensitive to climate change. If sea levels rise, land may be lost and sea walls will have to be built, but over 75 years the cost would be 0.1% of cumulative private investment. In the third world, some farmland may be lost to sea level rises and higher temperatures. But the fertilizing effect of more carbon dioxide may lift food output. Overall, he insists, there is "no strong presumption of substantial net economic damage."

Although the benefits of preventing global warming are easily overestimated, according to Nordhaus, the costs of curbing greenhouse gases will rise sharply as more are eliminated. He believes that perhaps one-sixth of greenhouse gas output could be prevented relatively inexpensively. That would include the elimination of CFCs, which are cost-effective to scrap partly because they have substitutes and partly because they harm the ozone layer as well as the climate. It would also include those cuts in carbon-dioxide output that might quickly pay for themselves through energy saving and an end to uneconomic deforestation. Beyond that point, the costs will rise rapidly. To halve greenhouse gas output, if it is done gradually, might cost about $200 billion a year, or about 1% of global output. If done quickly, it could cost much more. The sort of goal that European governments have set themselves, of stabilizing carbon-dioxide output by the year 2000 at 1990 levels, will cost much more than the world will gain from avoiding global warming, and this is assuming that the stabilization is permanent (a point on which all governments have been remarkably reticent).

Environmentalists greet such a conclusion with horrified disbelief. Certainly, Nordhaus has deliberately left a number of things out of the equation. He makes no allowance for the irreversible loss of species that will not be able to adjust to increased temperatures. Some of those species might be unmourned bugs; others might have commercial value, actual or (more probably) unexplored and unknown. The values that humanity ascribes to the other creatures that share the planet play no part in Nordhaus's equations.

Nor does he include a number for the possibility of catastrophe. What if warming causes polar ice caps to melt suddenly or the Gulf Stream to shift many miles south or an unprecedented drought? Each disaster has its band of scientific adherents; each might be worth paying an insurance premium to prevent. Curbing carbon-dioxide output is such a premium. Nor, again, do Nordhaus's numbers take account of the double benefit from some carbon-curbing measures. Using less fossil fuel will simultaneously reduce acid rain, oil spills, urban smog, and traffic jams. Nor yet—and this could be most important of all—do his calculations peer into the really distant future and consider the impact on the planet of a trebling, or a quadrupling, of greenhouse gases in the atmosphere.

Irritating though Nordhaus's arithmetic may be for environmentalists, it ought to concentrate attention on two points. First, as some carbon-cutting measures clearly pass the cost-benefit test, governments need to be persuaded to take these quickly. Second, environmentalists need to ask whether the money the world may yet spend to check global warming might not yield even larger environmental benefits if invested elsewhere: on population control or the preservation of endangered species, for example, both of which yield returns today rather than half a century hence.

Establishing Targets

Three questions will dominate all discussion of a climate convention. How far should the world aim to go in curbing greenhouse gases? How should the curbs be shared among countries? And how should potential free-riders be persuaded to pay their fares? Although the first question is logically the one to begin with, its answer is more likely to emerge as the sum of replies to the second two. Finding a way to share out the curbs will be an argument disguised in long wrangling over other points. Ought there to be a single target for stabilization (such as holding carbon-dioxide output at 1990 levels in the year 2000, as a clutch of industrial countries have promised)? If so, ought the target to be for carbon dioxide alone (that makes life easier for France, with its plentiful nuclear power), and should it take account only of carbon dioxide released by burning fossil fuels, or should it cover deforestation too? Brazil's burning forests send up carbon dioxide on a first world scale. Alternatively, should the target include all greenhouse gases? America wants to talk about all greenhouse gases, and will press for an allowance for the cuts it has already made in one of them by voluntarily banning CFCs in aerosols long before most European countries did.

But if all greenhouse gases are to be counted, ought there to be some mechanism for taking account of their varying power to trap the sun's returning rays? Methane is about 21 times more effective, molecule for molecule, than carbon dioxide, and CFCs about 12,000 times more effective. If "radiative forcing" is thus taken into account, so should be the lifetime of gases in the atmosphere. Methane does its damaging work for ten years, nitrogen oxide for 150. Allow for the differences, and what ought to be done about the wildly varying estimates of the durability of carbon dioxide at anything from 50 to 200 years?

Carbon dioxide accounts for roughly half the climate-changing impact of greenhouse gases, though its share is declining. Thus, setting goals in terms of carbon dioxide alone makes little sense. Yet measuring the output of other gases is fraught with difficulties. The amount of CFCs and of carbon dioxide released from burning fossil fuels may be relatively easy to calculate. Not so the carbon dioxide given off by deforestation, let alone each country's output of methane and nitrogen oxide. And if output of gases is to be measured, what about the creation of new sinks? Clearly, an allowance should be built in for reforestation, as growing trees will lock up carbon dioxide.

The choice of gases will give advantages to some countries, handicaps to others. So will the basis against which cuts or growth is measured. Japan has offered to stabilize its output of carbon dioxide per head at 1990 levels by the end of the century, but the number of Japanese heads is predicted to grow by 6% in that time. As Japan's population starts to decline in the next century, the world may not mind if Japan chooses such a basis, so long as it sticks to it. But what about third world countries, whose populations will double or treble as the century advances?

Third world countries, for their part, point out that almost all the man-made greenhouse gases now concentrated in the atmosphere have been put there by the activities of the rich world. As third world GDPs grow, so will their outputs of warming gases. But why should they be forced to rein in and restrict their future growth to accommodate the past misdeeds of the rich? The average person in a developing country annually uses the equivalent of one or two barrels of oil in the form of fuel bought on the market. In Europe and Japan, that number jumps to 10 to 30 barrels, and in America to more than 40. So third world countries will want to tie targets to population and the growth of GNP. Rich countries will insist that targets be "grandfathered," at least in the first instance: that each country's target approaches its present output of greenhouse gases.

Whatever is the basis for targets, how should they be adjusted? Should they aim for parity in percentage reductions or in absolute cuts? As energy-efficient Japan points out, a percentage cut would cost gas-guzzling America far less than its own frugal citizens.

Finally, many arguments will rage over the pace at which gases should be curbed. Already, the level of output commits the world to a warmer climate in the future; even if not a kilowatt of fossil fuel were burned from tomorrow on, the planet's temperature would still rise. Greenhouse gases will linger longer in the atmosphere. At present levels, each year of burning raises total concentration, and so the commitment to future warming. Stabilization merely means that temperatures may rise more slowly than they will if output of greenhouse gases continues relentlessly to increase.

Rapid adjustments will be expensive; gradual adjustments will invariably cost less. (Of course, no adjustment at all may eventually force panic-stricken nations to rush through even larger cuts, from a much higher base, than may be necessary if they start to change their habits soon.) Whatever target governments set themselves, its absolute level will matter more than the date on which it is first met. To aim for, say, a 20% cut in a country's carbon-dioxide output by 2025 will be far less expensive than to try to reach the same target by 2010. Yet thanks to the power of compound interest, it will be more important come the year 2100 to have achieved a cut of 20% on 1990 levels about the beginning of the twenty-first century than to have leveled off 5% below 1990 levels in 2005.

To make a treaty work, targets may have to be flexible. At the least, developing countries will need room for some growth in energy consumption. Other environmental treaties have allowed poorer countries to aim for easier goals. Indeed, the Montreal Protocol set third world countries a deadline for CFC reductions ten years later than it gave rich nations. By encouraging countries to do what is in their own economic interest (such as ending energy subsidies), a treaty is likely to bring more reluctant participants aboard and—equally important—keep them there.

To capture potential free-riders, a treaty will have to keep down the costs to them of joining. There are two principal ways of doing that. One is to set them easy targets; the other is for other countries to bribe them to join. Logical recalcitrants will trade off the cost of complying against the benefit of bribery. The tougher the targets they are set, the higher the bribes will need to be.

But paying bribes will drive up the cost of an agreement to other countries. They will then have to carry not only the costs of their own adjustment, but also a share of the cost of bribery. The more they need to spend on bribes, the weaker the targets they may want. Weaker targets will reduce not only the cost of an agreement to their own citizens but also the number of potential free-riders.

The Montreal Protocol set a precedent by promising third world countries cash to help them meet environmental goals. The money to help third world countries pay for the technology to live without CFCs will be doled out from a new global environment fund that is managed partly by the World Bank. The CFC fund was set up only after a long battle with the Americans who initially refused to contribute to it, principally on the grounds that it risked being an enormous new demand for aid cash. As the Americans foresaw, the money needed to bring countries into a global-warming treaty will be far greater than originally envisioned. And buying the participation of some third world countries will continue. Governments are already hoping to draw up a treaty on biological diversity, setting goals for species conservation. The possibilities for abuse are obvious. Most species are in a handful of developing countries. Yes, they will promise, we will be green—but only at a price.

The question of technology transfer will be even more complicated. Before they start haggling, third world countries will want assurances that they will have access to first world technology to cut their output of greenhouse gases. This has proved one of the hardest problems to resolve under the Montreal Protocol. At the London conference in June 1990, Maneka Gandhi, India's current environment minister and widow of Sanjay, insisted that her country be given not only cash but the technology to make CFC substitutes. When William Reilly, head of America's Environmental Protection Agency, pointed out that the technology was owned by companies and not by the government, she retorted: "Well then, you develop it and then you give it to us."

Gandhi was mollified by an executive from Du Pont who offered to explore a joint venture in making alternatives to CFCs, as long as Du Pont kept control of the technology and safety standards and was in some way paid for its involvement. He pointed out, however, that India might be wiser not to manufacture the entire expensive range of substitute gases for its tiny market, but to invest in the technology to apply them: redesigned air conditioners, refrigerators, and so on. This suggests plenty of future arguments about the precise mechanics of compensation. If India has to pay extra to buy the gases to be used in place of CFCs, that will clearly be a claim on the fund. But what if India decides to build a plant to make the substitute gases? Should the fund pay for that, however uneconomic?

Complicated and expensive though such questions will be for CFCs, they will be far more difficult for greenhouse gases. That is one of the reasons for considering, as part and parcel of any agreement on climate change, some machinery that would simultaneously discourage countries from producing greenhouse gases and transfer cash from those who might be willing to pay to those who might need to be bribed. Already schemes have been devised by academics for an international tax on the carbon dioxide produced by each country, with the proceeds to be spent to help poorer countries adapt, and for internationally traded permits to produce greenhouse gases, whose distribution would be designed to penalize some countries and bribe others.

Economic instruments have two important uses in international treaties. First, they offer a mechanism for transferring resources from the virtuous to the potentially wicked. Second, they hold down the cost of regulating global pollutants. Such measures will almost invariably deliver any given environmental benefit at a lower cost to society than will straight regulation. Simply setting each country a target for cutting its output of CFCs, carbon dioxide, and other harmful gases will be a more expensive—perhaps far more expensive—approach than using a mechanism that takes account of the costs of curbing.

This is doubly important for global pollutants such as greenhouse gases. What matters environmentally is not how much gas each individual country produces, but the overall world total. For the planet, therefore, the most efficient approach will be to allow some countries to curb less, and others more, than whatever global target the agreement lays down. To set a constant target for each country—say, stabilization at 1990 levels by the end of the century—may appear fair but will actually be deeply inefficient. Just as the costs of switching to lead-free gas are far higher for an ancient Ford than a nearly new BMW, so the costs of implementing an identical target will be far higher for, say, energy-efficient Japan than for wasteful Poland.

But there is a further point. With regulation alone, companies have a powerful incentive to move from participating countries to those that refuse to sign an agreement or that cheat. Because economic instruments reduce the costs of complying, they also reduce the incentive to move in order to break the agreement. Efficiency alone, in other words, offers some hope of keeping a grip on potential free-riders.

Taxes and tradable permits each have their advocates. Most of the advocates of an international carbon tax are politicians, including Carlo Ripa di Meana, the EC Commissioner for the Environment. He is keen on a tax levied by each member country, based on the amount of carbon dioxide it produces. Each country would keep the revenue it raised. Most schemes for global carbon taxes envisage one levied by a world agency on each country, according to the amount of gases it produces. The tax would be set at the same level for each country, but the revenues would be handed back on a formula designed to bribe noncooperators (developing countries or large energy producers).

Barrett is one of the few academics who have argued for a tax. He points out that if an international agreement laid down the total quantity of greenhouse gases that could safely be emitted and then distributed tradable permits among nations, the world would (in theory, at least) know with some certainty the total amount of gases that could be produced. It would not know the price at which such permits would change hands. That price would reflect the cost of curbing greenhouse gases (since no permit would be bought if its price were higher than the cost of suppressing an equivalent amount of greenhouse gas).

With a tax, on the other hand, humanity could be sure about the cost of reducing greenhouse gases, but not of the quantity that would be abated. It might even be safer to be sure about the cost than about the quantity. Suppose the cost of reducing greenhouse gas output rose steeply after the first 20% or so had been cut (and Nordhaus thinks that it would). In that case, a tough limit to quantity might mean that the costs of getting rid of extra greenhouse gases would soar. Rather than buy expensive permits, many countries would simply cheat.

A greenhouse tax might be imposed separately by individual countries. Indeed, that may well happen on a regional scale: in 1991, the EC Commission's environment directorate was drawing up plans for EC-wide carbon taxes. But some proponents of greenhouse taxes envisage a large international agency to collect and recycle the revenue. The sheer sums of cash such an agency would have at its disposal make that vision unworldly. David Pearce points out that a global carbon tax designed eventually to halve carbon-dioxide output could result in tax revenues of $600 billion, of which $480 billion would be paid back to developing countries.[9] To put that figure in perspective, $600 billion is six times as much as all aid disbursements to third world countries in 1989. "It is scarcely credible," argues Pearce, "that any single international agency would have the capability to manage such resource transfers."

The alternative might be a mechanism for allowing countries to trade permits to produce greenhouse gases. Under such a system, Japan (which would find it expensive to reduce its output of gases) might buy permits from Poland (which would find it inexpensive, as long as it had the cash that a permit sale would bring in). Or Britain's National Power might reforest a stretch of Brazil with trees that would mop up carbon dioxide in exchange for being able to build another coal-fired power station. One American utility, Applied Energy Services of Virginia, announced in 1988 that it would pay for the tree planting in Guatemala to absorb the equivalent of the carbon dioxide released by a new power station.

Best of all, a company in America making refrigerators might set up a subsidiary in India to make refrigerators there too. If its refrigerators were more efficient than average for new machines in India, it could earn permits there, which it could then use to make models in America that were less efficient than the American average. Or it could simply make money by selling its permits on the world market. Thus a system of tradable permits could, in theory, give companies with energy-efficient technologies a big incentive to transfer their technologies to less efficient countries in the third world and Eastern Europe.

Elegant though this idea may sound, it has problems. First, if the scheme covered (as it logically should) all greenhouse gases rather than just carbon dioxide, there is plenty of room for argument about how to trade off one gas against another. All those scientific uncertainties about the sources and durability of different gases would bubble to the surface.

Second, even if the agreement covered only carbon dioxide, the price of permits would be strongly influenced by the behavior of the three biggest producers of the gas: the United States, the former Soviet Union, and the European Community.

Third, there would be the question of what to do if a country exceeded its permits. That raises the awkward questions of penalizing cheats. But without a credible arrangement for punishing the uncooperative, no one would have an incentive to pay for a permit. That American refrigerator manufacturer would end up with worthless pieces of paper. This is simply another version of the free-rider problem described earlier in this chapter. Finally and most difficult of all, on what basis should permits be distributed? They cannot, as Table 7.2 clearly shows, be based on relative wealth: China and the Soviet Union would never agree. Ought they to be distributed, as Michael Grubb has argued, on the basis of the number of adults in each country (which would disproportionately reward the third world but recognize the moral principle that every adult has an equal right to the atmosphere)?[10] Or, as is more realistic, ought the initial apportionment to reflect fairly closely the existing output of gases, with perhaps a provision for changing the formula over time?

A convention on climate change may well be signed by the middle of 1992. If so, it will be a remarkable achievement. Together with the Montreal Protocol, it will mark an extraordinary willingness to talk seriously about the global environment in a way that was unimaginable as recently as 1980. Even more extraordinary, it will be an agreement based largely on the testimony of scientists: indeed, on scientific speculation rather than observable fact. Bear in mind that most politicians heard of the greenhouse effect for the first time in 1988. It will have taken four years to move from first fears to promises of policy change.

But what will those promises be worth? The Montreal Protocol involves a commitment to self-sacrifice by a handful of companies mainly in rich countries. Part of the reason most of those companies agreed is that they could see the prospect of a profitable alternative: the manufacture of CFC substitutes. A climate change convention, by contrast, threatens to deprive energy producers of their livelihood with no promise of alternative gain. It is hardly surprising that, at the Second World Climate Conference in Geneva in November 1990, Saudi Arabia agreed to start negotiations on a climate change convention but objected to every mention of carbon dioxide. It had some support from the United States.

To the extent that energy-consuming countries do indeed reduce their demands on fossil fuels, the price of those fuels will decline. It will probably fall, anyway, in the mid-1990s recession. That will give an incentive to some countries to increase their use of fuels, moving into the most energy-intensive industries such as metals manufacture, cement production, and heavy engineering. In more scrupulous countries, those industries will howl for special exemptions or tax relief.

Table 7.2 Shares of Global Carbon-Dioxide Emissions and Shares of Global GDP (%, rounded)

	Share of world carbon-dioxide (fossil fuels only[a])	Share of world GDP
USA	24	27
USSR	19	8
China	9	2
Japan	5	14
Germany (FRG)	4	7
UK	3	3.5
Poland	2	0.5
Other	34	
Regional groupings		
W. Europe	15	
E. Europe, incl. USSR	26	
LDCs	16	

[a]Excludes gas flaring, cement, and bunkers.
Source: David Pearce, "International Greenhouse Gas Agreements: Part 1—International Tradable Permits," Department of Economics, University College London, mimeo, 1990.

It may well be that the countries that need to be bribed to cooperate in a climate-change agreement are not mainly those of the third world. Most third world countries, living close to subsistence level and dependent on the whims of climate to feed their burgeoning populations, probably have more to gain from a successful treaty than the better insulated developed countries. For the rich, the costs of adapting to climate change may seem lower—and easier to share out—than the costs of trying to prevent it. Better, they may think, to build a few sea walls than to raise gas taxes.

It will be the big energy producers whose support most needs to be bought. Saudi Arabia and Iran, the Soviet Union and China, perhaps even the United States, will all face large losses of income from a successful climate treaty. The Soviet Union, the world's largest energy producer, will hate the idea of signing an agreement that potentially deprives it of its most promising source of hard-currency earnings—even if, in its newly fragmented state, its signature were likely to mean anything. Saudi Arabia, which dominates the world market for oil, has nothing else to sell.

For some energy producers there may be partial compensations. The energy-producing republics of the Soviet Union might gain if Europe bought its low-carbon natural gas for hard currency, even if they could sell less of their enormous reserves of coal. Sitting on 40% of the world's natural gas reserves, the Soviet Union would be in a powerful position to dictate that fuel's world price if it were able to speak with one voice. China has calculated that climate change could reduce its agricultural output, kill off four of its six main timber species, and wreak havoc with its water resources. It may therefore agree to try to cut the growth in its output of carbon dioxide even if that means it has to mine less of its coal stocks. It is hard to see such offsetting gains for the United States, which produces almost a quarter of all the carbon dioxide made by burning fossil fuels. As the world's second largest energy producer, it will lose revenue from exports and may also be expected to compensate other, poorer energy producers. Small wonder that the United States has been so unenthusiastic about negotiating a climate convention.

Probably the best that can be hoped for between now and the end of the century is an agreement to reduce those sources of greenhouse gases that cause other kinds of environmental harm or that cost the least to prevent. Making the Montreal Protocol work well should be one priority; finding better ways of advancing energy conservation, especially in the third world, Eastern Europe, and the Soviet Union, should be another. Without firm evidence of the warming impact of greenhouse gases—perhaps without some climatic catastrophe—it will probably be impossible to go further.

Only if technological advance significantly reduces the costs of curbing greenhouse gases will that prediction turn out to be wrong. Just as the development of CFC substitutes made possible the Montreal Protocol, so the development of substitutes for fossil fuels would give the best hope for a climate-change treaty, especially if the substitutes were no more expensive than the originals. Such magic matter may not be attainable; but if it is, only industry can invent it. In that sense, environmental progress depends crucially on giving the right incentives to industry. That is the theme of the second half of this book.

8

The Challenge to Companies

For most companies, the outbreak of environmentalism that began in the late 1980s is either a threat or an irrelevance. The managers who have been packing conferences on environmental law, pollution technology, and green auditing have been driven more by anxiety about the costs of getting an environmental decision wrong—an expensive lawsuit, a planning application refused, angry customers, or worried workers—than the opportunities from getting it right. Only in marketing departments has the advent of the green consumer caused a quiver of excitement.

Beyond a doubt the new greenery will impose costs on companies. Many of them are discussed in the following chapters. Yet it also represents an extraordinary opportunity, perhaps the biggest opportunity for enterprise and invention the industrial world has ever seen. Those who spot how to make the most of this will flourish.

The impact will be immense within companies. The demand for cleaner products and processes will change the way they think about innovation. Prodded by green consumers, companies will ask their suppliers quite new questions about the origins of their raw materials and the way they are handled; cornered by regulations, companies will give growing attention to ways of

177

disposing of waste. When a new product is conceived, an early question will be, "But what happens at the end of its life?"

The costs of green policies will be an extra burden on industry. Often, indeed, governments will load onto industry costs that they feel unwilling to impose directly on voters. Companies investing in the reduction of emissions will have less cash to spend on developing new products; management time spent monitoring environmental performance is time not available for corporate growth. To that extent, industry can become greener only by growing more slowly.

But this is an inadequate and dispiriting account of what is likely to happen. At a conference on sustainable development in Bergen in May 1990, Björn Stigson, head of ABB Fläkt, a Swedish engineering firm, produced an intriguing analogy. "We treat nature like we treated workers a hundred years ago," he said. "We included then no cost for the health and social security of workers in our calculations, and today we include no cost for the health and security of nature." Environmental protection may be to the next 50 years what government-financed public services have been to the past 50: a drag on growth, true, and a large burden on corporate costs; but also an enormous and hard-to-quantify source of increased human well-being.

It will also be the source of a radical shift in consumer tastes. Developing products that use nature most frugally at both ends of their lives will call forth whole new generations of technology. The change will be more pervasive than those that followed the invention of the steam engine or of the computer. Fortunes await those who devise less expensive ways to dispose of plastics or to clean up contaminated soil. The great engineering projects of the next century will not be the civil engineering of dams or bridges, but the bio-engineering of sewage works and waste tips. Industry has before it that most precious of prospects: a spur to innovate.

The world will not grow cleaner without the cooperation of industry; for only through industry can technologies be developed which will satisfy human needs while making fewer demands on the environment. The challenge for government and for environmentalists is to spot ways of creating the right incentives so that industry finds it profitable to be clean and unprofitable to be dirty.

Many environmentalists wince at the very mention of industry. As they rightly see it, industrial activity is the immediate cause of most environmental damage. It is industry that spews gases into the atmosphere, dumps poison in rivers, builds factories on open fields, and digs mines in rain forests. It is industry, too, that makes the products that pollute: the packaging and plastics, the cars, and the disposables. Much environmentalism is a new version of the old hatred of business by the utopian left. Many of the policies promoted by radical greens are more concerned with stopping companies from doing whatever makes money than with making the world a cleaner, greener place.

Such utopianism is foolish. Perhaps in the Middle Ages there was a time when human activity had little lasting impact on nature's balance. That day is gone for good. Today, 5.6 billion people live on the earth; within a century that number will climb past 10 billion, perhaps to 15 billion. Even in the poorest countries, where the lives of millions are barely touched by industry as the developed world knows it, the impact on the environment is already immense. Sheer numbers will inevitably make that impact greater still. And that even without the universal desire for the fruits of development. Bringing water supplies and electricity to villages are sure ways of increasing the demands the third world makes on the environment; yet they save women hours of walking to fetch water and find wood. These saved hours mean healthier mothers, better nourished children, and improved hygiene.

It is utopian, too, to think that the fairly poor will not want the trappings of Western wealth. Top of the shopping list of every liberated East European is a family car. A senior official of Britain's Friends of the Earth recalls with pain the hostile reception he got when he delivered his standard green lecture on the environmental damage done by cars to an audience of trade union officials. Many of the products that harm the environment have made life easier for people who can still remember that life was less pleasant before. Washing machines use more water than hand washing but mean less work; plastic packaging preserves food longer and means fewer shopping trips; chemical herbicides kill bugs more quickly than hoeing.

Above all, disposable products—be they diapers, plastic cups, or hospital gowns—have frequently brought huge increases in convenience, at the cost of extra pressure on the environment. Disposables save labor, and labor is a resource that will be increasingly scarce in rich countries if population growth does not revive. As labor costs go up, disposable products of all kinds will become more attractive. However much the greenest greens may bemoan the "throw-away" society, powerful economic forces will continue to encourage it.

Role of Technology

It is important for environmentalists to understand these forces. Rather than yearning for a world that can never be recreated, they need to help develop incentives for industry to support human needs in the least polluting way. The best hope for the environment lies in accepting what Paul Gray, former president of the Massachusetts Institute of Technology, has called "the paradox of technological development."[1] The industrial economy causes environmental damage, but it also offers ways to repair that damage.

From its earliest days technology has enabled mankind to use the earth's resources more frugally. The wheel requires less energy to shift a heavy weight than does the sledge. The closed stove delivers the same amount of heat as the open fire with far less fuel. Domesticated grain produces more protein from an acre of land than does wild grass.

Technology can still perform such ancient conjuring tricks. Indeed, the ability of technology to find ways of squeezing more and more output from the same volume of input, especially if given the right price signals, helps explain why pessimists, who prophesied environmental catastrophe through the exhaustion of a vital raw material, have so frequently turned out to be wrong. Consider, for instance, these words, delivered by President Theodore Roosevelt in 1905 when America's railways were gobbling wood for sleepers: "Unless the vast forests of the United States can be made ready to meet the vast demands which this [economic] growth will inevitably bring, commercial disaster, that means disaster to the whole country, is inevitable. The railroads must have ties. If the present rate of forest destruction is allowed to continue with nothing to offset it, a timber famine in the future is inevitable."[2]

Within a matter of years, the voracious demand for wooden sleepers by American railways had been slowed by the development of techniques for treating wood with creosote, then by the replacement of wooden ties with concrete ones.

President Roosevelt was not uniquely alarmist. Forty years earlier, a British economist, W.S. Jevons, had published a book called *The Coal Question* in which he expressed deep fears for the future for British industry:

> I draw the conclusion that I think anyone else would draw, that we cannot long maintain our present rate of consumption; that we can never advance to the higher amounts of consumption supposed . . . the check to our progress must become perceptible considerably within a century from the present time; that the cost of fuel must rise, perhaps within a lifetime, to a rate threatening our commercial and manufacturing supremacy; and the conclusion is inevitable; that our happy progressive condition is a thing of limited duration.[3]

That was in 1865, only five years after oil, now the world's largest single source of primary energy, was discovered. Calculations for 1968 reckoned that at current annual rates of demand, enough fossil fuels (coal, oil, and gas) remained for the next 2,500 years.

The erroneous pessimism of Roosevelt and Jevons ought to be a reminder to those who now forecast environmental catastrophe. It is, of course, extremely hard to guess correctly the course of technology. (Partha Dasgupta defends economists from charges of unique myopia by citing the proceedings of a gathering of British scientists in 1876: "Although we cannot say what remains to be invented, we can say that there seems no reason to believe that electricity will be used as a practical mode of power."[4]) But we need to be reminded that technologies have cycles, and that public alarm at their side effects may frequently coincide with the arrival of a new technology that does not have those side effects but may well have others. Technology, as this chapter discusses, tends to solve one environmental problem by creating another. But it retains the ability to deliver unexpected solutions to apparently insoluble dilemmas.

The past century has seen two particularly remarkable examples of the ability of technology to make more from less (see Figure 8.1). The first is energy. Between 1900 and the 1960s, the quantity of coal needed to generate a kilowatt hour of electricity fell from nearly 7 pounds to less than 1 pound. More striking still, the entire world's per head demand for commercial energy in the ten years to 1987, a period of fast population growth, did not change, while wealth per head rose by 12% in real terms.

A glance at car technology suggests there could be even more efficiency ahead, given the right price signals. Renault has already built a prototype of a car that can do 100km on 3 liters of

---

Figure 8.1 Primary Energy Consumption Relative to GNP

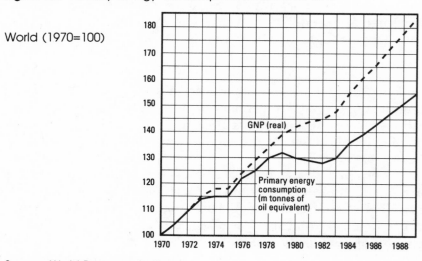

World (1970=100)

Source: World Resources Institute.

gas in town, 2.2 liters on the open road; Toyota is developing one that will do the same distance on 2.6 liters of diesel in the city, 2.1 liters on the open road. At present, the sales-weighted fuel economy of new cars in America is 8.4 liters per 100km. Remember that those prototypes were developed at a time when oil prices in real terms were declining worldwide. Calculations by General Motors suggest that the fuel price in America per vehicle mile, in 1989 prices, fell from 4 cents at the start of the 1980s to 2 cents by the end.

The increased ability of the world to feed itself has been even more striking. Anyone who looked at the terrifying projections for global population growth in the early 1960s found it unimaginable that the world could escape a devastating famine in the next three decades. There have indeed been some famines, although most, like the one in Ethiopia in the mid-1980s, have been partly linked to political disorder. But the appalling catastrophes that might have taken place have not. Instead, food output more than doubled in the world's poor countries between 1965 and 1988, well ahead of their soaring populations. The world's two most populous countries, China and India, have become self-sufficient in grain. The proportion of the world's people suffering from malnutrition has fallen (although the absolute number has increased). To a large extent, this transformation has been the accomplishment of the "green revolution," the breeding of new high-yielding strains of cereals, especially of rice. One reason for Africa's growing hunger is that there has been no green revolution in its staple food crops of cassava, millet, and corn.

The message is clear, and repeated often throughout history. It is that technology can often be environmentally helpful, finding substitutes for scarce natural resources or allowing existing resources to be stretched further. The task for government is to encourage industry to develop such technologies. One of the primary difficulties with this simple precept is the law of unintended consequences. Time and again, an apparently benign technology has turned out to have a sting in its tail.

Nothing sums up this point more poignantly than the life of Thomas Midgeley. A self-taught chemist on the research staff of General Motors, Midgeley and his team solved the problem of engine knock by discovering tetraethyl lead in 1921. This break-through led to the development of high-octane gas, which in turn made feasible more fuel-efficient high-compression gas engines.

Then in the late 1920s, Midgeley was given the task of finding a nontoxic, nonflammable substitute for the refrigerants in commercial use at the time. These were ammonia, methyl chloride, and sulphur dioxide, whose unpleasant characteristics made them unsuitable for use in the home. Midgeley came up with a compound called dichlorofluoromethane (freon 12). He demonstrated its safety to a meeting of the American Chemical Society in 1930 by inhaling a lungful of the gas, then using it to blow out a lighted candle. The product ensured the success of the Frigidaire division of General Motors and became invaluable in the Second World War as an aerosol propellant for insecticides such as DDT.

The life of the man who put lead into gas and chlorofluoro-carbons into the ozone layer ended in 1944. In 1940, he had been crippled by an attack of polio. He developed a pulley and harness contraption to help himself in and out of bed but strangled himself with the harness. It was a peculiarly appropriate demonstration of the unintended and malign consequence of even the most benign technological innovation.

Once a substance proves malign, moreover, it may be extremely difficult to get it out of the system. A side effect of the green revolution has been a large increase in world use of chemical pesticides and fertilizers. Yet the world cannot easily afford to return to the old varieties of grain that needed less of both, at least not without the development of new, genetically engineered varieties that may have other drawbacks. Even when industry agrees to get rid of a harmful product, the alternative may be much less convenient. Manufacturers of vacuum pumps voluntarily agreed to get rid of polychlorinated benzyls (PCBs), used in vacuum-pump oil, in 1971. Yet a suitable substitute has not been found. A small quantity of mercurials in emulsion paint provided excellent protection against mold. The alternative has been to use several different compounds in much higher concentrations, without being entirely sure about the ways in which those compounds react on each other.

Often, one environmental gain may be possible only if accompanied by a loss. Put a catalytic converter on a car and its fuel efficiency declines: the engine emits less nitrous oxide and sulphur dioxide but more global-warming carbon dioxide. Ban CFCs, and it becomes harder to insulate refrigerators and buildings. The ozone layer is protected but at the expense of higher greenhouse gas emissions. Biotechnology will pose many more questions of the same sort; for instance, is it better to have genetically engineered crops that require no pesticides, or may the environmental costs ultimately exceed the benefits?

Yet with all these reservations, the fact remains that industry has the ability to squeeze more output from natural resources. Inventive industry can find new ways of achieving the same impact on its market: to provide people with warmth, for instance, it may be more sensible to sell them better home insulation than more electricity. Increasingly, value is added by design, information, and quality; people spend more on attributes of a product that have nothing to do with the quantity of material in its manufacture and everything to do with the application of human ingenuity.

As manufacturing processes become better controlled, waste is reduced. As products from Coke cans to calculators become lighter, it takes less raw material and less energy to make them. Government needs to find ways of encouraging industry to use raw materials frugally. Such frugality brings double benefits. For every pound of raw material used is ultimately a pound of waste: use less water and there will be less dirty water; use less packaging and landfills will not be full of discarded paper and plastic.

The best way of ensuring that industry applies technology to solving environmental problems, rather than creating new ones, is to give the right price signals. Only if prices reflect the true cost of using environmental resources will companies start to value them as they value labor and capital, and aim to improve their productivity in the use of the environment as they strive for higher productivity of labor and capital.

A study by Robert Repetto of the WRI developed a measure of productivity for the American electricity industry which tries to take account of environmental productivity.[5] Making assumptions about the damage caused by power-station emissions, he reckoned that the cost of these unpriced outputs from the electricity industry in the mid-1980s was almost as great as the value of labor or the fuel the industry used. If the electricity industry had accounted for its success in cutting emissions, especially in the 1970s, when measuring its overall productivity, its performance would have been between two and three times as good as it appears from conventional estimates (see Figure 8.2).

Setting price signals, along with devising regulations or standards, is government's job. The green revolution is underpinned by governmental intervention. But industry and government have a common interest in making sure that such intervention leads to the greatest possible increase in the quality of the environment at the lowest possible cost. Companies want to try to make sure that environmental standards are set at levels they can reach but their competitors cannot; governments want to make sure that companies put cash and inventive energy into devising environmentally benign technologies. Once a company comes up with a green technology that allows it to meet a higher environmental standard than its competitors, government can insist that the higher standard become universal.

This is not what has happened in the past. Managers at environmental conferences are there because they have been trained to think of government regulation as a nuisance, not an oppor-

Figure 8.2 Single-Factor Productivity: United States Electricity Industry (1970=100)

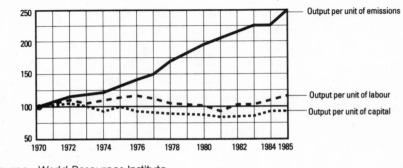

Source: World Resources Institute.

tunity. Yet when government intervenes, through regulation or through setting price signals, it creates new markets. Suddenly, electric cars become profitable; waste-management shares boom; desulphurization plants are in demand.

Both industry and government need to realize how far the market for environmental technology will be created and sustained by government intervention. Consumers' taste for green products will boom and fade, although always returning to a higher level of environmental consciousness from every trough. In the recession years of the mid-1990s, the green consumer will be replaced, at least at the mass market level, by the penny-pincher. Only the wealthier, trend-setting shoppers will pay a premium for green goods.

But the market for environmentally friendlier products will remain. It will be sustained by a number of things: by the rising legal penalties for polluting accidents, by the difficulty of persuading local communities to accept new factories that may pollute, and above all, by ever-tighter regulations about waste disposal. Governments, harried by voters, will continue to press for tighter standards for wastewater, for dirty air, and above all for solid rubbish, both hazardous and harmless. As these pressures will fall directly on companies (and on waste-disposal authorities), they will be largely hidden from voters, who will assume that they are being offered a free ride to greenery.

In fact, government regulations will raise the returns on all kinds of environmentally friendly investments. A water-treatment plant, uneconomical in the early 1980s, will look like a much better buy once the cost of sewage discharges goes up and the insurance premiums for an accidental spill become astronomical. A precipitator in the smokestack, once ridiculed by the finance director, will seem a bargain when the alternative is an entirely new plant.

For governments the trick will be to devise controls that foster green technology. That will be difficult. The temptation will be to regulate pollution by double-guessing companies: laying down the technologies they must use, instead of setting targets for the output of pollution and leaving corporate ingenuity to come up with answers. If governments seek the cooperation of the greenest companies, they will have to avoid protecting a particular technological solution to a given environmental problem.

There are dangers, of course, in relying on a confluence of interest between government and industry to raise environmental standards. Companies will always be tempted to press government to set standards in terms of a technology that they have devised, rather than in terms of its impact; and for government it will often be easier to do things that way. Large companies with political clout will see the alternative to, say, CFCs in terms of another chemical; or the alternative to cars running on leaded gas as cars running on lead-free gas.

But standards set in terms of specific technologies discourage innovation. That often comes not from the politically weighty giants, but from the minnows; environmental innovation, like many other kinds, tends to come from "outsiders," like small companies, suppliers, and foreign firms.

These are the companies for whom the environment presents the greatest opportunity. The new technologies that they invent are the world's best hope of enjoying a continued rise in living standards without putting greater pressure on the environment. The cleanest countries will be those whose environmental rules make it easiest for such companies to flourish. The most successful companies will be those that best turn such green rules to their own advantage.

9

The Green Consumer

What a fright the green consumer gave companies in the late 1980s. Retailers and manufacturers were knocked for a loop by the most dramatic change in customers' tastes that they had ever experienced. The shoppers' revolt broke out in Europe, but when it spread across the Atlantic, it found customers who were already used to throwing their purses behind every health scare at a moment's notice.

The companies that green consumers affected, primarily retailers and manufacturers of consumer goods, were traumatized. They learned that taking the environment seriously can be profitable. Managers who had long regarded environmentalists as a nuisance, pressing for product changes without appreciating their expense, suddenly discovered that ordinary people were willing to pay a premium for a product that they perceived as being better for the environment than a rival brand. Once the environment was upscale, it was worth worrying about.

The sheer speed with which green consumerism erupted in some countries will also have left its mark. A whole generation of managers will remember for the rest of their working lives how Americans suddenly panicked over Alar in apples, or how quickly British customers stopped buying aerosols containing CFCs. That will make companies more interested in the contents of their products, and more alert to the first whiff of a new environmental alarm.

Green consumerism has differed from country to country, and shoppers have concentrated on different products in different places. In America, customers fretted about packaging but were not much interested in the contents of mercury batteries; in Britain, "green" batteries sold wonderfully, but customers continued to accept plastic bags from supermarkets; and Germans worried about the plastics used to make drink bottles and ripped packaging from their purchases in supermarkets. The change in consumers' tastes was gradual in some countries, dramatic in others. Where it happened most suddenly, companies found it a hair-raising experience. Product markets collapsed or erupted in what sometimes seemed an arbitrary way. "At least with regulations," said Ron McLean, who runs environmental management in Europe for Arthur D. Little, an American consultancy, "you know what's coming for six months before and can lobby." Managers in some companies have been left scarred, vowing never to be caught out again. That alone is likely to ensure that some companies remain warily green even if the immediate pressure from the consumer fades.

In the United States, people worried in the early 1970s about issues, such as chlorine bleach in paper, that only dawned on some Europeans (including the British) in the late 1980s. The late 1980s saw a revival of environmental consciousness among consumers in America. A survey of Americans by Michael Peters (MPG), a British product-development consultancy, in the summer of 1989, found that 53% of those questioned had declined to buy a product during the previous year because they were worried about the effects the product or its packaging might have on the environment. Three-quarters of those surveyed said they would buy a product with biodegradable or recyclable packaging, and roughly as many were willing to pay a little more for such goods. A parallel survey the firm conducted in Canada found that the public's greenery quotient was just behind America's. Two-thirds of those questioned said they would be more likely to buy a product with recyclable or biodegradable packaging, and about 60% said they would be willing to pay more for such products. But in America, the relative weakness of retailers vis-à-vis manufacturers has meant that supermarkets have mainly followed, not led. Manufacturers of consumer goods, such as Procter & Gamble and Coca-Cola, and some companies in service industries, such as McDonald's, have been the leaders.

In Britain, where there had been less interest in the environment, the change was more dramatic. Within a few months, people learned to ask for aerosols that contained no CFCs, detergents free of phosphates, and beef that had not been grazed on cleared rain forest. The public, previously squeamish about using toilet paper made partly from recycled fiber, suddenly clamored for it. A poll by MORI, a British market research group, found that between November 1988 and May 1989 the proportion of respondents who said they had chosen a product because of its environmental friendliness soared from 19% to 42%.

The structure of British retailing, dominated by a few powerful chains, which dictate to manufacturers, also helps to explain what happened. Most of the supermarket chains reacted swiftly to the revolution in shoppers' tastes, forcing manufacturers to follow with equal speed. In other parts of Europe where retailers have strong market power, they have also picked up and amplified the change in shoppers' attitudes. But in northern Europe, green consumerism is old hat. Germans and Scandinavians have been buying phosphate-free detergent for years. Surveys by market researchers tend to show that Germans are in advance not just of the British, but even of the verdant Dutch, and that environmental awareness in Germany is the norm rather than the exception.

For the most ardent environmentalists, the green consumer is the ultimate oxymoron. Consumers are the problem, not the solution: consuming uses up the earth's capacity to produce materials and absorb waste. When, in September 1989, SustainAbility, a British environmental consulting firm, sponsored a Green Shopping Day, Friends of the Earth threatened to run a rival No Shopping Day. Beyond a doubt, the truly environmental should consume less, not differently. But until such a miraculous change in human disposition comes about, it is surely to the good that customers ask for more environmentally friendly products.

Origins of Consumer Consciousness

Environmentalism in the shops and at the polls grew mainly from the same roots. The atmosphere was ripe: in the summer of 1988, the press was full of stories of climate change, burning rain forests, and vanishing ozone. In Britain, the match to the fuse seems to have been the publication in September of *The Green Consumer Guide*.[1] Within four weeks it had shot to the top of the bestseller list in Britain. While other "green" guides tend to concentrate on general instructions to use bottle banks and insulate houses, the Elkington-Hailes guide in its British (though not its American) edition offered ratings for companies and products. It listed refrigerators by energy efficiency, dishwashers by water efficiency, and gas companies by the number of sites selling lead-free gas. Most influential of all, it gave grocery chains stars for greenery and listed a range of criteria on which they had been judged. A sign that consumers were ready for guidance of this sort was the success of a campaign by Friends of the Earth to persuade supermarket chains to introduce non-CFC propellants into generic-brand aerosols (something America had done years earlier).

Companies reacted in different ways to this sudden shift in tastes. Many buried their heads in the sand and hoped the whole upheaval would disappear. Others, more rationally, argued that environmental considerations would always influence consumers less than quality and price. Others realized that some customers saw environmental excellence as an aspect of quality and were willing to pay a premium for environmentally sound products. This was particularly true in North America and Britain. A study of American consumers by Abt Associates in November 1990 found that 90% of those interviewed said they would pay more for environmentally sound products.[2] The first quantitative study of Britain's green consumers was completed by Mintel, a market research firm, in June 1989.[3] The study excited boardrooms with its finding that some shoppers were willing to pay a premium of 25% or more for organically grown food and environmentally friendly products. For some time companies in continental Europe had viewed environmental issues as a way to move upscale. For instance, Germany's AEG, a producer of white goods, recovered from near bankruptcy in the early 1980s by manufacturing a washing machine that used less detergent, energy, and water than its rivals. Tengelmann, a large German retailer, began a campaign to attract green customers in 1984, when the German retail market was in the doldrums. In Britain, that example was seized on by Tesco, a chain attempting to change its shabby image. Tesco took environmental policy well beyond the supermarket shelves. By the end of 1989 it had become the first British retailer to install bottle banks at most of its stores, and the first to offer customers facilities for recycling plastics.

The link between environmental consciousness and the top of the market emerges from several pieces of market research. In America, a study by Cambridge Reports/Research International found that green consumers (defined by people's interest in green issues rather than their spending patterns) were almost twice as likely as the nongreen sort to earn over $50,000 a year and to be college graduates. The Mintel study found that a quarter of British adults could be described as "strong green." Although they exist across all social divisions, they were most common among the young, better off, and better educated, and in the economically buoyant south. One possible moral: the environment is chic.

Company Responses

A company that sets off down the environmental path soon finds it to be a long and tortuous one. Companies realize that if they are to boast about being environmentally friendly, they need to think not just about the impact of their product in the hands of the consumer, but about the process by which that product is made and sold. So the company that sells recycled paper towels soon wonders whether it should recycle its office paper; the company that boasts that its bottles can be recycled goes on to provide a bottle bank; the detergent manufacturer that begins by removing phosphates may end up analyzing the impact of a particular detergent on the environment right through its life cycle.

Some companies found that their initial response to the green consumer carried them further than they might have imagined at the outset. For instance, Coca-Cola, which has already cut the amount of raw materials used in its packaging, launched a joint venture with Hoechst Celanese early in 1991 to make bottles for soft drinks out of recycled plastics, thus closing the loop between initial product and eventual scrap. Gateway, a British supermarket chain, is now committed to developing new shops in urban centers and avoiding greenfield sites wherever possible.

Migros, Switzerland's biggest retailer, has a computer program to check the "eco-balance" or life cycle impact of its packaging: which kinds take most resources to make and to dispose of. Prodded partly by their customers, a growing number of companies on both sides of the Atlantic have become interested in studying the life cycle impact of products. They try to appraise the effect on the environment not only of the materials used to make a product and its packaging, but also of the energy involved from raw-material extraction through to delivery to the customer, and of the amount of a product a customer needs to use to produce a given effect. There may be no point in making an environmentally benign detergent if customers need to use three times as much to clean their clothes; or in producing a refillable container if it uses much more material than the nonrefillable kind and customers do not make the return trip.

As retailers' awareness of environmental issues grows, and as they find that their customers care about the environment, they pass the message up the line to their suppliers. When customers first began to think about the environment, supermarkets generally found that their conventional suppliers could not switch track fast enough, so they looked abroad, to countries where concern for the environment had taken root earlier. Three of the companies to benefit most in Britain's green boom were West German or Belgian: Varta, a German manufacturer of batteries, whose mercury-free and cadmium-free batteries increased their market share of sales through grocery stores from 7% to 17% in the space of six months in early 1989; AEG, whose sales rose by 30% in the year to May 1989, at a time when it was claiming to be "caring for the environment through technology"; and Ecover, a Belgian manufacturer of phosphate-free detergents, whose admittedly small sales increased from $1 million in autumn 1988 to $5 million just over a year later.

Similarly, when Loblaw, a Canadian grocery chain, deliberately decided to take a leaf out of Tesco's book and use environmental campaigns to smarten up its image, it found it hard to find suppliers in North America. Many of the 100 green products it put on its shelves in 1989 were imported from European firms, including Ecover. Not for the first time, it paid to have thought about the environment early. Loblaw's president, David Nichol, recalls the many years the Canadian government spent trying to persuade Procter & Gamble to introduce a phosphate-free detergent. "When we started selling a phosphate-free detergent, they got one on the market within six months."

Role of Suppliers

In a more radical departure, companies have begun to ask searching questions of their suppliers. America's three leading tuna canners, with 70% of the market, decided in April 1990 to ensure that their fish was caught only in "dolphin-friendly ways." As the Brazilian rain forest blazed in 1989, Marks and Spencer, a British retailer, sent a team there to find out whether their beef grazed on deforested pasture. McDonald's was attacked in *The Green Consumer Guide* for encouraging deforestation by its beef-buying policy and rebutted the criticism only after close scrutiny of its suppliers worldwide. British do-it-yourself chains began to cross-question suppliers about their policies: one, B&Q, looked at the peat bogs they use for garden fertilizers and eliminated one it thought was badly managed. Tengelmann wrote to suppliers in 1989 that all products and packaging containing cellulose must be chlorine-free.

Role of Marketing

The rise of the green consumer has been accompanied by the advent of the green advertisement. Casting around for green things to say about their companies, many marketing departments begin by describing what a company already does as "environmentally friendly." The delivery trucks use lead-free gas? The office has just been insulated to save electricity? The paper towels use a fair proportion of recycled material? Splendid. Call in the copywriters and think of a slogan. Or simply put a picture of a rabbit or a tree on the package and hope that some customers will infer a message that was never there.

Others, more reasonably, have adopted "cause-related marketing," an idea piloted in the early 1980s by American Express to raise money to repair the Statue of Liberty. Businesses such as banks or computer companies whose own activities do not impinge on the environment in ways that are obvious to consumers have offered to help support an environmental charity. The beneficiaries have tended to be the safer, middle-of-the-road charities, rather than aggressive ones like Greenpeace. Even so, such schemes have caused much soul-searching among some recipients. WWF (the Worldwide Fund for Nature, or the World Wildlife Fund, as it is still known in America), long skilled in raising cash from companies in exchange for the right to use its logo, suddenly found that many newly environmentally aware companies saw the familiar cuddly panda as the most distinctive of all environmental symbols. That brought benefits, as fund-raising grew easier. But with the money came qualms: WWF's supporters wanted to know whether the logo was going to companies whose environmentalism was impeccable or simply to those willing to bid for it.

So environmental marketing has rapidly turned out to be a morass. A heavily advertised American line of "biodegradable" plastic bags did not rot even when exposed to the air, and left small plastic pellets behind when they did. That enraged consumer lobbyists as well as environmentalists. The producer, Mobil, found itself sued by six states for misleading advertising. British companies have had their knuckles rapped by the Advertising Standards Association, the industry's watchdog, for calling their products "environmentally friendly" or "green," as food firms were once scolded for calling their cottage cheeses "slimming." Most have now switched to "environmentally friendlier." Nothing is gained by claiming that a drink can is "recyclable" if there are no facilities to recycle it. A bill in the California legislature in 1991 therefore proposed to outlaw the word "recyclable" on all labels unless consumers had easy access to a recycling facility.

Some advertising suggested that copywriters were more ignorant about the environment than the average consumer. A British ad for a new Rover car claimed it was "as ozone friendly as it is economical" because it used lead-free gas, disregarding the fact that gas, lead-free or not, has no direct effect on the ozone layer. BP Oil, falling into a similar trap, advertised its unleaded "Supergreen" gas by saying it caused "no pollution of the environment."

Such silliness, however, is merely peripheral. A far more difficult problem is that a product environmentally friendlier in one respect may not be in others. Procter & Gamble and Wal-Mart, America's second largest retailer, earned some derision for putting a green label on a brand of paper towels made from chlorine-bleached unrecycled paper packaged in plastic, simply because the inner tube was made of recycled material. ICI, a large British chemical company, launched a range of household cleaners early in 1990 with a claim that they were "environmentally friendly." Friends of the Earth promptly informed the press that, while the impact of the cleaners might be fairly benign when they were washed down the kitchen sink, their manufacturing process was a significant cause of water pollution and required a great deal of energy.

Whether a process meets the environmental claims made for it may be genuinely unclear. Or—and this will increasingly be the case—whether one product or process is less damaging to the environment than another may be impossible to tell. An example of the first sort ended up in the French courts. Rhône-Poulenc, the world's third largest phosphate producer, quarreled with Henkel, a German chemical manufacturer, over the impact of detergent phosphates on river life. Phosphate-free detergents account for 90% of the market in Germany, which is the largest user of cleaning preparations in all of Europe. In ungreen France, their share was only 6% until Henkel launched a product called Le Chat in 1989. Then sales tripled. Rhône-Poulenc retaliated with studies proving, it claimed, that phosphate-free detergents were more harmful than the old kind, and ran posters of dying fish supposedly killed by phosphate-free suds. Henkel took Rhône-Poulenc to court and succeeded in getting its campaign stopped.

It is not clear that detergents are an important source of phosphates in water supplies, though this has not stopped the phosphate-free share of the world detergent market from climbing from 6% in the early 1970s to 60% by 1988. Nor is it clear that mercury in discarded batteries is a source of water contamination; but this has not stopped battery manufacturers from eliminating mercury in zinc carbon and zinc chloride batteries and profiting handsomely from it, as Varta did.

Mercury-free and cadmium-free batteries still contain lead and harmful acids. Green advertising often tends to emphasize the nasty things taken out of a product without saying much about the nasty substances still there, or put in as substitutes. As Procter & Gamble put it,

> Too many environmental claims are currently based on the absence of particular ingredients. Users of such claims are thus able, in one phrase, to imply the safety of the ingredients they do use, and impugn the safety of those they do not use, without substantiation in either case. At the extreme, some such claims are based on the absence of ingredients which are not used in any product in the category.[4]

The argument over diapers has been even more muddling for the poor consumer. In America, Procter & Gamble commissioned work on the relative environmental impacts of disposable and cloth diapers. Add in the chemicals to soak the ones made of cloth, the hot water to wash them, and the gas for the vans that run diaper services, and Procter & Gamble, whose disposable diapers account for 18% of its sales, was able to mount a vigorous case for the environmental merits of the disposable. Environmentally conscious parents who want to swaddle their babies in cloth have begun to worry about the pesticides used to grow the cotton, so Seventh Generation, an American mail-order company specializing in products for green consumers, has a booming business in "green" cotton.

The proliferation of such environmental debates has had two effects. First, it has encouraged the formulation of advertising codes of conduct to set out what environmental benefits can and cannot be touted. The Federal Trade Commission and the Environmental Protection Agency, petitioned for guidance on green labeling by a coalition of trade associations, have been working to develop uniform national guidelines for environmental marketing claims. In Britain, the Department of Trade and Industry is considering bringing green advertising claims under the legal controls operated through the Trade Descriptions Act of 1968. The Advertising Standards Association, which monitors the truthfulness of advertising, has urged companies to produce documentary evidence to support broad claims.

At the same time, consumers have become more skeptical about environmental claims. Environmental Research Associates of Princeton, New Jersey, found in 1991 that nearly 47% of consumers dismissed environmental claims as "mere gimmickry." Hardly surprising: Marketing Intelligence Service of Naples, New York, simultaneously found that 26% of all new household items launched in 1990 boasted that they were ozone-friendly, recyclable, biodegradable, compostable, or some other shade of green.[5]

A survey of British consumers by the advertising agency Ogilvy & Mather found that between August 1989 and February 1990, the proportion of shoppers changing to a "greener" brand or switching to a different outlet to buy a greener product had stopped rising and was static at 23% and 14%, respectively. The agency also reported that the most "active" consumers, those most likely to make green purchases, were becoming disillusioned and making fewer of them.

Some shops find that people are reluctant to buy green products if they do not work as well as conventional alternatives. The chemicals that make a product "ungreen"—optical brighteners in detergents, mercury in long-life batteries—may be, at least so far, impossible to replace with something that does the job equally well. Never before (except perhaps in wartime) have manufacturers tried asking consumers to accept lower performance for the sake of a greater good.

The question companies most want answered is whether green consumerism is a passing fad or here to stay. In the same way as it arrived at a different pace in different countries, so experience will not be the same everywhere. Some survey evidence suggests that German consumers, besides having been environmentally conscious for longer than any others, also have a longer environmental memory than the more recently conscious Dutch or the British.[6]

Indeed, the longevity and effectiveness of green consumerism in Germany suggest a lesson for other countries. The media hype will fade, but consumer sensitivity will remain. Consumers will take it for granted that retailers and their suppliers care about the environment. Criticism from one of the environmental lobbying organizations, the self-appointed policemen of the environment, will cost sales. But good environmental behavior may simply become one of a bundle of indicators of quality that customers look for when they shop.

Advertising, which is an important medium of consumer education, has done much for green consumerism. Because companies spent so much in the late 1980s on advertising their environmentally friendlier products, consumers have been taught to think in new ways. For example, Procter & Gamble, one of America's biggest purchasers of advertising space, has worked hard to teach consumers about greener packaging and to promote the idea of refills. A generation of shoppers will have had their perception of packaging permanently altered by such campaigns.

The Need for Informed Consumers

Even those companies that have benefited from green consumers bewail their ignorance. If only, they sigh, it were possible to point out the slender links between phosphates and eutrophication or to spell out the finer points of the argument over bleach and water pollution. Then, perhaps, consumers might understand why one detergent is wrong when it claims it is better for the environment than its rivals, and stop switching their shopping habits with such maddening unpredictability.

Many shoppers are undoubtedly ill-informed. The November 1990 study by Abt Associates concluded that "consumers mean to do the right thing but don't always have the correct information with which to make purchase decisions." It found that second in popularity among all "green" purchases by American shoppers (after personal-care products) were those "biodegradable" plastic bags environmentalists so deplore. Research by Gerstman and Meyers, an American firm of packaging designers, found that 43% of those surveyed did not understand that a plastic ketchup bottle is not biodegradable and is unlikely to be recycled. In the early days of British green consumerism, in 1988, the market research firm of Gould Mattinson Associates found that "respondents were frequently unable to explain why products were harmful [but] there seemed to be an instinctive suspicion of clingfilm, burger boxes and pesticides." More dramatically, a survey carried out in the summer of 1989, when furious Americans were punishing Exxon for the *Exxon Valdez* oil spill by cutting up their account cards, found that British respondents rated Esso one of the greenest companies in the country.

Shoppers need to be well-informed about environmental cause and effect in order to be effectively green. Hence the attraction of "eco-labeling." In California, Scientific Certification Systems, a food and products testing company, has set up a scheme to award a "Green Cross" seal of approval to products that meet certain environmental criteria. The scheme has the backing of four big grocery chains. "Green Seal," a rival scheme based on the East Coast, also proposed to vet products. It decided to look at a restricted range of products, including household paint, facial tissues, and light bulbs, and assess their impact on the environment from every conceivable viewpoint. As of mid-1991, neither scheme had begun awarding labels. Both were still drafting criteria and sniping at each other. More limited private-sector schemes exist in various countries. Many supermarkets now have their own schemes, often based on sketchy criteria. So do some industries. Ten British paper merchants agreed on a labeling scheme to explain the contents of recycled paper. All such private

schemes, which do not employ uniform definitions or regulations, are inevitably second-best and confuse shoppers.

Governments too are beginning to run eco-labeling schemes.
Canada and Japan both established programs in 1989. Norway,
Sweden, and Finland all planned to launch schemes by the end
of 1991; France, Austria, and New Zealand also had plans,
though less well advanced. The European Commission, fearful
that the rival schemes of member states could make free trade
more difficult, is planning a scheme of its own. The prototype is
Germany's Blue Angel: in operation since 1977, it is now run by
the federal environment ministry and covers everything from
quiet lawnmowers to recycled wallpaper. At one point the Blue
Angel logo was recognized by four out of five German consumers. America has moved more slowly: federal definitions of what
"organic" means were introduced in the 1990 Farm Bill, and
there is a move to bring in a federal eco-seal, to be awarded by
the Environmental Protection Agency. But most of the initiative
has been at the state level: California has considered a statewide
plan, and a group of northeastern states have discussed common
regulations on labeling. The peculiarites of American law mean
that a government-backed scheme would be more open to legal
challenge than is possible in other industrial countries.

All these plans face problems, some of which crystallize the
difficulties facing even the most earnest green consumer. For
instance, should the basis for awarding the label be limited to
the way a product affects the environment when it is used, or
should the manufacturing process and its disposability also be
considered? The Blue Angel award is based on a limited range
of criteria, including the way in which a product scores on water,
air, and noise pollution and waste generation at four stages in
its life: production, distribution, use, and disposal. For instance,
anticorrosive coatings may qualify for the award if they have a
low lead and chromium content; and burners for central-heating
systems may be included if they have high energy efficiency and
low emissions of soot, sulphur dioxide, and nitrogen oxide. A
label states the reason for the award. Many of the 65 product
categories are not consumer goods. Only about 10% to 20% of
products in a particular category are likely to win an award.
More than 10% of environmental product labels in Germany are
held by foreign firms (including 14 from the Netherlands, 11

from Austria, 33 from ten other West European countries, and some Japanese car manufacturers and American chemical companies).[7]

As eco-labeling plans become more widespread, environmentally conscious companies may welcome them. But when the British government began to consider one such plan, the Confederation of British Industry attacked the idea. Procter & Gamble, however, argued that it would help protect firms that are scrupulous about their product claims against those that are not. It would also help with "the difficult problems of communicating environmental information, which is often complex and technical, in a way that consumers will understand." Other firms pray that the labeling will also lead to uniform standards. *Managing the Environment*, a study of the greening of European companies, quotes the lament of a manager from Perrier, a French soft-drink manufacturer, which has half its turnover outside France. "The rules change every day. Italy is changing its bottling rules; worse than that, some cities have different rules on plastic bottles. The Germans are taxing plastic bottles. The Swiss outlawed metal containers and are ahead in preferring carton boxes."[8]

But as more countries try to set up such schemes, the dilemmas they pose are also becoming clear. Should the label be restrictive or wide-ranging? If labels are to raise product standards, they need to be awarded sparingly. But if too few products qualify, then a second aim—educating consumers—may not be met. Ought the label to be available only to detergents and paper products, or to dog food and—why not?—bank accounts? Should the plans reward "best" technology or simply "better"? Few products actually benefit the environment. But some proposed schemes exclude whole groups of products—such as household chemicals—on the grounds that even the best cause too much harm. In general, schemes are likely to concentrate on products whose use environmentalists want to promote (biodegradable engine oil in Canada, building materials made from waste paper in Germany). The testers will tend to neglect more common items, whose effect on the environment may worry shoppers but be difficult to measure or simply bore environmentalists. Procter & Gamble claims that, with one small exception, not one of its products is covered by an environmental-labelling scheme anywhere in the world. Yet it is precisely Procter & Gamble's detergents, dishwashing powder, and disposable diapers on which consumers might most like an impartial view.

Eco-labeling, by highlighting the complexity of environmental choices, may encourage governments to think through their priorities. Is it more important to save paper by encouraging mothers to use cloth diapers than to save hot water and the energy it requires by encouraging the use of disposables? Should food and medicines be swathed in layers of tamper-proof packaging or sold with as little wrapping as possible? Such questions are too complicated to be left to even the most enthusiastic individual to resolve.

Green Investment

"Goodness is the only investment that never fails," said Thoreau. Not a maxim financiers often preach, but the success of the green consumer in turning managers into environmentalists has inspired others to bring environmental awareness to the stock exchange. The demand for green investments from individual investors on both sides of the Atlantic grew along with the demand for green products at the supermarket. One survey of 246 shareholders across America found that the two areas where they most wanted companies to put their money—even before paying higher dividends—were, first, cleaning up plants and stopping environmental pollution, and second, making safer products.[9] When Eagle Star, a large British financial group, surveyed some of its unit trust holders in 1989, it found that 72% rated the ecological stance of a fund manager as important while only 46% gave such weight to the manager's ideological views. The predictable result: a rush of new environmental funds, offering punters the hope of doing well by doing good. Some are run by idealists, hoping to use shareholders' votes to lean on companies. Others are more hard-nosed, and hope to match a new environmentally conscious kind of shareholder with the companies that profit from greenery.

The concept of "ethical" or "social" investment was originally developed in America, spurred by the desire of institutions such as churches and universities not to put money into companies doing business in South Africa. Since 1981 such investors and the institutions that advise them have had their own club, the Social Investment Forum (SIF). Most of its members apply at least one ethical criterion in selecting investments, generally connected with South Africa; but some also screen out companies involved in defense, nuclear power, tobacco, alcohol, and gambling, and those with bad employment and environmental records.

Partly to cater to such customers, a growing number of mutual funds offer ethically screened investments. Biggest is the Calvert Group, with assets at the end of 1990 of $500 million. By that date such funds in America had assets of $1 billion. The portfolios of such groups include the shares of companies that do not profit from environmental activities—banks, say, or computer manufacturers—and whose approach to environmental issues is regarded as virtuous. A different kind of "environmental" fund started to appear in America in the summer of 1989, investing in one of 100 or so firms that seemed likely to benefit from the boom in cleaning up pollution. These funds vary greatly in greenness. Typically they are run by one of the large securities houses such as Merrill Lynch. Some $600 million had flowed into such funds by the end of 1990. An older, purer version of this type of fund is New Alternatives, a small fund set up on Long Island in 1982. It invests primarily in companies developing alternative energy and pollution-control technology.

In Britain, the complexities of trust law make it harder for institutions to worry about the morality of their investments than about the rate of return. So the demand for ethical investment has come less from churches and universities (nowhere near as well-heeled as their transatlantic counterparts) and more from virtuous private individuals. The first screened unit trust in Britain was launched in 1984 by Friends Provident (a company, as its name suggests, with Quaker roots); Friends' Stewardship Unit Trust is by far the biggest social fund in Britain.

The Merlin Ecology Fund is the greenest of the British funds, launched in April 1989 by a group now known as Jupiter Tarbutt Merlin. The fund has a companion, Merlin International Investment Trust. Both initially steered clear of investments in businesses they deemed intrinsically polluting (such as oil), even if a firm was working hard at reducing the environmental damage it did. That austere attitude has now softened. Both groups look for the most environmentally responsible companies within each industrial sector, including, for example, Echo Bay Mines, a North American gold-mining company with a good environmental record.

All told, ethically screened unit trusts, pension funds, and investment trusts in Britain had assets of about £260 million in mid-1990, although the total of institutional investment with some ethical screening was several times larger. As investors moved out of unit trusts at the end of 1990, ethical and environmental funds seemed to be holding on to their cash better than the less virtuous.

Such funds are starting to spring up outside of America and Britain. Norway's leading investment company, Investa, has launched one. The Artus fund, launched in Cologne, Germany, in 1989, puts most of its cash into Merlin and New Alternatives. The idea has spread to banking in Germany: the Okobank of Frankfurt was founded in May 1988 to lend money to environmentally sound projects.

By and large, green funds aim to give their investors a return at least as good as they would earn on less virtuous investments. This is important for lawyers who, on both sides of the Atlantic, are likely to take the pragmatic view that as long as an ethically screened investment does better than the market average, then the use of the screen is unlikely to be challenged in the courts. Research on the performance of screened funds is sketchy, and is primarily conducted by true believers. But one study by Peter Kinder, a member of the SIF, of 400 stocks screened for a broad range of constraints, including South African operations and environmental virtue, found they did marginally better than the Standard & Poor's 500 index over five years from the start of 1984. In Britain, the Ethical Investment Research Service has constructed eight hypothetical portfolios of British shares over five years from October 1983, screened primarily for South Africa, nuclear weapons, and tobacco (though not greenery). Only two had yields worse—by a whisker—than the FTA all-share index.

Ethical investors have sometimes found it easier to weed out the unethical from their portfolios than to find solid virtue. Okobank, for instance, took in DM73 million ($46 million) of deposits in its first two years but could find borrowers for only DM25 million. In this case, the lack of a branch network made it hard to find suitable customers. But its problem is the same one faced by green consumers and green labelers: How green is green enough?

In America, a divide has opened up between the attitude taken by funds set up by conventional financial institutions, some of which see the environment primarily as an area of vigorous new growth, and that of more austere environmentalists. New funds set up in 1990 by, among others, Merrill Lynch, John Hancock, and Fidelity Investment rapidly attracted greenbacks: Merrill Lynch sold out its initial $50 million offering within three days, and $83 million more poured in before brokers were told to stop selling. But the more ardent environmentalists point out that all three funds invest in companies such as Waste Management, the world's biggest waste disposal firm, which has been involved in such environmentally unfriendly activities as incinerating toxic waste at sea and dumping recyclables in ordinary landfills. "Just because Waste Management picks up garbage does not make them a contributor to our environment," wrote one indignant investor in the Freedom Environment Fund, a subsidiary of John Hancock; on the contrary, retorted Dave Beckwith, the fund's manager, such companies "are socially positive by definition. They contribute to a clean environment by what they do."

Even the more verdant funds are embroiled in such issues. Calvert invested in Hawaii Electric, which wants to build a 500-megawatt geothermal power plant on Hawaii's Big Island. Geothermal power seems to be a good environmental issue, except that the plant will be built in a rain forest and is vigorously opposed by the Sierra Club, one of America's most aggressive environmental campaigners. Calvert eventually sold the stock, but for economic rather than environmental reasons.

A different approach is taken by the Global Environment Fund (GEF), a California-based fund launched in 1990. It is unusual in a number of ways. First, it is the brainchild of two environmentalists, Jeffrey Leonard and John Earhart, senior staff of the Worldwide Fund for Nature and the Conservation Foundation. Second, its aim is to invest in smallish companies with technologies that can be made to work in the United States but that might eventually solve environmental problems elsewhere. Some of the companies that pass for "green," Leonard argues, are beneficiaries of quirks of regulation: they might, for instance, have bought waste space that is now handy for dumping, or be willing to dispose of toxic waste that larger firms do not want to deal with. Meanwhile, small firms that are genuinely trying to develop more environmentally sound technologies often struggle to find capital. GEF is seeking out such companies, concentrating on those that are privately owned and aiming to invest long term where possible.

GEF raises cash from wealthy individuals and worthy institutional investors. When not helping the small and needy, GEF invests on the assumption that, as Leonard puts it, "There are no pure plays." For example, most environmental investment funds would put near the top of their lists Wellman, a New Jersey company that is the world's largest recycler of bottles made of PET plastics. The company keeps plastic bottles from cluttering landfills by recycling them into products such as plastic resins and nylon fibers. But Leonard claims that even Wellman is not pure green: the company, in which GEF holds shares, has some of the same problems with groundwater pollution as other plastics manufacturers. He argues that green investors should look not at whether a company is in a "clean" business, such as making computers, but at how hard it is trying to be cleaner. For environmental activists it is a short step from investing in greenish companies to trying to use shareholder muscle to make others greener.

Energetic green shareholders are more likely to pester managements with awkward questions. Merlin has a research department, the first of its kind in Britain, to improve the information available to environmental investors. Leonard uses his fund's shareholding to send long questionnaires to chief executives of companies like Wellman, saying, "Our intention is to maintain and provide for our investors a compendium of environmental information that we believe is important in assessing potential investments and monitoring the economic performance of our portfolio companies." If a company changes its behavior as a result of the inquisition, so much the better.

A broader attempt to mobilize shareholder power in this way was launched in the fall of 1989 by America's SIF. It brought together a number of environmentalists and investors to draw up a set of principles, which they hoped to persuade companies to sign, called the Valdez Principles (a name hardly calculated to endear them to companies). The Valdez Principles are broadly modeled on the Sullivan Principles, which laid down guidelines for firms operating in South Africa. The first six set out various rather woolly good intentions: to use natural resources sustainably and energy wisely, for instance, and to minimize waste creation. Many American companies already have environmental policies tougher than these. But the final four principles made corporate lawyers gulp. They committed signatories to make compensation for environmental damage; to disclose incidents of such damage; to have at least one environmentalist on the board; and annually to carry out and publish an independent environmental audit. The sponsors wanted to provide a rating of corporate environmental intent, with high marks for firms that were trying hard and low ones for the unrepentantly dirty.

The institutions backing the Valdez exercise, including the controllers of New York City and of the state of California, hoped to use that as a handy guide to greenery. But of the 3,000 American companies approached, only 28 (mainly tiny ones) had signed by the middle of 1991. The disclosure clause caused the greatest anguish: some companies felt that they might lose more by owning up to every polluting accident than by keeping mum. But the cleaner companies objected to being told to volunteer to be scrutinized by outsiders who might not assess them with understanding, while the dirtier had nothing to gain by participating. SIF therefore decided to try a different tack: in 1991, shareholders of 31 American companies voted on resolutions to adopt the Valdez principles; on average, 8% of shareholders voted for their company to sign.

The Limits of Market Power

By changing the climate in which companies operate, green consumers and investors have already altered the perception of many chief executives. Companies now know that just as it is "not done" to exploit their workers, it is not done to be dirty. A change in social attitudes does not instantly turn sinners into saints. But it raises the penalties for being caught doing environmental damage and the rewards of being seen as good. But neither green consumers nor green investors can substitute for government intervention. Their influence is too random, too poorly informed, to provide consistent pressure on companies to take the most cost-effective steps to be cleaner. Important though green consumers, in particular, have been, they are not the main force that will drive the greening of business through the 1990s. There are more durable pressures. This will come as a disappointment to those who hoped that environmentalism might not need much more government intervention, and who were encouraged by the sight of people voting with their wallets. If consumers could be left to decide what was environmentally sound and what was not, then governments could leave them to it. Dirty firms would be punished by the market. Environmentally harmful products would languish unsold. Companies would realize that the market would reward them for caring about their impact on the environment.

That first naive hope has quickly died. Consumers have an impact on a limited range of products: few people think about the environment when buying, say, a VCR or a pair of shoes. Yet the processes by which they are manufactured may have considerable impact on the environment. Moreover, many companies sell not to consumers but to other companies, which are unlikely to change their buying patterns as whimsically as end users. The farther upstream a company is, the more insulated it is either from green shoppers or from the scrutiny of suppliers by environmentally conscious supermarkets.

Deciding which products and processes are least harmful to the environment is immensely complicated. It may seem like a trade-off between apples and pears. The difficulty also besets that other kind of green consumer, the green investor, who will find it almost as difficult as the ordinary shopper to pick the truly virtuous company, and who will have to decide whether to prefer the dirty company in the plastics recycling business to the petrochemicals company earnestly trying to reduce the danger of oil spills.

The environment is much too complex to be saved by shoppers or investors. To be effectively green, both need guidance.

Giving them guidance is in the interests of government and companies alike. If, for instance, shopping power is to back energy conservation, people need reliable information about which domestic appliances use energy most frugally. Unknowledgeable people are a menace to companies, since they may believe every environmental guru who has a particular axe to grind.

Governments, aided by good research, are best placed to set environmental goals. But if consumers are to be truly effective, governments need to provide more than just information. Ultimately, the wariness of the most fervent environmentalists has some basis: the consumer may indeed be the "enemy" of the environment, not the friend. Protection of the environment may require people to accept less convenient ways of doing things: buying fewer throwaways, for instance, thus reversing the trend to replace individual labor with waste-creating disposables. In time, ingenious technology will make such choices less painful. But companies will be more likely to invest in such technology if government sets the ground rules.

So governments need to make sure that the market sets the right signals. An attraction of green products to producers is that they can be sold at a premium. That is the reverse of the polluter-pays principle. How much better if the burden of taxes and regulation on dirty products were to make them the expensive ones. Yet only with a few goods—such as lead-free gas or cars with catalytic converters—have some governments used taxation to tilt prices in order to give consumers the right message. Many more such incentives are needed if the power of the green shopper is to be harnessed properly.

The main forces driving companies to be better environmentalists—forces more durable and more powerful than green consumers—are the subject of the next chapter.

10

Waste Disposal

Corporate environmental policies are driven by pressures more lasting and potent than shoppers' whims. These forces will endure through the 1990s, even if a period of slow growth makes consumers more anxious to save money than to save the planet. Dominating these forces will be the attempts of governments to control the pollution caused by waste: by air emissions, water pollution, and most of all by solid waste. The evolution of policies on solid waste is the theme of this chapter; recycling, the most popular solution to the disposal of household waste, is the theme of the next. Subsequent chapters look at how companies are responding to pollution controls.

Waste and economic growth tend to rise in step with each other. This is not surprising, for waste is one of the most revealing indicators of consumption. All those natural resources the human race uses end up in the air or in water or on rubbish heaps; those that are not disposed of by factories or flushed down the drain usually end up in garbage cans. Some wastes, such as potato peelings and apple cores, decompose rapidly and harmlessly. Others, such as nuclear waste and certain chemicals, take many years to decompose, and, as they do so, may endanger human health or the ecology. Policies aimed at the safe disposal of waste tend to start with toxic substances released by industry; in time, public attention shifts from industrial to household waste, and from hazardous waste to ordinary garbage and litter. That shift is under way in many countries because of their growing recognition that refuse disposal may pose almost as many problems as the safe disposal of toxic waste.

The capacity of the planet to absorb waste, and the space to get rid of it, are exhaustible resources, just like oil and copper. In the case of oil and copper, the price will rise as the resource is used up. This will encourage people to economize in their use of it, or use technology to come up with other options. With waste, that does not usually happen. Society now needs to decouple waste from growth, just as the oil price increases of the mid-1970s decoupled energy use from economic growth. But decoupling waste will be harder. The rise in energy prices in the mid-1970s gave consumers a signal to economize on oil and gas. At present, the full costs of waste disposal are rarely reflected in the cost of the product to the customer, either in higher product prices or through charges for disposing of the waste people create. Indeed, neither the manufacturer nor the consumer of most products pays any of the disposal costs (directly, at least). Both will pay more in the future.

Why Waste Has Increased

Waste of all kinds has increased inordinately. In the United States between 1970 and 1988, the volume of municipal solid waste either landfilled or incinerated rose by 37%, and by 14% per head.[1] In total, Americans throw away 156 million tons of municipal waste a year. The volume of hazardous waste (some of which ends up in household trash cans—think of discarded batteries or old cans of paint) is larger still. Most estimates put the total at between 250 million and 500 million tons a year.[2] Most of that waste is generated, one way or another, by the chemical, metal, and petroleum industries.

Environmentalists think that waste is a bad thing. But for the human race as a whole, the increase in waste partially reflects improvements in living standards. Take packaging, which is easily the biggest single category of domestic trash. In America in 1988, packaging accounted for 43% of all municipal solid waste measured by weight. If the concept of "waste prevention" which companies have adopted also applies to consumers, it surely means reducing packaging.

Yes, but packaging frequently increases the value of a product, and not only in relatively unimportant ways—by looking nice, for instance—but by ensuring better hygiene. The increase in waste caused by the growth in packaging may have been balanced by a reduction in the amount of food people need to throw away.

Another reason for the rise in waste has been the pursuit of convenience. Take-out meals are an example of greater convenience bought at the expense of more packaging—and more litter in the streets. But the drive for greater convenience has affected not only the food industry. In a number of other respects, waste has been created by consumers' desire to buy products that save time. As customers shop less frequently, they want packaging that will extend, say, the shelf life of a perishable from a couple of days to two weeks. There has also been large growth in single-use products: from throw-away pens and cameras to paper cups and plates in restaurants.

The fastest growth in bulk of all single-use products in individual households is the disposable diaper, which makes up perhaps 4% of all the solid waste that American municipalities collect in domestic trash. One study puts the American market for disposable diapers at $4 billion a year, and their annual "life cycle" bill (which includes the landfill cost to receive them but not the pollution cost of their manufacture), at an additional $3.9 billion.[3] If the retail price of disposable diapers were doubled to reflect more of their true costs, would the market have grown as fast? The continued increase in waste will, of course, be driven partly by that most powerful force of all: demography. As the growth of populations in Western countries stagnates, the value of human labor will rise, relative to other resources, including natural ones. Both employers and individuals will have an incentive to substitute underpriced natural resources—underpriced because their retail price in no way reflects the costs to the environment of their use or their disposal—for their own increasingly valuable time.

If households put a high value on their time and convenience so, even more, do employers in labor-intensive industries. To Europeans one of the most extraordinary sights in an American café or fast-food restaurant is customers tipping a trayload of paper cups and plates or boxes into a bin at the end of a meal. In general, European restaurateurs still struggle to recruit washers. Hospitals are another labor-intensive industry that has substituted disposables for human time, with some garish results. American hospitals now generate on average some 13 pounds of waste per bed per day, ranging from disposable sheets and dressings to needles and syringes. Many of these objects have ensured higher standards of hygiene, now more essential than ever, given the public fear of AIDS; but hospital managers also jumped at the chance to cut laundry bills. Then in the summer of 1988, medical waste washed up on American beaches. Now, as Congress and state governments demand tougher standards for wrapping waste and keeping track of its eventual fate, the costs of disposables in terms of cash and of scarce managerial time are also starting to rise dramatically.

Incinerating medical waste (the method used to dispose of 80% of the stuff in America) already costs an average of 30 cents per pound before adding the costs of packaging and transporting. If the incineration is done off-site, as it increasingly is, a hospital can easily pay $600 a ton. Not surprisingly, some administrators look back nostalgically to the days of the hospital laundry. These examples suggest that if waste disposal is underpriced or (as for households) unpriced, people will substitute goods for time. Sometimes, as in the fast-food industry, disposables mean increased convenience for both staff and customers. Some fast-food chains have responded to pressure to do something about the litter in the streets not by reducing the number of burger boxes or chicken cartons, but (at times) by sending out litter patrols to collect discarded wrappings from the streets and (in the case of McDonald's) by encouraging customers to sort their wrappings into bins for recycling. Trying to make waste more manageable for consumers is easier than not creating it in the first place.

Finding a Site

While the volume of waste has been rising, the options for disposing of it have narrowed. People are increasingly reluctant to allow the establishment of new waste-disposal facilities near their home, especially if the facility is a dump or an incinerator for toxic waste. America's EPA reckons that 80% of existing landfills will shut by the early years of the next century (see Figure 10.1). Some 13 states, primarily on the East Coast, will run out of landfill capacity by the mid-1990s unless (improbably) they can open new ones. Japan will run out by 2005. The Netherlands has, in effect, run out already. In Los Angeles, furious citizens have campaigned to close the last remaining dump owned by the city at Lopez Canyon, and a project to build a new incinerator collapsed in the face of bitter local opposition. The Californian state legislature shut down almost one-third of its 623 landfills in 1989. West Germans, who in 1988 exported 2.1 million tons of garbage to East Germany, have lost that helpful outlet as the result of reunification.

In practice, the exhaustion of space is not so much geographical—in theory, much land still remains for waste dumps—but

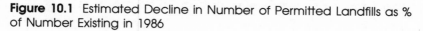

Figure 10.1 Estimated Decline in Number of Permitted Landfills as % of Number Existing in 1986

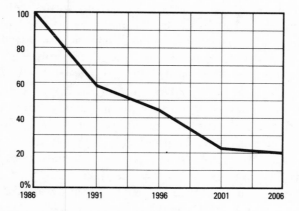

Source: U.S. Environmental Protection Agency.

regulatory. Governments, prodded by their voters, are steadily
reducing the number of options for disposing of waste and
raising the costs of using those options that remain. This problem
is worst for toxic waste. Exporting it was once the easiest way
to avoid thinking about it. The countries in Europe with the
noisiest environmental lobbies were the ones most likely to pay
somebody else to get rid of the muck. In 1985, West Germany
exported nearly 15% of its hazardous and special waste
(definitions and terminology vary from country to country, making it hard to compare what is happening in different countries),
much of it to Eastern Europe. The Swiss, who hold referendums
to decide where to put new incinerators, not surprisingly end up
exporting more than half their hazardous waste. The British have
been a rarity in the past, dealing with all their hazardous waste
at home and even importing waste from elsewhere (mainly Ireland and the Netherlands) to incinerate or dump (sometimes at
sea).

Rules on the disposal of hazardous waste within countries
have been growing tighter. Several European countries, including Germany, France, Belgium, and Britain, have traditionally
burned some of their waste on ships in the North Sea. A March
1990 conference agreed to stop that practice by the end of 1991.
The same conference tightened the rules on dumping dangerous
substances into the North Sea; they are to be cut by at least 50%
in the decade to 1995.

Most exports of hazardous waste from industrial countries
have ended up either in Eastern Europe or in the third world.
Either way, the technology for handling it is much less sophisticated than in the West. Perestroika will stop most dumping in
ex-Communist Europe. Cleaning the third world will be tougher.
Third world countries resent becoming dumps but may find it
hard to enforce their own environmental regulations to prevent
it. But under a convention drawn up by the United Nations
Environment Program and signed at Basel early in 1989, governments pledge not to move waste across borders unless the recip-
ient country has agreed to accept it and, more important, unless
the exporting country is satisfied that proper arrangements have
been made for its final disposal.

As the EC prepared to complete its internal market by 1992, Carlo Ripa di Meana, the EC environment commissioner, warned that "1992 must not turn into a tourist visa for wastes." The EC countries prepared for the barrier-free market by drawing up an agreement to become self-sufficient in the disposal of toxic waste. Shipments across borders between EC countries will not necessarily be prevented: it may sometimes be more economical for one country to dispose of the waste of another, such as Ireland, which generates too little to justify a large investment in treatment plants. Strict national self-sufficiency would also increase shipments of waste around Europe, as countries lugged the stuff not to the nearest treatment site but to the nearest national one, which might be much farther away. Electors are becoming more hostile to treating other people's toxic waste, even at a good profit. South Carolina and Alabama, which, like third world countries, see themselves treated as dumps for the prosperous North, have both tried to ban waste shipments from other states. There is a similar hostility toward disposing of other people's garbage in Europe. In 1989, a poll by MORI, a British market research firm, found that only 44% of the British saw toxic waste as one of the most important environmental issues, compared with 66% for nuclear waste. But three-quarters of those polled thought that Britain should not accept imports of toxic waste from other EC countries under any circumstances.

Ordinary garbage can still be exported—usually. The rubbish problem was crystallized in the minds of American voters by the adventures of the wandering garbage barge from the New York suburb of Islip. Ports as far away as Belize turned back the ship, loaded with 3,000 tons of Long Island muck, in the spring of 1987. That incident has had less dramatic parallels in other parts of America and in Europe.

The rules governing the disposal of ordinary garbage on land have also become tougher. In Europe, national governments have been ratcheting standards upward, as has the EC Commission. The commission sees an urgent need to adopt common standards for the disposal of waste of all kinds. Otherwise, waste will tend to seep toward the country with the lowest (i.e., least expensive) standards. So it has drawn up a directive that will turn landfill sites from inexpensive holes in the ground into expensive bits of civil engineering. It will also raise the costs of monitoring them after they are filled, and increase the amount of paperwork needed to keep track of what is dumped where. The commission has already produced two directives raising the standards for municipal incinerators, and is drawing up a draft directive to set stricter rules for all incinerators, including those that used waste as fuel.

All this will dramatically affect waste-disposal costs in some EC countries, including Britain. A study presented by two landfill specialists from Harwell Laboratory at their annual waste-management symposium in May 1990 makes horrifying reading.[4] Of 100 landfills studied, 62% had no measures to stop surface water from seeping in; 54% did not monitor leaching into groundwater in the surrounding area; 63% had no boreholes to monitor the potential buildup of dangerous gas; and 80% made no attempt to control their smell. Britain's local authorities, which operated almost three-quarters of the landfills surveyed, are clearly in for some nasty surprises, one of which will be a steep rise in the costs of getting rid of rubbish.

Already, the bill for disposing of trash in a city in California or New York can be as steep as $100 a ton. Disposal costs in some European countries are not much lower. In Germany, the Netherlands, and Italy, getting rid of waste can cost $80 to $100 a ton. Britain is one of the few industrial countries where waste disposal is not expensive. Costs range from around £3 to £4 ($5–$7) a ton to £30 to £40 ($50–$70). Britain's indigenous extractive industries have left plenty of old clay pits with naturally impermeable soil; the country's sloppy approach to waste regulation has also helped to hold down costs.

Inevitably, the costs of disposing of hazardous waste are higher still. In America, landfill costs for hazardous waste went from about $80 a ton at the start of the 1980s to about $255 a ton by the end of that decade, with the main increase being in costs of treatment rather than for dumping. Unpublished OECD figures for Western Europe show that the costs of landfill for asbestos in October 1989 ranged from $41 a ton to $338, perhaps ten times higher than a decade earlier. Incineration costs have probably risen still faster, although they vary less widely: from about $1,145 a ton for some of the nastier, high-chlorine wastes in West Germany up to $2,300 to $2,595 a ton in Britain, with a European average of about $1,825 a ton.

One effect in America, where the rules on waste disposal are probably the strictest and certainly the most complicated, has been to make landfills a highly attractive investment for any company willing to weave its way through the maze of Super-fund legislation (see below). The American arm of Hambro, a British merchant bank, has been buying up family-owned landfills, finding them high-quality management, and preparing them for flotation on the New York stock exchange. "They rarely think in terms of marketing, and may not have enough capital to develop the site. They tend to think of the site as a plot of land that brings in a steady income," says Fred Iseman of Ham-bro America. With good management and access to private cap-ital, Iseman reckons that the profitability of such sites may quintuple in a couple of years.

Tackling Toxic Waste

When European companies look at the way that legislators in the United States have controlled toxic waste, they shudder. One part of the American legal framework is intended to ensure the safe disposal of wastes being generated today—the Resource Conservation and Recovery Act, or RCRA, first passed in 1976 and amended in 1984. RCRA put the main responsibility for defining hazardous wastes and laying down their proper treat-ment into the hands of the EPA. It also established an elaborate tracking system, or "paper chase," for preventing illegal dump-ing. The sheer nuisance of this arrangement, now being copied by the European Commission, has encouraged some companies to reduce the amount of toxic waste they create.

RCRA also required the phasing out of many existing forms of disposal for hazardous waste, thus limiting the options avail-able to industry. And, although many industries that generate hazardous waste were exempted from its most expensive provis-ions, these exemptions are gradually being withdrawn. As a result, the stringent conditions that apply to the hazardous-waste management industry will increasingly apply to all companies that treat and dispose of their own waste. All these requirements will drive up the costs of compliance, which the EPA estimates at $23 billion in 1990, rising to $34 billion in the year 2000.

What most alarms Europeans, though, is the Comprehensive Environmental Response, Compensation and Liability Act (CERCLA, or "Superfund"), passed in 1980 in the wake of a public outcry over a toxic-waste dump at Love Canal, in New York state. This law was intended to compel the cleanup of thousands of abandoned and uncontrolled hazardous waste sites. To pay for the cleanup of toxic waste sites, the law set up a trust fund financed by taxes on the oil and chemical industries. This has become a behemoth, towering over American environmental policy, gobbling vast quantities of public and private cash and management time. The EPA aggressively chases companies held potentially responsible for the presence of waste on sites, to recoup from them the costs of cleaning up.

Under Superfund legislation (expanded in 1986 under the Superfund Amendments and Reauthorization Act) and subsequent court decisions, liability for these costs is extraordinarily wide. It may fall on almost anyone who has ever had anything to do with a toxic waste dump: the operator; the companies that transported the waste; the present owner of the site; the owner of the site at the time the contamination occurred; and indeed any company whose waste was ever dumped on the site, even if the dumping was perfectly legal at the time. The net spreads even wider. A lender who forecloses on a company and thereby assumes ownership for any contaminated properties acquires liability as part of the package. A 1990 court judgment frightened bankers by appearing to make a company's bankers liable even if they had not foreclosed, if they might have influenced their client's treatment of toxic waste. However, the 1990 savings and loan crisis might change this: as the federal government has become the reluctant owner of a large number of bankrupt thrifts, it has also acquired their exposure to Superfund claims.

The liability is strict, regardless of fault or negligence, as well as joint and several: cleanup costs can be assessed on the basis of a company's ability to pay, rather than on the volume or toxicity of the waste it has dumped. The only shred of protection accrues to companies that investigated a site before they acquired it and found no Superfund liability, a provision that does much to explain the rise of the environmental audit.

In spite of its ferocity, Superfund has not proved an efficient way to clean up toxic waste. True, fear of the huge penalties involved, and the rising costs of treating hazardous waste, have greatly encouraged companies to reduce the amount they create. In that sense, Superfund has been a clumsy way to impose on industry some of the social costs of pollution and thus change the way companies behave. But only 64 of the currently listed 1,200 Superfund sites have been completed since 1981, at a cost of $7.5 billion. The average cost of restoring the sites so far identified by the EPA is $25 million a site, with some running up to $100 million. Several companies have been forced to close as a result. Almost one-third of the $200 million spent by the federal government since 1988 went on the administrative expenses of private contractors.[5] Estimates of future costs vary hugely: the federal Office of Technology Assessment has calculated that the total costs of cleaning up all known toxic waste sites (not just those on the EPA's priority list) could be as much as $500 billion over the next 40 to 50 years. This does not include the costs of cleaning up sites contaminated by the Defense and Energy Departments, which may be just as expensive. The implications for federal spending are intimidating.

So are the implications for companies and their insurance providers. Chasing companies through the courts for their share of cleanup costs has now become a primary activity of the EPA. The biggest settlement so far, in May 1989, was for $66 million for a site in California, but the potential bills have soared into the *Exxon Valdez* category. Shell has been wrangling with the EPA since 1983 over a $1.9 billion bill for damage at a site in Colorado, in a case in which only the lawyers have cleaned up. In a broad range of industries—chemicals, petroleum, mining, pharmaceuticals, steel, heavy manufacturing, electronics, and electrical equipment—investors have begun to scrutinize company accounts carefully for information about potential liabilities. The Securities and Exchange Commission has strengthened its requirements for disclosure. The issue of how far insurers will have to pick up the eventual bills was still, in mid-1991, being fought through the courts.

Many states now have their own cleanup laws, every bit as tough as CERCLA. In early 1990, Occidental Petroleum and Maxus Energy agreed to clean up a number of chromium waste sites in northern New Jersey at a cost of about $51 million, to be spent over several years. The operations that had generated the waste had been shut down in 1972 by the then owner, Diamond Shamrock. Maxus Energy had taken over its oil and gas exploration business but had sold Diamond Shamrock's chemical operation to Occidental Petroleum in 1986.[6]

America's exorbitantly expensive approach to cleaning up toxic waste sites may alter as RCRA comes up for reauthorization in 1992. One possibility is the introduction of a no-fault system of compensation to prevent some of the interminable and expensive pursuits of companies through the courts. A more important question, though, is whether the standards for cleaning dumps should be set lower or whether cleaning up should maintain its present priority in environmental spending. Other environmental perils, some of them more threatening to human health or to the ecology, might be tackled more cheaply. The danger is that Superfund's vast budget gives it the inertia of vested interests: with such enormous sums of public money being spent each year (nearly $6 billion in fiscal 1989, for example), a Superfund site becomes a useful source of federal gravy. As that happens, the program will be as hard to reform in a cost-effective way as the defense budget has been.

No other country has anything as stringent as the Superfund legislation. But the idea may well spread. Once governments decide to clean up old waste dumps, they face an inevitable choice: Do taxpayers foot the bill, or does the government try to find private companies to pick up the tab? Draconian though the retroactive liability under Superfund may seem, it has a certain logic. Many European environmentalists argue that if the polluter-pays principle means what it says, then polluters must be liable for incidents for which they were responsible, even unintentionally, in the past. The alternative is to make the taxpayer responsible, and that is unfair. The implications of such a view are hair-raising: many polluting activities, from dumping nuclear waste to ploughing grassland (which releases nitrates into water courses), may take years to manifest themselves.

Germany has already considered plans that would make it easier to force companies to pay for cleaning waste sites. The EC is considering introducing civil liability for waste, although it is unlikely to come into effect before 1992 at the earliest. Under a draft directive issued by the European Commission in autumn 1989, companies that produce waste would carry strict civil liability for damage caused by their wastes to persons and property, and for injury to the environment, until the wastes were handed over to a properly licensed disposal firm. An individual plaintiff would be able to take a company to court to stop the damaging activity and to force the polluter to pay the costs of cleaning up the mess. In its draft form, the directive provides for joint and several liability to make banks or receivers liable if they acquire polluted land when a lender defaults. The directive also allows claims to be made for 30 years after polluting waste has been dumped, although that is being strongly contested by the insurance industry. American companies in Europe are taking no chances since some American states, led by New Jersey, have begun to impose even tighter laws on toxic dumps, forbidding the sale of a property that has not already been cleaned. Some companies even take seriously the prospect of such legislation in the third world. As Jill Shankleman of Environmental Resources, a British consultancy, puts it: "American managers say, 'Superfund has cost us millions of dollars. Upgrading our plants worldwide will cost us 10% of that. It's good insurance.'" Cornelius Smith, in charge of environmental policy at Union Carbide, takes the view that "It doesn't take a rocket scientist to figure that they'll have Superfund in five, ten, fifteen years."

A growing problem is that while industry has had to adopt more stringent policies to deal with toxic waste, much of what households throw out is just as lethal. A study by Britain's Hazardous Waste Inspectorate estimated that one-fifth of domestic refuse is hazardous. What happens to waste discarded by individuals may be much more dangerous than what well-run companies and institutions do. For instance, the medical waste that littered America's beaches seems to have come not from hospitals (which will carry most of the costs of tighter rules for waste), but from drug addicts and people using medical supplies at home. Stricter rules on the way industry handles products such as paint, batteries, and pesticides will look bizarre beside dustbins full of half-used tins of paint, discarded batteries, and almost-empty drums of garden chemicals. Even places (such as Massachusetts) that have laws on what can and cannot be thrown into the garbage can find it hard to enforce them.

Tackling Municipal Solid Waste

With toxic waste, the key problem for policy is to make sure it is safely disposed of. With municipal waste, at least the non-toxic sort, the key problem is to put right the imbalance between the amount created and the space to dispose of it. Governments in many developed countries began to worry increasingly about this toward the close of the 1980s. In the United States, more than 75 bills dealing with solid waste management were introduced by members of Congress in 1990.

"You can do four things with garbage," said Ed Koch, New York's colorful mayor of the late 1980s. "You can burn it. You can bury it. You can recycle it. Or you can send it on a Caribbean cruise." In the past, burning, burying, and the Caribbean cruise were the most common solutions. They are now becoming more difficult and more expensive. Instead, legislators see recycling as the most popular way to reduce the garbage piles.

Recycling was static for much of the 1980s after growing rapidly in the 1970s. But because governments consider that recycling is a popular way to reduce waste, they have begun to set themselves ambitious targets. The EPA in 1990 set a national goal of reducing the solid waste stream by 25% by 1992 and by 50% by 1997. Some American states have even more ambitious targets: Florida's goal is a 30% reduction in solid waste by 1994; New Jersey wants each county to recycle a quarter of its waste by 1991; New York aims to cut its waste stream in half by 1997. It sounds impressive; but in 1989 more than half of all American states recycled less than 5% of their waste streams. Britain's target is to recycle a quarter of household waste by the end of the century; the EC wants to raise the proportion from a third to half. For most governments, it will be hard to keep the size of the waste stream from growing, let alone to cut it.

The emphasis on recycling, as the next chapter argues, often represents a failure to think clearly about waste disposal. The political attention given to one waste material—plastics—shows a failure to understand what materials most clog up landfill space. In most industrial countries, paper is the biggest single item in garbage dumps: 40% of municipal waste in the United States, 33% of household refuse in Britain. "Dig a trench through a landfill," says William Rathje, an archaeologist from Arizona who has done just that (see Figure 10.2), "and you will see layers of phone books like geographical strata or layers of cake. Just as conspicuous as telephone books are newspapers, which make up 10% to 18% of the contents of a typical municipal landfill by volume. During a recent landfill dig in Phoenix, I found newspapers dating back to 1952 that looked so fresh you might read one over breakfast."

High standards for insulating landfills, designed to keep methane gas and nasty smells under control, make a nonsense of the word "biodegradable." Without air and moisture, trash simply

Figure 10.2 Average Volume of Materials Excavated from Landfills as % of All Municipal Solid Waste

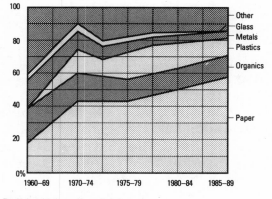

Source: W.L. Rathje, University of Arizona.

will not rot. Most people would not think of the contents of the
garden compost heap as a big part of the waste problem. Yet in
America nearly 18% of the weight of municipal waste is garden
refuse, and just over 7% is food (and the figure would be higher
if so many American kitchens did not have garbage-disposal
units). In most European countries the bonfire has not been
banned as polluting, and the art of the compost heap remains.
But "putrescibles," as the British authorities revoltingly call
them, still account for roughly 20% of household waste.

Cost-effective strategies for reducing the growth of municipal
waste obviously ought to concentrate on paper, food, and garden
sweepings. But they don't. Ask most people to define the waste
problem in a single word and they will generally say "plastics."
That is therefore the industry under the most pressure to think
about getting rid of its product, especially when it is used for
packaging. Plastics are undoubtedly a problem. They degrade
slowly; some of them give off toxic fumes when incinerated; and
they are rapidly increasing their share of all waste materials (a
direct reflection of the rapid increase in their use, especially in
products with short lives). Yet plastics still account for a small
part of total municipal waste: 7% by weight in Britain, 8% in the
United States. Some of the industry's leaders smell conspiracy.
"Newspapers don't seem so interested in the effect of paper on
landfills," says Ed Woolard, the chairman of Du Pont. He is right:
journalists rarely tell their readers that one way to produce less
rubbish is to buy fewer newspapers and magazines.

Such misunderstandings may lead to perverse policies. Consider this: Which is the more environmentally friendly container
for a pint of lemonade—glass or plastics? Glass, the recycler
would say without hesitation. America's Office of Technology
Assessment (OTA) estimates that glass made entirely from cullet
(glass scrap) saves about 15% of the energy needed to make the
product from virgin raw materials, and the same amount again
by avoiding the costs of mining and transporting the raw material. But the OTA also calculates that recycling pure plastic resins
can save 92% to 98% of the energy needed to produce single
virgin resins, although that sum excludes the costs of collecting
and transporting the recycled resins. Besides, plastics, with their
light weight relative to their strength, cut transport costs both of

raw materials and of retail distribution. They also take up less room in dumps. These considerations are deeply embedded in the arguments that will take place over government pressure on industry to recycle. If what matters is recyclability, then it may be that glass wins. But that implies that recycling is an end in itself, which is clearly wrong. If what matters is the overall impact of a product on the environment—the collection of raw materials, the use of energy to produce and transport it, and its final disposal—it is not at all clear that glass is superior to plastics; and per liter, paper cartons are friendlier than either.

With plastics, incineration may sometimes be a more efficient solution than recycling. A number of schemes either planned or in operation use waste to generate energy, and a virtue of plastics as a waste material is its high energy yield. Germany has many such schemes; at the start of 1991, the government announced an increase in the price paid by the national grid for electricity generated from landfills. German plastics producers think that incineration with heat recovery is the best way to dispose of their difficult product. In October 1990, National Power, Britain's biggest electricity generator, announced plans to burn almost 10% of Britain's domestic and commercial waste by the end of the century. The company plans to earn 60% of its revenue from waste-disposal fees paid by local councils, which will save the fees they would pay for landfill space, and most of the rest from selling electricity. One advantage of refuse is that, unlike other fuels, it piles up near centers of population, which in turn are the main markets for electricity. A disadvantage is that the neighbors of incinerators worry about the fumes; and disposing of the toxic ash left at the end of the process can be difficult.

Where legislators dictate the technology for reducing the waste stream, they may not choose the best technique; or they may make perverse decisions. Several American states have passed laws requiring the use of degradable plastics: Alaska for beer-can carriers, Florida for packaging for foodstuffs, and Oregon for backing for disposable diapers. Apart from markets for these products, created and sustained by regulation, degradable plastics have few uses in which they do better than conventional plastics (surgical sutures is one exception). That has not stopped several companies, including the Ferruzzi group, an Italian chemical giant, from developing new degradables that are based on cornstarch and so are a logical application of its agricultural interests to its chemical markets. Recyclers worry about the consequences if degradable plastics are swept up in mixed-bag recycling programs. Will that playground furniture start to droop? And legislators who know about Rathje's excavations are beginning to realize that "degradable" is a slippery concept.

Different materials have different optimum recycling rates, various points at which the marginal cost of recycling an extra tin can or glass bottle overtakes the marginal benefits to the environment. Probably the optimum recycling rate for any material has not yet been achieved, let alone passed. But a danger for the 1990s is that fervent enthusiasm among legislators for encouraging recycling will create targets that cost society more to meet—in terms of human time, say, and energy use—than they save by economizing on raw materials and waste disposal. This danger, and the alternatives to it, are explored in the next chapter.

11

Recycling

Many people love recycling trash. They have a comforting sense of virtue when sorting cans and bottles. A reason, perhaps, is that they are doing something concrete to feel they are being good citizens without spending extra money or making radical changes in their life style. The danger is that too much will be expected of a solution that, at best, can make only a modest dent in the accumulation of waste. Indeed, by forcing this fashionable solution on companies, governments may close off other options that might be more efficient economically—and even environmentally.

Recycling is not new. For example, people once bought many goods, from cookies to milk, in reusable cans or bottles. As manufacture became less local, and as the cost of labor to clean up the returned containers increased, reusable containers became less economical. They survived only where the rate at which they were returned by consumers was high, and where the cost of returning and cleaning the container was no higher than an alternative form of packaging. Thus, returnable bottles are widely used in home milk deliveries in Britain, where the average bottle makes a dozen trips, but less and less for soft drinks bought at grocery stores, where on average only two out of three bottles are returned. They survive in the British pub trade, where manufacturers can rely on the pub returning them repeatedly because the customer does not handle them. Japan does better still: two-thirds of all bottles are collected and used an average of three times, while beer and some sake bottles are reused an average of 20 times. (Though that is changing as the Japanese grow richer: they can now buy a can of sake that heats itself to the correct temperature.)

Left entirely to the market, some recycling will continue, but at rates that do not reflect the environmental costs of extracting raw materials or disposing of waste. It will take place only where demand for the recycled product is strong enough to cover collection costs. Even then, commodity markets are always volatile, and the market for recycled materials as a marginal material, even more so. In America in 1988, 90% of the lead in car batteries was recycled. That figure fell to 80% in 1989, a direct result of the fall in the price of lead, which reduced the incentive to recycle. The demand for recycled materials is vulnerable, like the demand for all products, to technical change. Technology, or the rising relative cost of human labor, can easily make market-led recycling uneconomical.

The pressure for recycling now comes not from companies, but from voters. Voters are not always entirely clear why they are keen on recycling. Sometimes they argue that recycling saves natural resources. Certainly it makes more sense to melt down an aluminum can than to mine bauxite and smelt it, which uses far more energy. But it is less clear that the environment is helped by making less paper from virgin timber: paper is made mainly from commercial forests, which are replanted as fast as they are destroyed.

It does make sense to price raw materials at levels that reflect the environmental harm done by their extraction and consumption. Left to itself, the market will generally prefer virgin to recycled materials, if only for their greater consistency of quality. In fact, much raw-material extraction is subsidized—for instance through special tax treatment to encourage exploration and development. Ending such subsidies would be much the least expensive way to reduce the consumption of raw materials: indeed, it would actually save government money.

As the costs of waste disposal have risen, so the economic arguments for recycling have advanced. But in many places even well-run landfills are a less expensive option than recycling. In that case, recycling schemes work only if taxpayers subsidize them or if governments force companies to make them work.

The Economics of Recycling

The costs of running a recycling scheme are determined by two factors. One is the cost of collection; the other, the market for the collected waste. The economics of collection depend on a number of factors. Who sorts the trash? If consumers will do so reliably for free, that is obviously much less expensive than doing so by machinery—and less expensive still than paying other people to do it more laboriously. Next, what proportion of the waste can be recovered? The high capital costs of reprocessing some materials (such as plastics) means they need big throughputs to make them worthwhile.

Collection is usually organized in one of three ways: the public sorts the trash and brings it to a collection site; or it is sorted into different bins and left on the curb for pickup; or it is collected together and sorted separately. Most North American schemes involve curb collection. The rubbish is further sorted—into bottles and cans, for instance—either as the collectors go along or at a special depot. At collection points, such as bottle banks, trash is picked up, often by specialized contractors. Such schemes are backed up by mechanical sorting of general trash: magnets, for instance, may remove steel cans. In Europe, where "bring" schemes are more common, a few experiments with collect schemes are now under way, including one in Sheffield and one in Dunkirk.

Collect schemes inevitably cost more than the bring type; in old cities, with apartment buildings and narrow streets, they may also be hard to organize. But collect schemes are obviously more convenient. The schemes have become increasingly popular in America, Germany, and Denmark, achieving cuts of 20% to 25% in household waste—and might perhaps manage 30%.

A study by Britain's Warren Spring Laboratory in January 1990 estimated that bring arrangements could probably recover 10% to 15% of Britain's household refuse, or maybe 20% in the longer term.[1] Central sorting is probably practicable only for metals and glass, and might therefore recover no more than 15%. All told, perhaps a maximum weight of about 40% of the contents of Britain's domestic rubbish bins are technically recoverable for recycling.

Recycling will be less expensive if it draws on the cooperation of a well-motivated public. That is an attraction of involving environmental groups in such proposals. In Britain, Friends of the Earth helped to launch a collect scheme in Sheffield. In France and Germany, voluntary groups have run campaigns to persuade the public to recycle trash; the companies that collect the sorted trash pay the groups so much per ton.

Individuals in many countries, including America, Japan, and Germany, show an extraordinary willingness to take part voluntarily in schemes to reduce the burden of waste. In one Japanese municipality, Zentsuji, citizens sort their waste into 32 separate categories, from rags to paper to appliances, and take it to appropriate collection sites. Sometimes the pressure comes from state laws or from neighbors. More often, it seems to be simply a sense of civic duty that makes people willing to sort trash into different space-consuming heaps, to rinse out tin cans, to lug bottles to bottle banks and newspapers to recycling depots. Far from recycling to save themselves money, people are willing to spend time and effort to do it. Many must derive a rewarding sense of virtue, or even pleasure, from making an individual effort to be environmentally responsible.

Indeed, where people are required by law to recycle trash, instead of doing it out of altruism, it may be that the quality of recycling will suffer. Garden State Paper, a customer for New Jersey's mandatory newspaper recycling program, has reported problems with contamination of supplies. A famous book, *The Gift Relationship*, by British sociologist Richard Titmuss, argued that the quality of blood donated under Britain's voluntary scheme was higher than that provided under American schemes that paid donors.[2] So it may be that recycling schemes work best if cities or voluntary bodies make it as easy as possible for households, and then allow a warm glow of self-righteousness to be their chief reward.

The Market for Waste

Persuading citizens to sort their trash is only a first step. The other big factor in the economics of recycling schemes is the market for what is collected. If the sorted waste ends up in a landfill with the rest of the trash, then the expense of sorting and transporting (the primary cost of all rubbish-disposal systems) will be wasted. Recycling is pointless without a market for reusing materials.

At present, the waste that commercial recyclers want to buy is not the waste that costs municipalities most to dispose of. In America, some 55% of aluminum cans are recycled and 43% of all aluminum that towns would otherwise have to get rid of. The comparable figures for all aluminum vary from 18% to 40% in Europe and Japan, partly because aluminum is less widely used in drink containers; Sweden, with the aid of a deposit system, has managed to recover 70% of all aluminum drink cans. The economic incentives are there because recycling aluminum uses only 5% of the energy needed to extract the stuff from raw bauxite in the first place. So in Britain, where Alcan announced the first plan for recycling aluminum cans in April 1989, recycled scrap already accounts for a third of production.

But although recycling aluminum is highly profitable, it is a minute part of the contents of trash bins. Even in America, the world's biggest market for aluminum products, with packaging and cans accounting for a quarter of the industry's output, aluminum makes up only 1% of the weight of municipal solid waste.

Precisely the opposite is true of garden waste and discarded food. Together they account for about a quarter of the weight of waste discarded by American households and a tenth of what the British throw away. Even as compost they have precious little value, although some American cities have set up municipal compost heaps to try to recycle garden waste. A constant problem is that pesticides and other chemicals tend to get mixed up in lawn clippings and fallen leaves. In some states, including New Jersey, people are not allowed to throw out their leaves with their ordinary refuse. Few projects are as ambitious as the one begun in Fairfield, Connecticut, where a $3 million composting center was opened in autumn 1989 to create topsoil for parks and landscaping.

The market for the collected waste and for recycled products can change, like any other market, with new technology and consumer tastes. An example was given at the annual convention in 1989 of the Bureau International de la Récupération, the trade association of the world recycling industry, by Henri Ubogi, president of the textile-recycling division. Ubogi bemoaned the advent of self-cleaning machinery in the printing and car industries, which had knocked the bottom out of the demand for wiping cloths.

A more dramatic illustration of the same phenomenon is provided by the auto industry itself. In the late 1960s, the usual practice of dumping cars in hideous junkyards was becoming more difficult: space was in short supply, and the junkyards were ugly. In 1970, President Richard Nixon's environmental message to Congress called for some system to encourage the recycling of junked automobiles. In fact, no government action was needed. The market devised its own system, thanks to the development of two technologies that turned unwanted car hulks into a useful raw material. The late 1960s saw the transition from open-hearth steel-making to the basic oxygen furnace, a process that uses less steel scrap (typically, 28% compared with 45%). But at the same time, another steel-making process, the electric-arc furnace, came into commercial use. It was capable of making steel almost entirely from scrap. It could be used on a smaller scale, which meant the capital costs were lower. Minimills, using electric-arc furnace technology, gradually emerged as the most profitable part of the American steel industry (see Figure 11.1). Unlike traditional mills, they tended to be set up near sources of scrap, which kept down the costs of raw materials and of their transport.

The second new technology was the automobile shredder, a machine that takes a complete car, minus tires, radiator, gas tank, and battery, and shreds it into fist-sized pieces. Separators then remove the nonmetallic bits and the nonferrous metals. Put minimills and shredders together, and add the boom in demand for steel scrap in 1973–1974, and the market had serendipitously devised a solution to the problem of car junkyards. As Joel P. Clark and Frank R. Field say:

> In retrospect, the resolution of this automobile dumping problem seems almost magical. This is perhaps unfortunate, since it perpetuates the myth that technology will always find a solution to any situation, and thus all that is needed is to push technology along through regulatory mandates. As this case shows, while there was much in the way of legislative and regulatory discussion, technological and economic pressures resulted in an efficient solution with essentially no intrusion upon the private sector.[3]

The magic may now be wearing off. The main concern of car makers during the 1980s has increasingly been to meet foreign competition and to comply with ever-tighter regulations on emissions and fuel economy. A good way to increase fuel economy is to reduce a car's weight; a good way to reduce weight is to substitute plastic compounds for ferrous metal. This solution

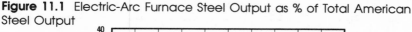

Figure 11.1 Electric-Arc Furnace Steel Output as % of Total American Steel Output

Source: J.P. Clark and F.R. Field III, "Recycling: Boon or Bane of Advanced Materials Technologies?" (Washington, DC: World Resources Institute, 1990).

increases the amount of plastics ending up in the waste stream, but the more dangerous problem is that it reduces the value of, and thus the incentive to recycle, car hulks. Car shredders will find that each hulk yields less steel scrap and more shredded plastics (see Table 11.1). The cost of disposing of the unwanted plastics, often toxic, will go up.

The tale of junk cars demonstrates the two qualities a material needs to be readily and economically recycled: low collection costs and strong final demand. Steel benefits from both—even steel thrown out by ordinary households can be magnetically extracted from trash heaps—with the result that recycling is general everywhere. In Britain, for instance, scrap accounts for 44% of production, although not much of that comes from municipal waste. If recycling is to make a big dent in the amount of rubbish that ordinary consumers throw away, the magic that kept American cars out of junkyards for 20 years needs to work for other materials, too.

Making the magic work has proved hardest, so far, for paper and plastic. Paper is a good example of the sheer complexity of recycling and the number of things that have to go right to sustain an effective market. It is far and away the largest single component of landfills: 41% of America's municipal solid waste by weight and 33% of Britain's. Its recycling rate is just under a quarter in America, if industrial scrap paper such as returned newspapers and printing offcuts are not counted. In Europe,

Table 11.1 Scrap Value of Car Hulks

Typical hulk weight	**3,150 lb**
Steel scrap: 2,250 lb @ $125.00 net ton	$135.00
Nonferrous: 150 lb @ $0.12 per pound	$18.00
Fluff: 750 lb @ $125.00 net ton disposal	($47.00)
Freight	($10.00)
Processing costs: 3,150 lb @ $30 net ton	($47.00)
Scrap value of hulk	$48.75

Source: J.P. Clark and F.R. Field III, "Recycling: Boon or Bane of Advanced Materials Technologies? Automotive Materials Substituion" (Annapolis, MD: World Resources Institute, 1990).

figures collected on a different basis show quite large variations in the rate at which waste paper is recovered.

The less homogeneous the paper collected, the greater the cost of sorting. High-quality office paper is worth money to recyclers but takes up far less room in dumps than newsprint, whose value is low and highly variable. But collecting waste paper is a minor difficulty compared with that of finding uses for it. In the 1980s on both sides of the Atlantic, popular enthusiasm for collecting newspapers for recycling caused a sharp fall in the price. West Germany made waste paper collection mandatory without first setting up end uses for it. The entirely predictable result was a glut and a collapse in the world price. A surge in collection in America in 1989 led to vast stocks of unwanted old newspapers accumulating in warehouses. The glut spilled over into foreign markets. America, already the world's biggest exporter of waste paper, enormously increased its overseas sales of waste paper in the 1980s. In 1970, only 3% of America's recovered waste paper was sold abroad; by 1987, the amount had risen to 18%. American exports to Europe have been falling, a direct result of a rise in local recycling.

The green consumer's demand for products labeled "recycled paper" has helped to create new markets, and 1989 saw a 20% rise in the amount of waste paper used by British industry. A growing demand for recycled paper could reduce the pressure on landfills. The story so far suggests that two main changes are likely. First, in industrial countries, paper mills may increasingly be located near centers of population, rather than forests, to keep down transport costs. Even mills set up near trees may often have the capacity to use waste paper as well as virgin pulp. They will invest heavily in de-inking plant and other equipment to improve their ability to salvage waste. As of 1988 in the United States, seven newsprint mills using recycled paper were already in operation, with the capacity to produce almost a quarter of the country's annual output of newsprint.

A second possibility is that third-world paper industries may grow up on the basis of paper reclaimed in richer countries. Some 60% of America's exports go to markets in three newly industrialized countries: Taiwan, South Korea, and Mexico. They have low labor costs, which allows them to sort paper more

finely than richer countries can afford to. They also have relatively new and efficient mills. In Taiwan and South Korea, rising
labor costs are likely to limit the competitive advantage in sorting
waste. But other countries with still lower labor costs may take
over where they leave off.

No industry has given as much anxious thought to the market
for its recycled product as plastics. At present only 1% of what
is thrown away is recycled in America and hardly any in Britain.
The reason is partly that the industry is in its infancy. The plastics
industry started to think more about recycling in the mid-1980s,
not because it was cheaper (as with steel scrap) but to fend off
popular criticism. But recycling plastic also poses some funda-
mental problems. Plastic's high weight-to-strength ratio means
that a vast volume of, say, empty plastic lemonade bottles may
have to be collected to provide a modest quantity of material for
recycling. Worse, plastic products are often made of several
different resins bonded together. This is especially true for plastic
used in food packaging. A ketchup bottle may use one plastic on
the outside for appearance and strength, another for the middle,
and a third designed to resist fats and acids. Not surprisingly,
separating this club sandwich for recycling may be nearly impossible, certainly for the householder and probably for the
industry. Yet single resins are much more valuable than the
mixed variety.

A great deal of research is being done on developing technologies for separating different plastics, with German and Italian
companies leading the field. Wellman, the company that accounts for 75% of polyethylene terephthalate (PET) bottles recycled in America, has embarked on a large program to develop
sorting technologies for mixed resins.

Although most plastic available for recycling has a mixture of
resins, few companies can handle it. A study by the Environmental Protection Agency in 1990 identified only 16 plants worldwide (three in the United States) that were turning mixed resins
into structural products such as plastic "timber," although other
plants, some using different technologies, are rapidly being or-
dered or built.[4] The end-products from mixed resins until now
have tended to be replacements not for other plastics, but for
timber, concrete, and metals to make things like park benches

and building materials. The city of Chicago has already awarded a contract for recycled plastic timbers and equipment for its city playgrounds. A sound-baffling wall, 320 meters long, has been built with mixed-resin blocks in Cologne. Bales of mixed plastics are being used to build bridge abutments and to protect underground pipes in France.

Recycled plastics will be different from other recycled materials, which usually become substitutes for the virgin product. Moreover, while a bottle made from recycled glass can be made into another glass bottle, it is not possible with present technology and rules on food packaging to use recycled plastic to replace food containers made from the virgin material. That may change, but the effect at present is to postpone the eventual problem of disposal, not to solve it.

Who Pays?

If landfill is sufficiently expensive, if collection costs are low enough, and if the value of the scrap is high enough, recycling schemes can be economical. Indeed, some of the big American waste-management companies have already spotted municipal recycling as a growth industry, less fraught with legal pitfalls than toxic waste disposal. Waste Management, an American giant that runs more recycling plans than any other private firm, estimates that the most efficient curb collection schemes cost $70 a ton. Add to that perhaps $40 a ton for a materials recovery facility, to sort and clean the waste, and the costs of a collect scheme start at $110 a ton. Of that, perhaps $30 to $40 can be recovered by selling the scrap. But the remainder has to be met through a system of shared savings or "diversionary credits": the municipality pays the recycler part of the money saved by avoiding landfill costs. If landfill costs $100 a ton, the sums clearly work; if it costs $20, they do not.

Several American cities now use such concepts to spread the cost of recycling. The Waste Management scheme in Seattle pays because it costs the city $75 a ton to dispose of trash: it can therefore cheerfully pay Waste Management $51 a ton to collect some for recycling. Chicago and Newark separate out their paper and split the money they save in landfill costs between the recycling business and their own coffers. Britain's Environment Protection Act, passed in autumn 1990, provided for a scheme of diversionary credits. The idea is similar to the concept of shared savings used to promote energy conservation.

But where landfill costs are not high enough to pay for recycling, governments face a choice. They can use tax revenue to bridge the gap (as some American cities do), or they can make companies meet the deficit. Of course, such subsidies from taxpayers or companies beg an obvious question. If the point of recycling is to save landfill costs, why do it if it costs more than a well-run landfill does? But that is a question voters rarely ask.

Government Intervention

Sensible policies to promote recycling will start from a basic proposition. Price signals are flawed: neither producers nor consumers understand the true costs of throwing things away. Households, which generally pay for garbage collection through taxation, may regard waste disposal as free. Governments can change that in at least three ways.

One is to charge people in proportion to the amount of refuse they put out for collection. That may encourage households to think about the kinds of goods they buy and be more willing to separate refuse for recycling, either at home (through the compost heap, say) or at curbside. Some municipal authorities will hesitate, for fear of encouraging customers to get rid of their waste in socially nasty ways (like dumping it on the town hall steps, perhaps). But in America some already have such a system. For example, Seattle, Washington, charges a small flat-rate fee for waste services and a larger amount for the bin load, or even the half-bin load, as a way of encouraging people to take part in its recycling scheme.

The scheme is run by Waste Management; 90% of eligible households take part. Nick Harbert, who was running the scheme in 1991, doubts whether Seattle's carefully calibrated scheme of charges is the main influence on participation. In San Jose, California, where he previously worked, 55% to 60% of households took part even though it made no difference in their garbage collection bill. "That makes me think that a sense of moral obligation is the main thing that drives this program," he says. Perhaps, but in another scheme, in Perkasie, Pennsylvania, households get rid of unseparated refuse only in specially marked bags sold by the municipality. While Seattle customers register in advance for a fixed number of bins, households in Perkasie can decide each week how many bags to fill. In the program's first year, the total amount of unseparated waste in Perkasie fell by 60%, and total collection and disposal costs by 40%.[5]

Such schemes may work best in spacious suburbs, where collection costs are low and people are less likely to dump their rubbish illegally. In other areas, other measures may work better or serve as a useful reinforcement. One possibility is a charge on products when they are bought, rather than when they are thrown away. Often, such charges take the form of returnable deposits.

An example of a tax to encourage recycling is America's imposition of a $1.37 a pound levy on virgin CFCs. More widespread taxation in this form might solve the problem faced by Britain's Bird Group, a metals recycler. It has teamed up with Germany's Lindemann, a machinery maker, to develop a technology for extracting all the CFCs from domestic refrigerators— not only from the compressor, but also from the insulating foam. In 1990, it estimated that the scheme would work only if customers were charged a compulsory deposit of $29 per refrigerator. In time, the phasing out of the manufacture of CFCs will drive up their price; a tax or deposit scheme is one way to accelerate what the market should eventually achieve unaided.

There is less urgency about ordinary waste. Still, some American states have tried levies on products that cannot be recycled: in 1988, Florida announced that a disposal fee of a penny would be levied from October 1992 on any container sold through retail outlets that does not achieve a recycling rate of at least 50%. That fee will go up to 2 cents if the 50% target is not met by 1995. Others have tried banning products, for instance disposable diapers in three American states, and in Minnesota, plastic drink containers, polystyrene-foam food packaging containing CFCs, and food packaging that will not biodegrade and cannot be recycled.

Deposit refund schemes are an older idea. When children scavenged for lemonade bottles to augment their pocket money, manufacturers found it less expensive to use refillable bottles and government had no need to intervene. But once one-trip bottles become less expensive, a new logic emerges: deposits offer a way to recoup some of the environmental costs that such containers impose on the environment. The consumer has a choice: take the time to return the bottle or lose the value of the deposit. Deposit schemes seem to work well with drink bottles. In Sweden, a deposit scheme of about 10 cents on PET bottles brought a return rate of 60% to 70%. Experience with aluminum cans suggests that a recovery rate of 80% to 90% could be obtained by raising the deposit to around 30 cents a bottle. Studies in the United States quoted in a 1989 report from the Office of Technology Assessment suggest that such plans result in the return of 70% to 90% of targeted containers and are especially good at reducing litter.[6] Several states report that they have cut the number of drink containers dropped along the roadside by as much as 80%.

That the government imposes a deposit system does not mean it has to run or finance it. But allow manufacturers to choose whether to charge deposits and they may well decide not to do so. In that case, their products will appear less expensive than those of their neighbors. In Switzerland, where deposits are imposed on glass containers, the market share of aluminum ones, which carry no deposit, seems to be growing.

A problem with deposit schemes on ordinary containers, though, is that the deposit may have to be out of all proportion to the environmental costs saved by recycling, if it is to affect behavior. Deposit schemes are much more appropriate as ways of discouraging people from throwing away toxic waste with ordinary garbage. In the United States, where lead in paint is banned (except in the yellow paint used to paint lines on roads) and lead-free gas is the norm, the primary way lead gets into the atmosphere is through car batteries that are dumped illegally. The proportion of batteries that are recycled has been declining. Two states, Rhode Island and Maine, have introduced deposit schemes for lead-acid batteries.

A third possibility is a charge on virgin materials. Before governments consider such refinements, they should make sure they do not favor the use of virgin products over recycled ones. One way or another, they frequently do, and so are indirectly damaging the market for recycled goods. As the first half of this book makes plain, the cost of virgin materials is subsidized in many countries: inexpensive electricity cuts the price of aluminum; depletion allowances for mining hold down the price of minerals; tax relief for forestry makes timber less expensive. One study put the value of such reliefs in the United States at nearly $7 billion in the 1982 fiscal year, although that figure declined dramatically as a result of the tax reductions in 1986.[7]

Such subsidies, by encouraging consumption, encourage waste. They also affect the demand for recycled materials. Recycling schemes will always have a better chance of working if raw materials are properly priced, and an even better one if the costs of environmental damage, for instance by mining, pulp-making, or commercial forestry, are also included. If raw materials are not properly priced, then subsidies for recycling will operate like subsidies for environmentally friendly agriculture: governments will spend one part of tax revenue to offset the harm done by spending another part.

All of these measures are intended to influence the amount of waste that people generate. Other measures may specifically encourage recycling. For example, governments may underwrite the market for recycled products: the converse of subsidizing virgin products. Some American states are considering proposals for favorable tax treatment for purchases of recycled goods. The Dutch government supports the market for recycled paper, just as governments support commodity markets for virgin products in order to ensure stable supply.

A study of market-based approaches to environmental problems suggests a system of recycling credits.[8] These might, for example, be applied to newsprint. Most American newspapers contain some recycled fiber (although the rates achieved by the *Los Angeles Times* and the *Chicago News*, of 50% and 45%, respectively, are unique). But overall demand has not kept pace with growing supply. A recycling credit program would first establish some minimum aggregate content for newsprint and perhaps for paper board. Producers and importers could choose whether to meet the minimum requirement; or to do better, and sell a credit for the amount by which they exceeded the baseline; or do worse, and buy a credit for the amount by which they fell short. The effect would be to allow an individual firm to choose the course that was most efficient for it, while ensuring that the industry overall achieved a set goal. Similar schemes might encourage the content of recycled lead in lead-acid batteries and of used oil in motor-vehicle lubricating oil.

Corporate Responsibility

Companies have a strong interest in demanding economically efficient approaches to waste disposal, because the trend in Europe and Japan may be to load the entire cost of recycling onto companies. The pressure in Europe began to build after the European Court threw out a case brought against Denmark by the European Commission. Denmark banned nonrefillable drink containers, a policy that the commission deemed protectionist. Drink manufacturers from other EC countries would hardly bother to use the special bottles demanded by Danish law for so tiny a market. In 1988, the court ruled that this was an area where the interests of the environment should take precedence over those of free trade.

The ruling opened the way for other EC members to pursue their own policies on packaging. Member states with vociferous environmental lobbies had been frustrated by the ineffectualism of the commission's efforts to put together a directive on drink containers since 1974. The directive, finally passed in 1985, feebly told member states to draw up whatever program each thought best to minimize the impact of drink containers on the environment, by voluntary or legal means, as they preferred.

With carte blanche from the European Court, Germany protected its market for refillable bottles, which conveniently also meant protecting myriad small bottlers of beer and soft drinks, many of them in politically sensitive Bavaria. For some time, the German government had been struggling to prevent a growth in the volume of one-trip containers, especially nonrefillable plastic bottles. To protect the local beverage industries and to please Germany's powerful environmental lobby, the government fought to keep plastic bottles out of the market. In 1977, the government and beverage industries reached a voluntary agreement to try to halt the decline in the use of refillable bottles. When, in spite of the 1977 agreement, use of one-trip bottles began to rise in the mid-1980s, the government established quotas for different refillable bottles and deposits on the larger plastic ones, and made it obligatory for industry to accept bottles when consumers returned them. Liberated by the decision of the European Court, Germany went further. In 1989, a mandatory deposit was put on plastic bottles, which crippled the market for bottled water from France and Belgium: EC rules say that mineral waters must be bottled at source, and lightweight plastic greatly reduces transport costs. France and Belgium now produce mineral water in special glass bottles for the German market.

When the deposit scheme for plastic bottles passed in Germany's parliament, the public demanded to know why only one kind of packaging was under attack. In 1990, the government obliged. Under a proposal passed in parliament in April 1991, tough new obligations were imposed. Retailers were made responsible for recycling packaging. They have to remove outer packaging before offering a product for sale, or else provide a receptacle so that customers can leave it at the shop rather than take it home. There will be signs in shops to make customers aware of their rights to remove packaging on the spot. These obligations will be waived for manufacturers and distributors who take part in a "voluntary" recycling scheme, which will pick up used packaging, sort it, and pass it free of charge for recycling.

The government has laid down tough targets. By the middle of 1995, half of all packaging materials must be collected and recycled. Thereafter, the proportion rises to 80% or more for plastics, paper, board, glass, tinplate, and aluminum. No recycling scheme anywhere has ever achieved such targets. Moreover, the system will be paid for entirely by industry. There will be no recycling credits, as in Seattle, to help split the cost with municipal taxpayers who no longer have to pay tipping charges. Instead, companies will pay a levy linked to the number of dots on their product packages. The cost is likely to be enormous. In theory, it will cost DM10 billion to DM15 billion ($6 billion to $9 billion) to set up the scheme and then DM2 billion a year to run it. That sum will be met by selling companies the right to put a green spot on their packaging, guaranteeing that it can be recycled. Companies in turn will add 2 pfennigs to the cost of each product marked with the spot.

Manufacturers fear that in practice the cost may be vastly greater and that they may end up carrying it. They also argue that the scheme covers all packaging (while North American ones tend to go for three or four easily handled wastes); all households (while North American schemes concentrate on houses rather than apartments); and starts with no guarantee of final markets for the recyclables. Germany's glutting of the European market for recycled paper may be repeated in many other commodity markets. Foreign manufacturers fear that the scheme may be protectionist. German retailers have undertaken to do their best to encourage their suppliers to join the scheme, and may eventually be reluctant to carry products not marked with the green spot. They have not, however, explicitly agreed to exclude nonparticipants for fear of breaking the cartel laws.

What Germany does, Japan has been considering. Desperately short of dumping grounds, Tokyo metropolitan district has been refusing to accept large items of domestic waste such as television sets or refrigerators. A rash of illegal dumping has followed. Private contractors have been shipping waste to Japan's northern island, and local authorities there are up in arms. So the Japanese ministry of health and welfare has tried to persuade manufacturers to take more responsibility for the final fate of bulky electrical appliances such as old fridges, washing machines, and television sets, either by recovering the appliances themselves or by sharing the disposal costs. In April 1991, the government announced a new law that would require the Diet to designate manufacturers that will have to recycle under government guidelines. Manufacturers of glass bottles and large household appliances may be asked to design products that they or dealers can recycle.

Other European countries are racing after Germany. Denmark, which already taxes one-trip packaging, plans to increase the tax and is debating a ban on PVC. Italy is threatening to introduce taxes starting in 1993 on materials that do not meet recycling targets of 50% for metals and glass and 40% for plastics. Unlike the German targets, the Italian ones will partly count incineration toward the recycling total. Switzerland has recently introduced regulations for drink bottles, laying down recycling targets that must be met by 1993. Sweden is proposing a ban on one-trip bottles made of PET. In 1991, Dutch industry drew up an elaborate plan for a 10% cut in packaging by the end of the century. What frightens Europe's industry most is the prospect that the EC Commission, anxious to improve on its earlier directive on beverage containers, might seize on Germany's scheme as a model.

The community has already taken a tougher line on manufacturers' responsibilities for the final fate of their products: plastics manufacturers have been told to take "voluntary" responsibility for the collection and recycling of plastic bags. Plastics manufacturers were invited by the EC Commission in 1987 to come up with credible ideas for managing plastics waste. In 1989, a sense of self-preservation drove the Association of Plastics Manufacturers in Europe to put together a plan for recycling all separately collected plastics by 1995, backing the target with an investment in recycling plants.

In 1991, the commission had yet to give its blessing to the German scheme, although Dr. Klaus Töpfer, Germany's environment minister, said he would not ask for it and would take no notice if EC approval were withheld. Several EC countries complained bitterly that the German measure would interfere with trade. They were particularly enraged by a last-minute concession to Bavarian brewers, insisting that one-trip bottles should account for no more than 28% of the market. To contain the German initiative, the commission had decided to draw up a directive to cover all packaging, rather than just drink containers. A draft directive finished in the fall of 1991 proposed that 60% of all packaging should be recycled within ten years and that, meanwhile, the output of packaging should not increase. It caused almost as much industrial annoyance as the German measures.

Germany's recycling plan is a clear demonstration of the danger of putting too much emphasis on the most complicated of all answers to waste disposal. It is the equivalent of America's command-and-control regulation of air pollution: government lays down a single technological solution to a problem that might more economically be solved in other ways. If carried beyond a certain level, recycling begins to generate large economic and environmental costs of its own.

The largest gap in the present headlong rush to recycle is that governments act on one side of the market without keeping an eye on the other. It is easy to set deposits at a rate that encourages consumers to return bottles or batteries; harder to make sure that there is a sensible way to recycle them. Developing markets for recycled products will be a greater challenge to both government and industry than getting people to sort their rubbish or to bring it back.

The Spread of Recycling

Recycling is starting to spread beyond packaging to other consumer goods. The determined Töpfer has announced plans to introduce compulsory deposits on cars. The German government will eventually consider a plan to make manufacturers take back used cars if the industry meanwhile fails to think up a recycling scheme of its own. Manufacturers have begun to think harder about ways of dealing with the plastics they use. General Electric reached an agreement with European car dismantlers to take back GE plastics from junk cars. America's Society of Automotive Engineers developed a standard labeling system for polymeric components to help identify parts when a car is dismantled. Volvo has done the same thing with the plastic components of its cars. Several car makers, including Volkswagen, Renault, and BMW, are experimenting with reverse assembly or dismantling plants, which separate car components according to their construction material. BMW is building a special plant in southern Germany to produce a recyclable car.

After cars, computers. The German Association of Computer Manufacturers formed a project group to think about disassembly before Töpfer does so that it can put a proposal to him rather than vice versa. The idea is not as farfetched as it sounds: already

a group of four companies in America have set up a joint experiment to recycle plastic computer housings: General Electric's
plastic, used to make Digital Equipment's computer housings, is
being reclaimed, mixed with virgin plastic, and turned into roof
shingles by Naillite for McDonald's restaurants. Another proposal on the German government's drawing board would force
tire manufacturers to take back and recycle used tires.

These proposals would be more impressive if governments
were clearer about their reasons for encouraging companies to
recycle. When, in 1987, a commission set up by the Australian
government looked at a proposal to levy deposits on glass drink
bottles, it found that a scheme costing industry and consumers
A$200 million to A$350 million ($154 million to $270 million)
would cut the costs of litter collection by A$2 million to A$4
million and reduce waste-disposal costs by about A$26 million.
"For consumers to judge that container-deposit legislation would
be worthwhile," commented the commission with masterly understatement, "they would need to place a high value on the total
of those benefits which the commission could not quantify." If
governments are doing what the voters want, people must be
willing to pay plenty for the pleasures of recycling rubbish rather
than disposing of it in other ways.

Cleaner Processes, Cleaner Products

Companies face many pressures to think seriously about the environment. Most will resent them. A wise minority will see the opportunities they present and think creatively about ways to respond. They will make two kinds of changes: in their manufacturing processes and in the products they make.

Previous chapters have described two of the strongest pressures on companies: the rise of the green consumer and the need to reduce waste, whether the by-product of industrial activity or the final fate of a product. Other forces will also influence companies. One will be the growing desire of ordinary voters not to live next to an environmental eyesore. Call them NIMBYs—Not In My Back Yard—and consider them as exemplars of environmental property rights. Voters think they own the rights to quiet streets, clean air, safe water. Place an airport or an incinerator or a chemical plant in their home town, and you diminish the value of those rights. A second force will be the cost of making mistakes, both in terms of lost reputation and hard cash. A third will be regulation. Voters will continue to press for tougher green regulations on companies, especially as their costs will be largely hidden. They will be encouraged by the bureaucrats who staff environmental agencies around the world. Like bureaucrats everywhere, they will see it as part of their job to expand the amount of work they have to do.

This list ignores one more influence, which is harder to gauge than the rest: the price of energy. Even without carbon taxes, environmental regulations will continue to push it up. But while energy prices will be influenced by environmental considerations, slow economic growth in the first half of the 1990s will probably cause a continued decline.

Siting

Where companies and roads and airports are located will be determined more and more by the power of local NIMBYs. Who wants a chemical plant across the road from their house? Or a landfill half a mile from their children's school? Who wants an incinerator or an oil rig as a neighbor? Nothing will drive the greening of world industry faster than the growing hostility of people to installations they consider to be polluters. Mention the possibility that the pollution may be carcinogenic, and the back-yard gates slam shut for good.

NIMBYs are often rich: they can afford to put calm before jobs. Some are the old, or at least the retired middle classes, who no longer have much reason to care about local employment and have plenty of time to lobby their younger friends in government and the media. NIMBYs will help to redistribute wealth, as exasperated companies site new plants in poorer regions, where jobs still matter most, or in poorer countries. But they will also force those companies that have no choice to work hard at their green image. And they will make it much more expensive to get rid of waste. NIMBYs will thus raise the costs of dirty processes and the rewards of being clean.

NIMBY squeamishness imposes real costs on companies that are thought of as potential polluters. When they want to build a new plant or to expand an existing one, they have less choice of sites than other firms. Their managers have to spend more time searching for solutions and winning planning permission. Such costs are higher in America than almost anywhere else.

Frank Blake, a lawyer specializing in environmental law, sums it up. "Companies can't do much without getting a permit, which is given mainly on environmental grounds," he says. "So industries that want to get permits need to have a good green reputation. For many of my clients, my advice is simply, 'Forget it.' The larger companies can afford to negotiate through the very expensive and time-consuming process, but not the small. Companies tend to rebuild on existing sites, rather than trying to find new ones. And they don't go to places where getting permits is hardest, like the Northeast." Do frustrated companies go abroad? "I'm sure it happens all the time."

Legal Penalties

Nothing will do more damage to a company that hopes to cultivate a reputation for greenery than a polluting accident. But an accident may cost a company more than its reputation. It also may mean an immense bill. For other firms in the same industry, it will mean an increase in insurance premiums and another click in the ratchet of environmental regulations. Like the siting problem, fear of accidents will be a constant pressure on companies to become greener.

Accidents can often transform a company's—or a country's or an industry's—attitude to environmental safety. Bhopal taught American chemical companies to set high standards in the third world; Seveso led the EC to tighten rules to prevent industrial accidents; a fire at a warehouse belonging to Sandoz, a Swiss chemical company, transformed that company's environmental policies. Accidents also carry financial penalties, especially in the United States, where courts impose ferocious punishments. Exxon spent over $2 billion cleaning up the Alaskan oil spill. As a result, many American shipowners raised their liability insurance from $100 million or $150 million to $750 million or so. The difficulty of obtaining coverage for pollution risks of over $1 billion led Shell to announce that it would no longer ship oil to many American ports.

In Europe, the size of compensatory settlements of all kinds is converging upward, although it still tends to be only a fifth of those awarded in American courts. When, in August 1989, Shell UK accidentally allowed 156 tons of crude oil to escape into the river Mersey, Britain's new National Rivers Authority promptly took the company to court, where it was fined £1 million, many times the biggest fine previously awarded against a polluting company in the British courts. Shell had already spent £1.4 million cleaning up the mess. Ominously, the judge said that he had weighed Shell's good environmental record against its large resources. Oil companies will have spotted two morals: large companies are more likely to be hit hard by the courts *pour encourager les autres;* and time and money spent on conservation before an accident give some protection against even heavier punishments when one occurs. The legal liabilities that frighten American companies most, though, are not for dramatic accidents. Environmental statutes generally provide for criminal as well as civil penalties. As a result, managers now quite often go to prison for breaking environmental laws, such as failing to get a permit for some activity or to fulfill its terms. Often, the offense involves the inappropriate disposal of toxic waste. In one notorious case, a Hungarian entrepreneur, a former freedom fighter, was imprisoned for failing to get a permit to dump used tires in a bog beside a road. Penalties are getting heavier. In the 1988–1989 fiscal year, the Environmental Protection Agency imposed some $37 million in fines for environmental crimes. That was a quarter of the entire amount levied by the agency since 1974. Furthermore, 50 people were fined and given prison sentences of eight years each.

Pollution Control

Given the rising costs of being dirty, more companies see the benefits of being clean. The traditional approach has been "end-of-pipe" solutions, approaches that tackle effluents or gases just before, or even after, they leave the plant. But a new approach is now being developed: one of preventing pollution in the first place. It is less expensive in the long run to rethink the whole of an industrial process than to tack on a bit of extra technology at the end. As a result, "waste minimization" has become a catchphrase among the greenest companies, whose names are rarely found on labels on supermarket shelves. Of the 100 to 200 companies worldwide that have made environmental performance their top concern, most are chemical companies. The most radical corporate thinking on the environment is taking place in large chemical companies such as Du Pont, Monsanto, Dow, Hoechst, ICI, and Ciba-Geigy. Realizing that the environment is one of the three or four most important issues facing their industry, their boards have formulated green strategies and set up sophisticated management systems to carry them out. This is hardly surprising: chemical companies in industrial countries typically produce 50% to 70% of all hazardous waste, either in the course of manufacturing or in the form of their final product. In other industries—especially oil and cars—there are companies that take greenery equally seriously, although they are rarer. But the number of companies and industries in the former category will rise as the costs of polluting increase.

These companies have tended to be more interested in making the manufacturing process cleaner than in producing goods for green consumers. They have focused mainly on the pollution that comes from smokestacks and sewage outflows. They have been driven much less by the buying power of shoppers than by the many costs of polluting, especially by the risks of handling and the costs of disposing of toxic waste. Many also claim that being greener has saved them money. Now, just as companies driven mainly by green consumerism have widened their attention from cleaner products to cleaner processes, so these businesses have begun to think more about their products.

A striking aspect of these environmental strategies is the extent to which they move far ahead of local regulatory requirements. For example, a number of companies have set themselves targets for toxic emissions and for waste generation far more stringent than anything the law requires. Monsanto has pledged itself to cut toxic air emissions by 90% by the end of 1992 and then to work toward a goal of zero emissions. Du Pont has promised to cut toxic air emissions by 60% from 1987 levels by 1993, to cut carcinogens by a further 90% before the end of the century, and eventually to stop emitting them entirely. These "green leaders" also frequently set standards for their overseas subsidiaries that may be even higher when measured against local norms. Frequently they insist that the company's standards be applied worldwide. For example, Union Carbide stipulates that its facilities in Africa stick to standards consistent with America's Clean Water Act, even though there is no such act in Africa. Johnson & Johnson applies the same standards all over the world. If standards rise in one country, the company claims, they are adopted universally. Dow Chemical has technology centers for various products, part of whose job is to ensure that the same technological standards are applied wherever a new plant is built. One effect is to raise standards in third world countries.

These policies have their critics. Few economists regard the goal of zero emissions as a wise one. Better to aim for the point at which the cost of getting rid of an extra molecule of nasty substance overtakes a rational estimate of the benefits to human health or to the environment. That point might come after a few puffs of carcinogens, especially from a plant in a densely populated area. It might be reasonable to set a much higher level of emissions in the case of less harmful gases, especially from a plant in the middle of nowhere. Some industrialists, even in the chemical industry, think that zero emissions are fine as an ideal but ludicrous as a practical goal. Robin Paul, managing director of Albright & Wilson, a British-based, American-owned chemicals-to-household goods group, is one such person: "Science," he points out, "is getting better all the time at measuring traces of substances in emissions." The chairman of Du Pont, Ed Woolard, made a broader point in a speech in December 1989:

> As we move closer to zero, the economic cost which society must ultimately bear may be very high. Or the energy expenditure necessary to eliminate a given emission may have more ecological impact than trade emissions themselves. Society will have to decide where the balance should be struck, and may conclude

in some cases that zero emissions is neither in the environment's nor the public's best interest.

Imposing world standards has other drawbacks, especially in third world countries, where it may be harder than simply aiming to be a bit cleaner than the locals. It may indeed sometimes be worse for third world countries than playing by local rules. Excessive virtue may lead Western companies to invest less than they might otherwise do, leaving the door open to local firms more interested in evading than exceeding their country's green standards. A company's partner may be the government, which may balk at paying for higher emission standards than its own laws require. Or there may simply be no local facilities. IBM found no site in Argentina able to meet its tough requirements for waste disposal. Its Argentine plants therefore recycle three-quarters of the waste they generate.

Pollution control still mostly means adding bits and pieces. It may mean installing a dust filter or building a purification plant, essentially transforming one type of waste into another that is less harmful and more manageable. For instance, a dust filter may convert uncontrolled clouds of filthy smoke into clean smoke and a heap of dirt that can be disposed of in a properly run landfill. Such an approach involves no change in the manufacturing process.

For companies in the industries most sensitive to the charge of polluting, add-on technology is not enough; the costs of being dirty and the benefits of being clean are so high that a new approach becomes worthwhile. The sums being spent on pollution control, especially in the chemical industry, are staggering. Bayer, a German chemical group, spends 20% of its manufacturing costs on environmental protection, about the same as it does on energy or labor. In the United States, Chevron expects environmental spending to grow by 10% a year, and sees it glumly as "the only growth area of the oil industry." Albright & Wilson spends half its capital program on environmental protection projects or products. As a result, these companies find that it pays to take a radical approach to environmental protection. They have been seeking ways to ensure that, in the phrase coined by 3M, Pollution Prevention Pays (PPP). Proving its point, 3M claims to have saved well over $482 million in the 15 years that its PPP policy has been in effect. Other companies have acronyms of their own: Chevron has SMART (Save Money and Reduce Toxics), Texaco has WOW (Wipe Out Waste), and Dow Chemical has WRAP (Waste Reduction Always Pays).

Often simple improvements in process efficiency are looked for at first. Chris Hampson, board director of ICI responsible for the environment, says that about a quarter of the company's current environmental costs came from "losses in containment and less than optimum operation of plant."[1] Robert Muirhead, formerly Exxon Chemicals' European safety and environmental control manager, reckons that waste-disposal costs are double the actual cost to the company when account is made of lost production and operating costs. When future liability for waste is added in, the cost could be doubled again.

Having first popularized the idea of waste minimization, 3M now thinks through the concept in four stages, as follows.

1. *Reformulation.* Can a product be made with fewer raw materials so that the company warehouses are not full of dangerous substances? Can it be made with fewer toxic materials? For instance, can a solvent-based coating be replaced with a water-based one?

2. *Equipment redesign.* Can steam from one process, for instance, be used to drive another?

3. *Process modification.* Is it helpful to change, say, from batch feeding, which may mean readjusting the pollution-control systems with each new batch, to continuous feeding, with fewer quality-control problems?

4. *Resource recovery.* Can a waste product be salvaged and reused—as a raw material in another process or as a fuel or as a product?

Union Carbide breaks down the pattern in a different way. It is one of several companies that insist that each plant draw up its own waste-minimization policy. Since 1987, every big capital-investment project at Union Carbide has been reviewed for its potential in reducing waste. The company reckons that most of the measures it takes to minimize waste fall into one of three categories: good housekeeping, which includes reductions in spillages and leaks as well as better inventory control so that, for instance, chemicals are bought in smaller quantities; changes in the materials used, for example, switching to less hazardous substitutes; and changes in technology.

The simplest waste-minimization techniques are often of the good-housekeeping variety. Stopping day-to-day accidents may not be as dramatic as preventing another Bhopal, but the cumulative effect on the environment may be as great. Some companies adopt techniques to stop accidents after they have had one. Sandoz, for example, Switzerland's second largest chemical company, spent Sfr150 million ($100 million) on measures to prevent a repetition of the disastrous Schweizerhalle fire in 1986, including installing two catchment basins to stop water used in firefighting from draining into the Rhine. Shell UK spent £100,000 ($177,000) on a new leak-detection system after its spill in the Mersey in 1989. It is better, of course, to make such investments before accidents occur.

Better still is simple waste prevention. Union Carbide found that one of the best ways to stop the escape of polluted air from its plants was to set up a regular schedule of checks on components such as pumps, valves, and flanges. Keeping these promptly and properly repaired has allowed the chemical company to cut fugitive emissions down to a minute fraction of the levels judged acceptable by the Environmental Protection Agency. Utah-based Geneva Steel estimates it has been able to reduce its emissions to a quarter or a fifth of the allowable maximum primarily through the simple device of teaching workers to take proper care of the doors of its coke ovens. "The workers baby the things," says Joe Canon, its chairman.

Such good housekeeping is likely to be the least expensive kind of pollution prevention. Indeed, it is most likely to be the kind that shows a profit. "Most waste happens because something is not being used properly," argues ICI's Hampson. "Waste may happen because a plant is only 90% efficient in its use of raw materials. The rest is going out in waste. A lot of pollution is associated with inefficiency." As an example, he cites the production of fine denier nylon yarn by ICI's fibers division. The yarn is wound in a continuous thread several miles long onto a 25-pound bobbin. Each time the yarn snaps, ICI loses money— and creates waste, because the half-filled bobbin has to be disposed of. "Our efficiency is currently around 85%," Hampson says. "If we can get that up to the low 90s, we will make a 30% increase in profits."

Good housekeeping may stop waste being created in the first place. Beyond that, waste minimization becomes more complicated. It may involve changes in the quantity or quality of raw materials used in order to prevent waste being created in the first place. Thus Volvo is cutting solvent emissions from car plants by switching to water-based paints. Sigvard Höggren, vice president for environmental affairs, believes that "In the long run we must use materials in our processes that do not give rise at all to hazardous emissions." Polaroid is trying to find ways to substitute water for organic solvents in the manufacture of films for cameras. Exxon Chemicals, unhappy about the amount of hazardous waste caused by soil contamination, is rethinking the design of some of its plants. Often, simply using less air or water dramatically reduces the amount of polluted air or water that a plant has to dispose of. The volume of really nasty toxics may be no lower, but it may be easier to handle. Sandoz has been trying to reduce the amount of wastewater it generates. Handling fewer dangerous materials is one protection against accidents. Richard Mahoney, head of Monsanto, describes how his company reached that conclusion: "After Bhopal, we found we were handling far more hazardous materials than we needed to."

Uses for Waste

Many of the companies that have tried to reduce waste have found ways of recovering and reusing it. This means that the company not only has to dispose of less waste; it may also need less raw material. For example, Chevron produces 10,000 oil samples a month, each contained in a tiny glass vial. Because even a trace of oil on the glass puts the used vials in the category of hazardous waste, the company used to pack them with absorbent material in 55-gallon drums and send them to hazardous-waste landfills at a cost of $5,000 a month. In June 1988, a vial crusher was installed, which broke down the vials and recovered the traces of oil. The oil could be reused, the glass recycled. The equipment cost $20,000, paying for itself by the end of the year.

Chevron also spent huge sums disposing of the mucky emulsion of oil and water left from a plant's wastewater system. It installed a mobile centrifuge to spin the sludge, separating the oil and water and leaving a small cake of solid gunge. The oil is reused as feedstock, the water purified and discharged, and the cake of muck, its volume less than 5% that of the original sludge, is all that needs to be sent to a hazardous-waste dump.

Polaroid used to use freon, a liquid solvent whose evaporating vapors seem to damage the ozone layer, for cleaning the plastic parts and electronic circuit boards that go into its cameras. In 1988, as the possibility of a ban on chlorofluorocarbons approached, Polaroid installed new degreasers at one of its plants, which captured and recycled escaping freon vapors. Polaroid saved a net $75,000 a year by cutting the bill for new freon.

Several companies have found markets for wastes that they could not use themselves. Thus Du Pont formerly got rid of 3,600 tons a year of a chemical called hexamethyleneimine (HMI), used in making nylon. When it started to look for other methods, it discovered a market for HMI in the pharmaceuticals and coating industries. Now, demand exceeds by-product supply. In 1989, Du Pont had to find a way to make HMI on purpose.

Some companies rely on the ingenuity of local managers to find ways of disposing of waste. Others take a more structured approach. In 1986, Dow Chemical set up a management team to pick out potential by-products that were being thrown away and find ways of reusing them. It examined five plants to see how far primary feedstocks could be replaced with by-product feedstocks. It planned the plant modifications that had to be made and sorted out transport difficulties. As a result, it cut purchases of hydrocarbons for feedstock; made it possible for those plants that had found it hard to get enough feedstock to produce at higher capacity; reduced the company's demand for expensive incineration of waste; and marketed spare ethylene dichloride to other companies.

A Chevron subsidiary, Warren Petroleum Company, found another outlet for its waste. About twice a month it sends used caustic to nearby pulp and paper manufacturers, which use the corrosive liquid in their treatment of wood products. Chevron found these buyers by adding the chemical by-product to a list published each month by the Houston Chamber of Commerce Industry Surplus Chemical Inventory Program. But it is not always the company that finds the outlet. In France, waste glucose from the manufacture of prunes d'Agens caused an enormous water-pollution problem. The river-basin authority solved it by suggesting that the manufacturers bottle and sell the juice.

A powerful argument for preventing pollution at the earliest possible stage in a process is that it is likely to be less expensive in the long run. Some work by America's Electric Power Research Institute found that pollution-control equipment—cooling towers, scrubbers, electrostatic precipitators—added to a coal-fired power plant after it was built could add 45% to the capital cost and 30% to the operating cost. Integrating controls into the plant at the design stage could save up to half these costs. The plant's complexity was also reduced, and its flexibility and reliability increased.

A practical example of this arithmetic comes from Novo-Nordisk, Denmark's largest pharmaceutical company.[2] In 1987, the Danish parliament decided that total discharges of nitrogen compounds should be cut by 50% of their current levels by 1993. The company had large quantities of waste nitrogen compounds from its Kalundborg plant. One option was to build a large wastewater treatment plant to convert the dissolved nitrogen compounds into gas that could be evaporated into the atmosphere. The company thought that would cost Dkr100 million ($16 million) in initial capital investment and Dkr20 million to 40 million in running costs.

"The cleanup solution didn't feel right," says Torben Schjidt Jensen, manager of environmental affairs. "It's a waste to convert nitrogen that could otherwise be used as fertilizer into gaseous nitrogen, which just evaporates into the atmosphere." Instead, the company halved its nitrogen emissions within two years, at a capital cost of Dkr10 million, primarily by converting the leftover nitrogen into fertilizer and distributing it free to farmers. The separated wastewater is sent to the local coal-fired power plant and mixed with lime to neutralize sulphur emissions.

These money-saving initiatives raise the unavoidable question: If pollution prevention always paid, why would anybody pollute? One EPA official provides this answer: "We have a data base with a thousand examples of companies doing pollution prevention that pays—but we could clearly do the opposite and collect examples of where it doesn't pay."

Much pollution prevention yields genuinely high returns that may have gone unnoticed for years. As with energy conservation, much pollution prevention may well cover its cash costs in two or three years. Yet companies may still not undertake it because the yields may be small in absolute terms compared with those from other more central, nonenvironmental investments. And managers may not want to be bothered with finding out about the best ways of cutting pollution, or implementing them. Unless companies have other good reasons for making pollution prevention a priority, the costs may mean they see no reward in cleaning up.

In fact, the farther the road is traveled toward zero emissions, the smaller the financial returns become. The cost of each bit of pollution prevention will rise relative to the amount of cleanness it buys. The "green leaders" are frank about this. "We're going to test the public's willingness to pay," says Monsanto's Mahoney. "There will be a price tag for all this, and in my company it will be hundreds of millions of dollars." Monsanto argues that the main reason that, in spite of large increases in productivity, its gross profit margin has remained stuck at 25% is the cost of the many social programs (including environmental) it has introduced. The latest initiative from 3M, called Pollution Prevention Plus, comes with a warning that not all future cleaning up will be profitable.

Many companies have hardly begun to think about switching to clean technology. An OECD study estimated that clean technologies accounted for barely one-fifth of pollution-control investments.[3] Companies, it argued, are most likely to adopt clean technologies when they are changing the production process.

Volvo, for example, combined its program to reduce solvent emissions from paint spraying with the construction of a new paint shop, at Torslanda. This will have a capacity of 130,000 car bodies, half Volvo's annual capacity at Gothenburg, and will cut solvent emissions by 80% to 85% as compared with a conventional paint shop. The OECD study argues that changes in the production process will be made only if the new process is more profitable than the old.

Clean technology is easier to introduce in new and fast-growing industries. Indeed, because new technology is almost always cleaner than the old sort, a country with low levels of capital investment (such as Poland and Britain) will tend to be relatively dirty. Fast-growing industries have the opportunity and flexibility to build in new technology. But with the important exception of chemicals, the fast-growing industries are often those, such as office machinery or electronics equipment, that are only moderately polluting. The big polluters—industries such as metals, textiles, clothing and leather, and food—are ones where slow growth discourages new investment. By contrast, end-of-pipe equipment has attractions for polluters, the pollution-control industry, and regulators. The technology is tried and tested, easily available from suppliers and easily applied. The risks are fewer: if the device does not work, the company can continue to produce; if, on the other hand, a new process gives trouble, the company's survival may be threatened. Installing add-on technology is a neat public statement of a company's commitment to a better environment, and may be easier for people to appreciate than the adoption of a new technology. This may partially explain why those companies that have pursued strategies of waste minimization spend so much time talking about what they have achieved.

Measuring the costs of environmental protection relative to its benefits is easier with end-of-pipe technology too. As Höggren of Volvo points out when discussing the clean technology of Volvo's new paint shop at Torslanda, "Let's say it's a total cost of some Skr1.7 billion—how much of that amount is devoted to purely environmental matters? I could never define that."[4] The person in charge of environmental issues may find it hard to persuade those who head the production process of the need for change. That is, of course, why dramatic action is often taken after an environmental accident: at that point, the manager in charge of environmental affairs suddenly has more clout.

In the pollution-control industry, the drawbacks are different. A few small companies specialize in developing waste-minimization technology. Generally, though, companies want to sell products that are highly standardized and easily recognizable, rather than processes that require long, specific studies and may be difficult to market. Industry case studies made by the OECD show that new clean technologies may be hard to transfer from one user to another. They may be highly specific to particular installations and production techniques. Worse, they lack the advantage of add-on technologies, which are likely to be maintained by the company that provides them. The maintenance contract may be worth more than the original product to the company that supplies it. A clean process, by contrast, is simply handed over to the customer. If things go wrong with it, the necessary repairs and adjustments may be much less profitable to the installer.

Many countries offer various kinds of financial aid for pollution control. In Germany, for instance, accelerated depreciation is possible on investments of which at least 70% goes to pollution control. It is often easier for a company to get aid if it uses add-on treatment rather than changes in the production process that hide the treatment technique.

Even regulators may effectively discourage the adoption of clean technologies. In industrial countries, permits tend to be given for "best available or practicable technologies" and often include an incentive or even an obligation to use proven "conventional" processes. An industry may see the choice as unpalatable: if it experiments with an unproven process and gets it wrong, the regulator will grumble; if it gets it right and achieves a much higher level of pollution control, the regulator will ratchet up the standards to meet the new level of performance.

Building Incentives

Government attitudes are beginning to change. Countries like France and the Netherlands have set up special agencies to promote clean technologies. The Dutch offer a higher level of state subsidy for clean technologies and product than for add-on technologies, although many of the higher grants have tended to go toward the development of quieter vehicles rather than cleaner processes. Denmark offers state cash to pay for pilot projects in clean technology. In 1983, the year reported by the OECD, only 1.3% of the available cash was used by industry, "which reflects," as the OECD says with masterly understatement, "some circumspection on its part."

Probably the most important incentives to the spread of clean technologies are government measures to check pollution. Until now, such measures have had two characteristics: they deal with one type of pollution at a time, and they require industry to use a method rather than achieve a result. This is starting to change. Interest is increasing in the concept of "integrated pollution control," the idea that regulators should take account of all the ways in which a plant generates waste, rather than looking at one medium at a time. Why cut air emissions if the net result is more water pollution or more muck dumped in landfills? This attempt to build waste minimization into the structure of regulation is a cornerstone of the Environmental Protection Act passed by the British government in autumn 1990. Permission for some 5,000 of the largest and most polluting industrial processes will have to be obtained from Her Majesty's Inspectorate of Pollution (HMIP). Its inspectors will expect new investments to use "best available techniques not involving excessive cost," and HMIP intends to keep an eye on technologies developed in other countries as well. Existing plant will gradually have to be brought up to a set of standards decided by HMIP. Once companies began to understand what they were in for—and a survey by KPMG Peat Marwick McLintock in May and June 1990 found that even in chemical companies, nearly a quarter of senior managers had never heard of the impending legislation—they began to complain about what it would cost them. The challenge for HMIP will be to teach British companies that cleaner technology may frequently be less expensive in the long run than the add-on kind.

At the same time, a growing number of countries are talking about setting mandatory waste reduction goals. The American Congress has repeatedly threatened to introduce them. Several states, led by Massachusetts, are in the throes of introducing toxics-use reduction laws, aimed at restricting the amount of toxic chemicals that companies use, rather than the amount they emit. A common provision of such legislation is the requirement that companies produce plans for reduction. What happens in America may soon happen in other parts of the world.

Making industry clean up is easy compared with the task of making individuals change their behavior. In the EC, some 60% of industrial waste is already being reused. But 60% of household waste is dumped. The cleaner large companies make their processes, the more they will be urged to help consumers be clean, too. The focus will shift from minimizing corporate waste to minimizing the contents of the household trash can. That, too, will be seen primarily as a task for companies.

Cleaner Products

The better companies get at reducing waste, the clearer it becomes that the problem is the product, not just the process. In the best chemical companies, effluent accounts for perhaps 4% of output. It is the final user that creates large amounts of waste. Throughout the 1980s, companies like Dow and BASF steadily cut effluent per ton of product sold, but their final sales increased. So the next obligation on companies will be to consider the impact on the environment of their products all through their lives. That means thinking not only about the extraction of raw materials and the production process, but also about the way in which a product is packaged and transported. More important, it means thinking about what will happen to a product when the consumer no longer wants it.

Because most of the goods people buy eventually end up as garbage, reducing waste can mean one of only a few things: buying products that use less raw material to serve their function; buying products that can be recycled or reused; buying products that last longer; or simply buying less. Radical environmentalists would see only one answer: consuming less. Although most people are unlikely to accept it, deep green logic is impeccable. For instance, the Dutch government at one stage was considering whether to alter the code of conduct for advertisers in order to discourage consumption.

More likely, people will go on consuming as much as ever but demand new technologies and new materials. Consider an analogy from the food industry. Some people, finding that sugar and fat are bad for them, manage to drop both from their diets. But others continue to have their cake and eat it, thanks to food technologists who have invented ways of making things sweet and creamy without sugar, milk fat, or calories. Rather than make massive changes in consumption patterns, people and governments will look to industry to help them consume in less environmentally harmful ways. The attitude of governments to companies will be: "You created this problem. Now you solve it." That may mean looking for products that disintegrate more quickly. "We're looking for products guaranteed not to last," was the slogan of Wal-Mart. Or, conversely, it may mean finding products that last longer, or ways to make products more easily recyclable. It could mean selling less—especially of packaging, the obvious way for consumers to minimize waste—or selling products that are less toxic. Or, most radical of all, it may mean thinking in terms of selling an "impact" rather than a product: if a consumer wants a warm house, say, does that mean selling electricity or insulation?

Waste Minimization for Consumers

The greenest way to reduce waste ought to be to get people to buy fewer products, or products made with less material. Technology can create products that need to be replaced less frequently. For instance, car tires are a particularly difficult kind of waste to dispose of. Production of tires in the United States has risen, as people have bought more cars and driven more miles. But the number of tires per million vehicle miles of travel has declined, mainly because they are more sturdily made. A boon to harassed rubbish collectors? Only partly. The new blends of natural and synthetic rubbers that have strengthened tires mean less recycling of rubber from old tires. And steel-belted tires, while more durable than the old kind, are also more difficult to recycle. While technology also can devise ways to produce more goods from less raw material, it will not come up with waste-saving products unless the costs of waste disposal are reflected in the price. Tires are more durable not because the costs of disposing of them have risen (although they are one of the hardest products to destroy), but because consumers wanted fewer punctures. Without clear signals from the market, technologies that appear to be based on fewer raw materials may actually include more. For instance, the widespread assumption of the 1970s that electronics would reduce the use of paper now seems ludicrous.[5] The use of paper by American businesses rose from 850 billion pages to 1.4 trillion between 1981 and 1984.

Indeed, without the guidance of a price structure, new technology is as likely to create more waste as less. For example, microwave ovens have created a new market for film-wrapped packages of items that would once have come in paper bags. In the days when people bought a pound of green beans in a paper bag, the wrappings accounted for 0.6% of the weight. When they bought the same quantity in a can, the container was 13.5% of the weight. Once they changed to microwave cooking, the packaging was more than 16% of the total weight. A general trend has been to sell more individual portions of food, which reduces wasted food but means more wrapping, both around each portion and around several portions in a pack.

Technology has created convenience and saved people time, but increased waste. The advances of technology, however, do mean economies in raw materials. Products become smaller and lighter. Think of toasters, irons, and television sets. New smaller products replace bigger old ones: pocket calculators, microwave ovens. The ultimate small-is-powerful is the microchip. The entire global annual production of microchips could fit in a single 747 jumbo jet. But lighter products are often produced on the assumption that if they break down, they will be replaced rather than repaired, another example of the substitution of environmental resources for human labor. Also, the small new products may be additional, not alternative: few kitchens use a microwave to replace a conventional oven rather than complement it. And the tiny microchip, whose manufacture generates a surprisingly large volume of nasty chemicals, sits in a large plastic or metal box. If the number-one priority for reducing municipal waste is cutting the weight of products, then the simplest solution is to reduce the weight of packaging materials. This is already happening. Reynolds Metal, one of the biggest manufacturers of aluminum cans, has cut the weight of its product by 45% over the years. Some figures produced by Britain's Industry Council for Packaging and the Environment show how dramatically the weight of various other kinds of packaging has declined (Table 12.1).[6]

But there are still problems. One of the easiest ways to cut the weight and bulk of paper packaging is to substitute plastic. The EPA reckons that corrugated cardboard boxes account for 12% of the weight of America's municipal rubbish; many of these boxes could be replaced with shrink-wrap film and a plastic base. Several companies are doing just that. Nordyne, a subsidiary of Nortek, an American energy company, transports mobile home air-conditioner and furnace units that are shrink-wrapped with plastic onto pallets, with corners, tops, and bottoms protected by corrugated cardboard. The glass jars Gerber uses for its baby food are distributed in shrink-wrapping on a corrugated base, without cardboard partitions between the bottles. A German study calculated that switching from plastic to other materials would quadruple the weight of packaging and double the use

Table 12.1 How Packaging Gets Lighter (oz)

	pre-1939	1950	1960	1970	1980	1983	1985	1990
Baked beans can	...	...	...	2.4	2.1	...	...	2.0
Glass milk bottle	18.9	14.0	12.0	...	...	...	...	8.6
Beer can	...	3.2	...	...	...	...	0.7	0.6
1.5 liter PET bottle	...	...	...	...	...	2.3[a]	...	1.5[b]

[a]Including base cup.
[b]No base cup.
Source: INCPEN, "Packaging and Resources," 1989.

of energy during production. As is so often the case with environmental questions, there is no single virtuous answer (apart, deep greens would claim, from simply not consuming): a choice has to be made between two second-bests.

A few manufacturers have found that they can do away with some kinds of packaging entirely. Hertie, a German department store, no longer requires each imported shirt to be packed separately in a plastic bag. In the first five months of 1990, that saved 2.7 million plastic bags. In 1985, Migros began selling toothpaste tubes without an outer plastic box. The company's marketing executives were aghast. Unboxed toothpaste tubes would look awful on the shelves. They were right: toothpaste sales dived in the first six months after the change was made. Gradually, in-store signs educated customers, and Migros went on to remove excess packaging from everything from yoghurt to drinks.

Reducing the toxicity of municipal waste may prove even harder than slowing its growth. People toss old bottles of garden pesticide or paint solvents into garbage cans without thinking of the consequences. Manufacturers will be asked to find answers. Some are already doing so. Polaroid has developed mercury-free batteries for film cassettes; Safer (gardening products) markets pesticides based on naturally occurring fatty acids rather than petrochemicals, which it claims are far less toxic; Procter & Gamble has eliminated metal-based inks for printing on packaging.

Recycling

As the previous chapter explained, governments increasingly want companies to make the arithmetic of recycling add up. The pattern has been repeated in several parts of North America: suggest that a ban may be put on a product, such as disposable diapers or soft-drink bottles, unless the industry that makes them "voluntarily" sets up a recycling scheme. This sort of green blackmail has persuaded packaging industries to pay for, or even organize, recycling schemes. It has been used to try to create markets for recycled products. Its effect has been most dramatic on the plastics industry. Hostility to plastics in legislatures in many countries has led to frantic efforts by manufacturers to find ways of saving their materials from the trash can.

Because they realize that the future acceptability of their product may depend on whether it can be recycled, plastics manufacturers are making heroic efforts to find ways of recycling their materials. Manufacturers have rarely become involved in the recycling of less problematic materials. One exception is a joint venture announced in January 1990 between Waste Management and Jefferson Smurfit, one of America's biggest manufacturers of paper and packaging products, to process and market recycled paper fiber. Such deals are likely to be more common in the plastics industry, where manufacturers have a direct interest in showing that their product can be recycled. In April 1989, Waste Management had already set up a similar arrangement with Du Pont, America's largest plastics manufacturer, to collect, separate, and process recovered plastics. Du Pont has also been working to develop markets for recycled plastics. It has, for instance, persuaded the state of Illinois to test a variety of road-building products made from recycled plastics.

Other plastics manufacturers are also moving rapidly into recycling. Dow Chemical was one of the first. With seven other plastics manufacturers it formed the National Polystyrene Recycling Company to recycle polystyrene into nonfood packaging. Part of the company's raw materials come from 450 McDonald's restaurants, which have installed separate bins to encourage customers to recycle their food containers. The aim is to recycle a quarter of all disposable polystyrene products by 1995, a proportion that would exceed current recycling rates for glass and paper. Reynolds Metal, which already recycles as well as manufactures aluminum, aims to recycle at least as much plastics as it produces. Union Carbide, another plastics manufacturer, is building a plant to recycle plastics retrieved from the states of New Jersey, New York, and Connecticut.

In congressional hearings on pollution prevention in April 1990, Ronald van Mynen, the vice president in charge of environmental affairs at Union Carbide, gave a neat example of how to turn the tables on the public sector by complaining that Connecticut had not made it mandatory for consumers to recycle plastic waste. "Union Carbide wants to make plastics recycling work," he told the Senate subcommittee on environmental protection. "And we want Connecticut's plastic waste. We have the experience, the technology, and the markets—but we need a steady supply of plastic waste. That's where elected officials and other opinion leaders must exert their influence to educate and stimulate the public to participate."

Other creators of plastic waste are trying different approaches, for instance trying to create a market for the recycled waste. Several schemes for recycling have foundered when voters discovered that their recycled bottles and newspapers were being buried or burned rather than reused. Another strategy is designing the initial product to make it more suitable for recycling at the end of its life. Plastics are a special problem: New York, Iowa, and Massachusetts all admit that less than half of all plastic containers collected are recycled. Procter & Gamble insists that containers for their liquid soap and bleach are made with a 25% minimum of recycled resins. McDonald's hopes eventually to use recycled burger boxes to make furniture for new restaurants.

Plastics recycling in some European countries has been made simpler than in the United States by the more widespread use of bottles made from PET, a plastic that is relatively easy to recycle. For instance, Colgate-Palmolive is experimenting with bottles made from recycled PET for liquid soap. Coca-Cola has been working with a bottle producer and governments in the Netherlands and Germany to develop a single-resin bottle that will be easier to recycle. McDonald's is considering whether all the plastic it uses should be polystyrene, and Heinz has replaced its multilayered ketchup bottle with one made of PET alone.

An initiative by 25 British firms with an interest in plastic containers is the most dramatic recycling program. In 1990, they set up a joint venture called Recoup, aimed at making it possible to recycle half of Britain's plastic containers by 1995. It will help pay for a number of collection schemes for sorted domestic waste, which will then be sorted as far as possible into pure polymers by a sister company, Reprise, at a separation plant that aims to have the world's first automatic process for separating PET and PVC. If Britain's plastics industry meets its target (extremely tight, considering that in 1990 hardly any plastics were recycled), it will leap far ahead of the recycling rates for other containers such as glass and aluminum. An interesting question is whether that will make a large difference in the acceptability of plastic containers. Will an investment in recycling old bottles turn out to be really an investment in market share for the new ones?

In North America, it has become common for recycling schemes to involve three partners: the consumer, the municipality, and the manufacturers of the products perceived to cause most of the problem. Companies become involved for fear of incurring worse penalties if they do not. Thus it was to save themselves from even heavier obligations that companies in Ontario, Canada, supported a pioneering recycling scheme. In 1986, the provincial government threatened to ban some products, such as disposable diapers and some soft-drink bottles, if industry did not "voluntarily" support recycling. The soft-drink industry and its container and container-material suppliers therefore decided to set up a plan. More arm-twisting subsequently brought in the newspaper industry, grocery manufacturers and distributors, and the plastics and packaging industries.

Governments play many versions of the Ontario approach: threaten a ban or stiff regulations and the costs of not running a recycling scheme suddenly overtake the costs of doing so. The threat of regulation changes the arithmetic. Newspapers offer one example of such legislation. Californian newspaper publishers must make sure that a quarter of the newsprint they use is recycled. That target will rise to half by the end of the century. In some parts of East Coast America, publishers face an even tighter timetable: Suffolk County, on Long Island, passed the toughest recycling law in the United States in June 1990. It would compel newspapers with circulations of 20,000 or more that are printed or sold in the county to be published only on newsprint containing at least 40% recycled fibers by the end of 1996 or face a $500-a-day fine. New York state's newspapers, including the mighty *New York Times,* are angry: 64 of them had already signed a voluntary agreement with the state to increase the amount of recycled paper they used to 40% by the end of the century—a good example of companies asking to be allowed to do voluntarily what they would otherwise be compelled to do.

New Attitudes toward Production

Companies' obligation to dispose of products will encourage them to band together, as plastics manufacturers have done in America and Europe, to form joint ventures for research, recovery, and recycling. New alliances will emerge. For example, several plastics manufacturers, in America and in Germany, have teamed up with waste-management companies to collect and recycle plastics: Du Pont with Waste Management, as mentioned earlier; BASF, Bayer, and Hoechst with a number of smaller German waste collectors.

Companies are starting to take into account the final fate of a product when it is being designed. Plastics manufacturers and their customers are moving away from complex bonded layers of resins, which are lightweight but hard to recycle, and away from composites, designed to do specific jobs efficiently, toward heavier, less efficient, single resins. Some mail-order companies in America now pack their goods in popcorn rather than polystyrene foam beads. Enlightened car manufacturers are trying to use a narrower range of materials, especially plastics. GE is making some of its appliances easier to dismantle. The integration of final fate into initial design is new: How many manufacturers in the 1970s considered whether their wrappings could become filler for ski jackets or bedding for farm animals? As Eberhard von Kuenheim, chairman of BMW, puts it, automotive engineers will have to become concerned "not only with the construction, but with the destruction" of cars. They need to find ways "to reduce the need to extract new raw materials from the earth, and to reduce the amount of material which we must dispose of." Many manufacturers of many different products may eventually find that strategy thrust upon them.

Given the pressure behind recycling, one of the big entrepreneurial opportunities of the 1990s is likely to be the need to find new uses for waste. As in all new markets, there will be a time lag while companies adjust. It will take time to develop new technologies, build new markets, and establish new sources of supply. But by the end of the century corporate activity in some industries, from plant location to the colors on the package, will be influenced in one way or another by the garbage glut. Smart companies can see that all environmental regulations are likely to grow tighter. Governments, realizing that companies would prefer to clean up in their own way, voluntarily, will increasingly hold out legislation as a threat. To wait for the regulations before acting may be more expensive than anticipating them and building them into new investments. "Our job is to do it our way, before we have a sword hanging over our heads," says Richard Mahoney, chief executive of Monsanto. A company that takes environmental responsibility more seriously than its rivals may find it can introduce new technology at its own pace, rather than having to do it quickly and therefore expensively. It may be able to do the market research for a more environmentally friendly product before it becomes compulsory. It may be able to persuade legislators that rules should be tightened to raise environmental standards in ways that it can meet better than its competitors. All this requires imaginative management. That is the theme of the next chapter.

13

Environmental Management

Companies that take the environment seriously change not only their processes and products but also the way they run themselves. Often these changes go hand in hand with improvements in the general quality of management. Badly managed companies are rarely kind to the environment; conversely, companies that try hardest to reduce the damage they do to the environment are usually well managed. Why the link? Perhaps the main reason is that concern for the environment means adding a new layer to management. Companies whose strategy was maximizing profits and ensuring survival now find they have social obligations and need to worry about their impact on the natural world. These ends may conflict with each other. What happens, for instance, when the demands of the environment turn out to be incompatible with the demands of the consumer for price, quality, or convenience?

Even when there is no conflict, the goals demand a tolerance for ambiguity that irritates conventional managers. Ulrich Steger, whose Institute for Environmental Management at the European Business School in Oestrich-Winkel, Germany, is the first of its kind in the world, argues that "environmental management needs state-of-the-art management tools to manage complexity."

Another management guru, Don Simpson of the Banff Centre for Management in Canada, speaks of the need to develop "the skills to deal with multiple stakeholders" and to "think in networks, not hierarchies."

The Search for Total Quality

The directors of those companies that have tried hardest to improve their environmental image speak with an impressive conviction. Ralph Saemann, a director of Ciba-Geigy, sets out his vision of corporate environmental responsibilities in language as emotional as a green politician. He speaks of the need for a new corporate culture to foster environmental conviction from the bottom up, and of the need for "empowerment," a term beloved by green activists but alarming to conventional businesspeople because it implies increasing the influence of lobbyists on corporations. Some directors of American (but not British) companies speak with equal openness and passion.

In American management terms, environmental responsibility has become an aspect of the search for total quality. The concept that defects in the production process cost most to remedy if a product has left the factory gates was born in America, exported to Japan, and reimported into best managerial practice. Recalling faulty cars, for instance, is costly and embarrassing. Less embarrassing, though still inefficient, is to correct the defects before the car is shipped. Best of all is to aim for total quality and zero defects: to prevent mistakes from occurring in the first place.

Close parallels may be drawn between aiming for total quality and cradle-to-grave environmental management. For example, as remedying defects is most expensive once a product has left the factory, so cleaning up after an environmental accident is most expensive and costly in terms of reputation. Less expensive is end-of-pipe technology to remove pollutants at the end of the manufacturing process. Least expensive in the long run, and safest, too, is pollution prevention: cutting down on the toxics used in a plant. An important aspect of the quality of a manufactured product, so some business gurus argue, is the total loss caused by that product to society. Companies should aim to minimize the "societal loss" incurred by each product. One kind of "loss" is the failure to satisfy customer needs; another is the loss suffered by the environment as a result of the production, use, and disposal of a product. Indeed, some managers wonder whether traditional definitions of quality that apply to customer satisfaction should be broadened to incorporate environmental criteria and extend to all who are affected by a product from its cradle to its grave.

Such visionary thoughts help managers to estimate all those costs that are otherwise not captured in the price mechanism. Many of these costs, as previous chapters have argued, are already incurred by companies, in the form of siting problems, potential damage to reputation, and sudden changes in regulations and customer tastes. Such costs are expected to rise, and they need to be incorporated into management strategies. The pursuit of total environmental quality helps to explain why so many of the most earnestly green companies (especially American) search for the Holy Grail of zero emissions, the green equivalent of zero defects. Those companies that do not feel comfortable with the policy of zero defects ("I prefer 'continuous improvement,'" said the chairman of one large British chemical company) do not like the idea of aiming for zero emissions either.

The pursuit of quality may also explain why some companies insist on setting common environmental guidelines for subsidiaries all over the world. As a well-run company would not willingly set lower quality targets for third world plants, so those that take environmental management seriously want common goals for greenery. That strategy is possible only where environmental policy is a centralized responsibility. American multinationals often impose detailed environmental operating disciplines on their subsidiaries, both in the United States and abroad. British companies, which often have more decentralized managerial structures, find such an approach too rigid. That may change. ICI, whose decentralized approach thwarted top management's desire to take the lead in phasing out CFCs, decided in 1990 to ask each of its sites to draw up an environmental improvement program and to report regularly to headquarters on their performance against a set of quantifiable objectives.

An Effective Corporate Policy

In practice, how does management differ in the most environmentally serious companies from the rest? The answer is complicated by the fact that there is no single set of rules that tells managers how to be truly environmental. (This may be the case because it has taken business schools, at least outside Germany, so long to grasp the importance of environmental management as a subject.) Certainly the number of packed conferences on the subject suggests that managers are eager to learn.

The first and essential step is a clear statement of corporate principles and objectives spelled out with the full backing of the board. These then need to be broken down into detailed rules to cover all activities. Compliance with the rules must be regularly monitored and the results presented to a senior executive who has responsibility for environmental performance. The gathering and dissemination of information are central. A key element in this strategy is the environmental audit and its integration into corporate policy.

But would-be-green companies have other characteristics that set them apart from the dirtier kind. One interesting example is Johnson & Johnson, which demonstrates the close links between a company's environmental policy and its attitude to its employees. Johnson & Johnson's policy grew out of its "credo," a statement of corporate goals laid down in the 1940s by General Johnson, a remarkable man who founded the company in the 1930s. He believed that "factories can be beautiful" and that "we ought to pay our employees what they are worth." His credo said that the company's first responsibility was to its customers, its second to its employees. The community came third, and shareholders last of all.

This fine vision became clouded over the years. In 1978 at a series of meetings, its managers around the world said, "The credo is all very well, but all the chairman wants to know about is the profit for the past quarter." In 1982, the company had a traumatic experience when some of its Tylenol was found to have been tampered with and contaminated.

Part of the company's recovery was driven by the development of a new environmental program based on the "credo." It starts with the proposition that, in the words of Jack Mullen, vice president in charge of corporate affairs, "If you are in the health-care business, you can't play games with your employees' health and safety." A program has been set up that involves making sure that all parts of the company are obeying government and corporate environmental rules. It is now building links (some educational, some financial) with local communities and continuing the environmental education of employees. It is also trying to cut packaging and make as much use of recycled and recyclable materials as possible. New products are studied for their impact on the environment from every point of view, including their use of raw materials, manufacturing process, and packaging.

Johnson & Johnson's experience illustrates a number of features common to companies anxious to improve environmental performance. It has built its environmental program on the foundations of a corporate disaster. Near-catastrophe influences boards to accept large budgets for environmental protection programs. It shows, too, how environmentally conscious companies attend to employees' welfare, since these are the people most likely to be hurt by a sloppy environmental policy. Bad employers probably cannot be good environmentalists. Finally, Johnson & Johnson's example demonstrates the crucial importance of securing the wholehearted backing of the board and putting a board-level director in charge of environmental policy. No company can pursue a coherent environmental policy unless everyone sees that the board backs it up to the hilt.

Employee Involvement

A prerequisite for effective corporate environmental policy is the enthusiasm of employees. A company's employees may also be its neighbors. For example, most of the people who work for Geneva Steel in Utah also live near it. They use the ski resort 15 minutes away from the mill's coke ovens. They must be the world's best-educated steelworkers, with an average of one year of college education each. Many of them, like their chairman, Joe Canon, are hard-working Mormons. All told, the workers have a strong sense of environmental responsibility. The company is one of the few steelmakers in the world with a good environmental reputation—and one of the world's most profitable.

Canon is unusual in the steel world in many ways. First, he is in his early forties, like most of his managers, and so 20 years younger than most steel bosses. His managerial style is flexible and informal. Second, he began his career as a regulator at the EPA. So he understands how regulators work—even if he finds them as maddening as other industrialists do. Third, his company is profitable, and he has a controlling stake in it. All these factors may explain why he has been able to bring forward the timing of some large investments—replacing an old and inefficient open-hearth furnace with newer and much less polluting technology—mainly on environmental grounds. "We began more than a year before the state wanted us to," he says, "but we would have had to make the change eventually. The alternative would be to sue and fight. Litigation is expensive."

One consequence of Canon's known enthusiasm for the environment is that employees have found some good answers to environmental problems. The company used to cool its steel in freon, an ozone-depleting substance. One of the laboratory workers waged a war with the purchasing department to persuade them to try using a much more expensive silicon-based alternative. Her trump card was to argue, "Joe Canon wants us to think about the environment." When the department capitulated, it emerged that a barrel of freon evaporated within a month but the silicon-based coolant could be used over and over again. "It turned out to be cheaper, after all, and we're no longer discharging 55 gallons of freon a month," said Canon triumphantly.

Involving employees in environmental policy is not only a way for a company to appear as a caring employer. It may also make it possible to push through policy changes that would otherwise meet with inertia or resistance. Board enthusiasm may be hard to translate into action by middle management, but once workers become environmentally committed, the constituency backing reform in a company will be larger and more powerful. Workers may start to make new environmental demands. Employees at Hercules BV's Rijswijk offices are given a folder each day in which to put paper for recycling. Hercules is a company that takes the environment seriously. As its employees grew more environmentally conscious, they began to press management to do something about phenol emissions, which smelled nasty but were not considered threatening to health. The company managed to eliminate them within a year.

The links between employee care and environmental care will become more important as the number of new workers stops growing. "The two top corporate priorities for the 1990s are the environment and recruitment," points out Tom Burke, director of Britain's Green Alliance, a British environmental lobbying group. "I tell firms that they are linked. Good people don't like working for a company with a bad environmental image."

That point is confirmed in a small survey by KPH Marketing carried out in Britain in the summer of 1990. The respondents were 117 graduates and 27 postgraduates at the University of Surrey, primarily in engineering and science disciplines. When asked what factors they would take into account in choosing future employers, the students put connections with oppressive regimes at the top of the list. Equally important were companies' environmental policies and their record on personnel. More than half the students described their concern about green issues as either "strong" or "very strong." The firms thought to have the worst environmental records included Exxon (34%), British Nuclear Fuels (28%), Shell and Union Carbide (both 12%), and McDonald's (11%). All these companies have been making strenuous efforts to improve their environmental image. Companies that succeed in convincing students and young managers that they are genuinely interested in their impact on the environment will find it easier to recruit. Even in those industries that the bright young regard as grubbiest—chemicals, petrochemicals, heavy industry—companies that work hardest at being green may do better than rivals in the same business.

The Community

Employees may be the people most affected by companies' environmental policies, but its other neighbors follow close behind. Environmental issues have brought a new emphasis to the ways companies handle their links with those who live around their plants as well as with pressure groups.

As ICI's Chris Hampson said: "We've had operations on Teesside for more than 50 years. Once, people were grateful for the wealth we brought. Now, they are pleased with the jobs, but don't want dirt in their rivers. Our own people find they get attacked by their neighbors if we are regarded as polluting." Large amounts of management time are devoted to building links with local people. When, for instance, British Petroleum wanted to build an oil platform in Poole Harbour, a beauty spot in the south of England, the development director of the oil field spent more than a third of his time trying to allay the worries of local people. Giving people a sense that they have some control over what happens to their environment is a way to win friends and planning permissions. The company won over local people by carrying out extensive environmental research, running computer simulations to study tidal flows and sand movements, and drawing up six different options for public debate.

One American waste-management company found sites in six towns, then told each one that they were one of the options. Were they interested? Approached this way, a couple of towns said yes. In France, there is much less public opposition to the sites of new nuclear-power plants than there is in America or in the rest of Europe. In 1978–1980, local people were offered inexpensive electricity. Envious American companies fear that such a tactic, if they tried it, would be called bribery. So it is; but it can also be perceived as a rational bargaining away of some environmental rights for cut-rate fuel.

The bargaining is usually of a more discreet sort. Sensitive companies may invest management time and some cash in being nice to the local community: a donation to the local boys' club here, visitor's day there, a sports center across the road. Most companies do a bit of this sort of thing; but chemical companies tend to try harder. Dow Chemical, for instance, adopts sections of beaches and highways to keep them litter-free and runs special collections of household hazardous waste. Its Michigan division has given $25,000 to the local Audubon Society to study bird populations on the Great Lakes. Companies also produce as much public information as they can. All Dow Chemical's main sites have visitor centers and run plant tours. In the north of England, the visitor center at Sellafield, British Nuclear Fuel's main site, has become the biggest tourist attraction for miles around.

Lobbyists

The groups most courted and most feared by managers are the environmental lobbying organizations like Greenpeace and Friends of the Earth, which can, with a single press release, condemn a product or a company. The more responsible groups realize that this kind of power is both a strength and a weakness. After years of protesting, they find themselves suddenly asked by companies and governments, "All right, then, what do you want us to do?" Enumerating practical environmental priorities is much harder than demonstrating or boycotting products.

Some environmental groups have begun to build links with companies. Raymond van Ermen of the European Environmental Bureau, an umbrella body for Europe's environmental lobby, says that his organization is often approached by business federations and European companies with requests for a dialogue. Environmentalists and businesses are already talking at the national level; the new emphasis is at the EC level. Environmental groups want better access to corporate information, and to product research at an early stage; companies want to get a feel for the way environmental groups will be pushing regulators.

Such rapprochements pose delicate problems for both sides. Environmental groups proliferate: American companies face—by one estimate—18,000 of them. Which to talk to? Pick the wrong one, and jealousy may make the others more hostile. The environmental groups also walk a narrow line. When Loblaw, a Canadian retail chain, introduced a line of 100 environmentally friendlier products early in 1990, many of them were endorsed by Friends of the Earth and Pollution Probe. David Nichol, president of Loblaw, argues that the cooperation of environmental groups was what brought green consumerism to Canada within a matter of months. The executive director of Pollution Probe did television commercials with Loblaw, arguing that nondisposable diapers were the greenest way to wrap up a baby, but that Loblaw's disposables were the next best thing. In the uproar that followed, he was forced to resign.

In America, many environmental groups still suspect anything a company wants to do. Some lobbying groups deliberately target environmental leaders. Jerry Martin, director of environmental affairs at Dow Chemical, claims that his company was told by Greenpeace: "We're picking on you because you're a leader. If we can move you, we can move the whole industry." Subsequently, he says with relief, Greenpeace shifted its attentions to Du Pont.

Other groups—notably the Environmental Defense Fund (EDF), the Natural Resources Defense Council, and the Conservation Law Foundation of New England—have begun to negotiate with companies to help them devise better environmental strategies. As a result, they have helped to work out some path-breaking schemes to improve the environment, often at minimum cost to regulators and to companies. For instance, the Conservation Law Foundation (CLF) helped devise financial incentives for New England Electric, a Massachusetts utility, to invest in energy conservation. "CLF found that it knew how to beat up utilities but not how to make good things happen," says New England Electric's chief executive officer, John Rowe. "We began as adversaries, but then realized we weren't getting anywhere by fighting."

In another instance, in August 1990, the EDF set up a six-month task force with McDonald's to look for ways to reduce the amount of waste the company creates. The agreement specified that EDF should receive no money for its work and be free to use whatever means it liked, including litigation, to pursue solutions it believed in, whatever McDonald's decided; it also precluded McDonald's from using the agreement with EDF in advertising. The deal was promptly attacked by the grandfather of consumer campaigns, Ralph Nader. "Grassroots environmental groups are not convinced that McDonald's is serious about creating a better environment," he announced.

In the future, environmental groups will diversify. Some will concentrate on providing services to their members, in the form of information, recycling, or campaigning; others on building bridges with companies. Indeed, companies may come to see that they have something to offer the campaigners. Shell has drawn up an elaborate range of scenarios for future energy demand, including one picturing a sustainable world, which it intends to share with interested environmental groups. Well-informed campaigning is in everybody's interest.

Customers

The green consumer is essentially a retail market. But some companies claim that their industrial customers are beginning to put a value on greenery. In a survey in the late 1980s of business attitudes toward suppliers, 3M found that nearly 20% of respondents rated "concern for the environment" as the most important quality, followed (17%) by value for money. In some industries the pressure to care about the environment is changing the relationship between companies and their customers. ICI, for instance, now offers to take back contaminated sulphuric acid from its customers in the oil industry and clean it up. Hampson sees this as a chance to strengthen ties with customers: "Customers will increasingly want to deal with suppliers who can solve their environmental problems. Disposing of our customers' waste products is a way for us to link ourselves more closely with them."

Dow Chemical has also turned responsibility into opportunity. It is developing a concept called "product stewardship," designed to ensure that its products are safely distributed, stored, and used by its customers. In 1989, Dow launched an even bolder scheme. Most of the chlorinated solvents the company sells are replacements for ones that have leaked into the air or water. Dow's Chemaware solvent-recovery project is designed to help customers reduce this leakage and to collect and reprocess used solvent, getting rid of the residue in an environmentally acceptable way. The company reckons that the Chemaware program will eventually mean a big drop in its solvent sales. Even so, it went ahead with the project partly because it saw what had happened with CFCs. A failure to prevent leakage has led to a ban and to the development of other products that will do the same jobs at much higher cost and less efficiency.

Some companies have seen a chance to offer customers a new, greener service for CFCs. Toyota has pioneered a scheme to drain and reprocess the CFCs in their car air-conditioning systems for free, rather than let them leak out to damage the ozone layer. ICI and Du Pont both have schemes to recycle CFCs. Du Pont will ship containers anywhere in America to collect CFC-11 and CFC-12 (the two main kinds used in refrigeration and air conditioning) as long as there is a minimum load of 500 pounds. The customer simply has to meet the cost of filling the containers. Neither Du Pont nor its customers make money from recycling— yet; though Du Pont expects to do so as the supply of CFCs dwindles and recycling becomes more profitable. Suppliers realize that they may be able to offer customers a service that will tie them in more closely, and thus they will eventually increase profits even as the volume of sales diminishes.

Environmental concerns are also encouraging companies to build links with one another. Ed Woolard of Du Pont points out that "One alternative to recycling waste ourselves is to form relations with other companies: we won't lose responsibility for the waste, but they will help us handle it." The search for an alternative to ozone-gobbling CFCs has led to new levels of corporate cooperation: product companies have come together to test toxicity and have run joint recycling ventures. Plastics manufacturers have established some research cooperatives to look for better ways to recycle their materials. The problem of disposing of heavy metals in batteries has led Philips, an electronics group, and other companies in the Netherlands involved in battery manufacture and distribution to consider ways to recycle 80% of nickel cadmium batteries.

Such cooperation may also make it easier for small companies to make room for the environment. Big profitable companies with spare room and management capacity understandably find it easier to be environmentally conscious than small ones, although the most ingenious technology for cleaning the environment often comes from small firms. A survey by Baum, a German club for companies that aims to spread environmental ideas, found that many small companies were not even obeying environmental rules, let alone pursuing green policies. One of Baum's aims is to spread environmental awareness by getting bigger firms to persuade their smaller suppliers.

The Power of Information

No management tool is more powerful than information. When boards of directors realize what volumes of waste are being emitted, their attitude toward environmental issues often changes dramatically. The British subsidiary of Rhône-Poulenc decided to build a computerized waste-accounting system to keep track of the waste each plant generates and the costs of disposing of it. The data go back to each plant every month. "The first time I did this," the manager in charge of the system told the newsletter ENDS, "there was quite a sensation. I was besieged by calls saying, 'Are you absolutely sure?' It was a revelation. They were jolted from blissful ignorance about their true product costs."

In America, nothing has galvanized senior management as much as Title III of the 1986 Superfund Amendments and Reauthorization Act (SARA). Title III insists that companies report all the pollutants they emit. This goes further than the draft directive on environmental information agreed upon in 1990 by the EC council of ministers, which will affect new plants but leave existing ones largely unaffected. Complying with SARA Title III was an eye-opener for many chief executives. "It is painfully clear," says Fran Irwin of the Conservation Foundation, "that companies had no idea what they were releasing—no idea."

"Unless you measure something, you don't really control it," says ICI's Hampson. The environment directors of some European companies wish that their firms were obliged to collect and publish as much data as their American rivals. Quite apart from opening eyes, the data are formidable management aids. They set out sensitive figures in a form that directors can translate into corporate policy. They make it possible for chief executives to set goals for subsidiaries: get your reported emissions down to such-and-such a level or lose some of your bonus.

Union Carbide, for example, sets managers targets for health, safety, and environment. Failure to meet them can mean loss of pay. "One guy failed twice and is no longer with us," says Cornelius Smith, the vice president in charge of the environment. "Another is rumored to have lost 80% of his bonus when he got a fail. But the measurement is a litmus test of good management. Good environmental programs usually point to the presence of a good manager." ICI has also decided to make environmental performance a factor in management rewards.

Companies are developing new ways to build environmental considerations into accounting procedures. At 3M, Robert Bringer, vice president in charge of environmental engineering, has been looking at setting prices for raw materials, such as hydrocarbon solvents that cause particular pollution problems, to reflect more closely their environmental costs. And General Motors, as part of a broad review of the way internal pricing affects incentives, has been considering charging prices that reflect the high costs of disposing of pollutants. In the paint shop, for instance, such a system might encourage engineers to look more closely at the way paint guns are purged. As companies do more work on activity-based costing in order to set better price signals, environmental costs are likely to fall closer to the point at which they are incurred. "That way," points out Bringer, "at least the company gets to keep the money."

Environmental Audits

For most green companies an environmental audit is essential. This process was first developed in the United States in the early 1970s as a way for a company to check on compliance with environmental legislation. Specialist environmental auditors check compliance and examine sites or plants that are being bought or sold to ensure that they carry no surprise Superfund liabilities. After the Bhopal disaster, companies were anxious to ensure that their overseas subsidiaries met the same standards as their parent company. American multinationals started to audit abroad. That has brought the practice to Europe, where it has acquired a different role. Because environmental liabilities are less severe in Europe, companies see auditing as a way of discovering how they could improve their environmental record, and demonstrating to the outside world that they take their responsibilities seriously. They may also want to look at broader environmental issues, particularly at where their raw materials come from. In America, too, environmental auditing is increasingly seen as a way to make sure that a company is protecting itself against criticism, rather than merely as a defense against legal liabilities.

First into the field were chemical and petrochemical companies. Arthur D. Little developed environmental, health, and safety auditing for Allied-Signal, an American chemical giant, after a series of pollution incidents involving a pesticide called Kepone. In the early 1980s, chemical and petrochemical companies accounted for four-fifths of Arthur D. Little's worldwide clientele. The range of companies calling in environmental auditors widened in the late 1980s, although most are still in manufacturing. Ron McLean of Arthur D. Little says that in 1988 all his clients were subsidiaries of American firms. By 1990, homegrown European firms accounted for a third to a half of his business. One British consultant, SustainAbility, found that 30 to 40 companies had asked for help within a month of starting to undertake audits (with PA Consulting Group, a management consultancy).

An example of the way audits work in practice is provided by Union Carbide. A bureaucratic, stuffily managed company, Union Carbide was scarred by the Bhopal disaster and then frightened by a takeover bid. Part of a dramatic improvement in management has been a strong emphasis on environmental policy, which has been a corporate requirement since 1987. Responsibility for day-to-day environmental management is in the hands of individual plant managers, who may spend more than half their time working on health, safety, and the environment. The objectives they pursue are monitored and enforced through a system of audits, presided over by Cornelius Smith, who in turn reports directly to the company chairman.

Union Carbide's auditing teams look not only at subsidiaries but also at some facilities used by the company, such as overseas terminals. Sometimes the company pools auditing of hazardous waste sites or terminals with other chemical companies. This is another example of the joint enterprise that environmental policy encourages. A tough follow-up procedure ensures that the auditors' recommendations are systematically put into effect.

The auditors may be retired senior members of staff. Companies that have done this auditing prefer to use either their own staff or a mixture of employees and outside consultants. Allied-Signal puts its high-flyers to work with hired consultants, seeing auditing as a wonderful way to get to know how the whole company operates. BP creates teams of people drawn from different parts of the firm in different countries. Besides reviewing compliance and environmental management, BP conducts "issue audits." In 1989, it examined its activities in tropical rain forests; in 1990, its impact on wetlands.

The number of consultants eager to offer audits has increased. In 1988, Environmental Data Services drew up a directory of environmental consultants operating in Britain. There were 125. In 1990, the number had almost doubled. Accountants see this as a splendid new opportunity. Every European conference on environmental auditing is now either promoted or attended by a bevy of men in pin-striped suits eagerly discussing sustainable development and waste minimization.

The trouble with the loose use of the term "audit," argues Nigel Haigh, director of the London office of the Institute for European Environmental Policy, is that it "gives the whole process an imprimatur of respectability by drawing a false analogy with financial audits." People have widely different expectations of the process. The International Chamber of Commerce argued in a position paper published in 1989 that the purpose of environmental audits "is to provide an indication to company management of how well environmental organisation, systems and equipment are performing."[1] Conventional auditors tend to see it as a tool for testing how well a management system works, to make sure that national and corporate regulations are being properly applied and to check on exposure to environmental risks. Some companies see it in terms of laboratories, technologists in white coats, and emission figures—as a way, in other words, to monitor the reduction in sources of pollutants. Some audits do both. For instance, at Royal Dutch/Shell, an oil and petrochemical group, the auditing looks at environmental management systems and performance as well as at various environmental indicators, such as the quantity of wastes produced, the number of spills reported, and deviations from effluent or emissions limits.

In the future, audits may look more closely at the life cycle of products. Retailers, anxious to buy environmentally, will want information from suppliers about the environmental impact of the raw materials and manufacturing processes used to make the products on their shelves. Similar information will be needed for eco-labeling plans. Investors in green equities will start to demand environmental information at annual meetings and in company reports.

Environmental lobbyists are interested in environmental audits. They see them as political, rather than management tools. The proponents of the Valdez principles want signatories to carry out an audit and then to publish the results. Britain's Labour Party is wondering whether to make audits compulsory for companies. The European Commission is working on a proposal to encourage them, due for publication by the end of 1991. The commission is thinking of limiting the obligation to large firms and suggesting a three-year reporting cycle.

The question of who should be allowed to conduct an audit is also important. Growth of environmental auditing on both sides of the Atlantic has meant that firms with no expertise have come into the business. Established firms, anxious to preserve their reputations (and profits), are thinking about drawing up a common methodology, agreed-upon standards, and even lists of accredited practitioners. But auditors at Arthur D. Little think it may be easier to standardize the methodology of audits than to draw up an agreed-upon checklist of environmental standards.

Accountants have begun to think about external environmental auditing. In Britain, the Chartered Association of Certified Accountants sponsored a report on the greening of accountancy by Rob Gray of the University of East Anglia.[2] He suggested two possibilities. One cautious version proposed disclosure in the annual report of a firm's environmental policy; its spending on environmental protection; future spending, including contingent liabilities; compliance with legal standards; and statistics for discharges, emissions, and waste. A more radical alternative, beginning with the concept of sustainable development, would try to build on the distinction between man-made and natural capital. Environmental accountancy might recategorize business assets, so that annual accounts would reflect diminutions in natural capital as well as depreciation of the more conventional sort. The association has asked Gray to develop criteria that could form the basis of new environmental accounting standards, which might eventually be prepared by the Accounting Standards Committee.

Perhaps a report from the environmental auditors will become as much a part of a company's annual report by the end of the century as the report from its financial auditors. A few bold companies have already begun to publish external accounts of their environmental achievements. In 1989, the Caird Group, a British waste-disposal company, distributed to its shareholders a summary of an independent environmental audit of all its waste management operations. Even more dramatic was the publication in 1990 of two reports by Norway's Norsk Hydro, a large chemical and fertilizer manufacturer, one for Norwegian readers and the other for an international audience. The more detailed Norwegian report (according to Environmental Data Services) sets out the numbers of emissions and discharges against authorized limits; describes environmental impact assessments carried out by the company and by official bodies on corporate activities; and discloses some potential liabilities, such as serious mercury contamination in the soil beneath one plant. The company has subsequently asked each of its plants to prepare inventories of overall waste generation. These will provide a baseline for subsequent improvements. Quarterly reports of plant emissions and of spills or incidents are also being centrally collected. In this way, the collection of information for publication is likely to serve as an impetus to better environmental management.

An even more dramatic innovation was the 1990 annual report of BSO, a Dutch information technology company. It attached financial numbers to the environmental damage done by its operations: emissions from its energy consumption, pollution from cars and airline flights, dirt from water treatment, incineration, and power generation on the company's behalf. The money values represented the marginal cost of reducing emissions to the point where they would equal the marginal benefits of doing so. Different pollutants required different rules: the cost of treating wastewater, for instance, was taken to be that of turning it back into drinking water.

All told, BSO reckoned that it did environmental damage worth 2.2 million guilders ($1.2 million) in 1990. From this, it subtracted "environmental expenditures" such as fuel levies and water and refuse charges. It virtuously deducted the remaining 2m guilders of "value lost" from conventional value-added, to produce a figure of 253.6 million guilders of net value-added.

Not many companies are likely to see the compulsory publication of reports such as Norsk Hydro's or BSO's as an opportunity. Indeed, insisting on the publication of audits, or even on their conduct, will undoubtedly alter their effect. Auditors and audited both claim that audits are far more useful when senior management backs them than when they are considered merely an obligation. What matters, after all, is not whether an environmental audit is carried out, but what action is taken to follow up on its findings. Further, just as no company would append to its annual report the full details of its auditors' review of its financial position, so none would willingly publish a full review of its environmental activities. The EPA, pressed by the environmental lobby to insist on the publication of environmental audits, takes the view that published ones would be less frank than those conducted for internal consumption.

In time, companies may come to do one audit for public consumption and another, or several more, as aids to internal management. Rather than press for compulsory auditing, politicians and lobbyists would do better to press for more disclosure of information on the materials companies use and the wastes they create. No single policy is likely to have so large an effect on corporate attitudes to the environment, at so little expense, as the enforced disclosure of such information. It is the best and least expensive way of bringing to the attention of each company, at the most senior level, the impact its operations are having on the planet. While it may lack the glamor of green taxation or new environmental standards, the power of public information, in a readily comparable form, should never be underestimated as a way of influencing corporate behavior.

14

Industry and the Global Environment

A s environmental standards grow tighter, companies will become increasingly concerned about the impact of these standards on international competitiveness. They will fret that tough rules in their own country will give them a disadvantage in international trade; and they will grumble that other countries are using their environmental standards to handicap foreign competitors. These worries will increase as global, rather than national, environmental issues come to the fore: trade may become the mechanism by which some countries seek to persuade others to adopt common environmental policies. The complex links between environmental policy and international trade are the theme of this final chapter.

Since companies are not altruists, most will be only as green as governments compel them to be. They will do what is required of them and what they perceive to be in their self-interest. That is as it should be. It is not the job of companies to decide what values ought to be attached to natural resources and what the priorities of environmental policy ought to be, any more than it is their job to decide what share of national income should go into education or what the speed limit should be. The setting of environmental priorities and their translation into price signals and regulation is government's role.

But government can do its job more effectively, and clever companies can profit, if both understand their mutual interest in environmental regulation. The rules government sets—whether through market-based or command-and-control instruments— are essentially a form of domestic protectionism. They work like customs barriers. They keep out of the economy those companies that cannot meet them. Dirty power stations are penalized, just as customs barriers penalize third-world textile manufacturers. They raise prices in much the same way as customs barriers do: electricity becomes more expensive if power stations have to invest in scrubbers, just as shirts are more expensive because Bangladeshi imports are kept out.

Here, though, the similarities end. The companies that lobby most vigorously for protection from cheap foreign imports are the weakest: those that cannot cope with competition at the bottom end of the market. The weakest companies will be those lobbying hardest against environmental intervention. They will be the ones to shout loudest that tough environmental rules will make it impossible for them to compete with companies from dirty countries abroad.

Market leaders will see things rather differently. The challenge is to get government to set standards at a level that they can meet but their competitors cannot. They will see foreign competition differently, too. Realizing that worldwide environmental standards will tighten over the years, they will see the advantage of an assured home market, protected by tough standards, in which to develop path-breaking environmental technologies. These will then have eager markets abroad, as other countries raise their own standards.

Governments in countries with a tradition of state corporatism understand this function of regulation. In Japan and Germany, the concept of technology-forcing regulation is familiar. In countries such as Britain and America, where government has become wary of intervening to tell industry how to do its job, the concept seems more novel. Only gradually are governments coming to realize how industry's environmental leaders can reduce the costs of raising standards. If one company has developed a cleaner technology, then it costs a country less to raise standards to the level that technology can deliver. From the company's point of view, the past costs of investing in developing the technology have to be offset against future benefits from selling it. From the government's point of view, though, the balance of costs and benefits looks better: the costs of a standard that can be met with an existing technology are far lower than the costs of one for which no appropriate technology has yet been developed.

Take one example. In smoggy southern California, regulators have set tough emission standards that new cars will have to meet by the end of the century. At first, it appeared that meeting the standards might call for new fuels, such as ethanol and methanol, which in turn could be used only in cars with redesigned engines. That threat drove the oil companies to devise new formulas for gasoline which, they argue, will achieve emission levels as good as alternative fuels in the engines of existing cars. The snag: the best brands of reformulated gasoline cost some 15 to 20 cents a gallon more than the unreformulated sort. The company that first developed the gasoline, Arco, was arguing in the summer of 1991 that regulators should mandate it. That way, the regulators would get cleaner air at a lower cost to society—and the makers of reformulated gasoline would have an assured market.

The potential green alliance between companies and governments is a delicate one. Protectionism is always a dangerous path, and environmental protectionism is no exception. The most environmentally conscious companies will want government intervention designed to give as much support as possible to their particular answers to environmental problems. Government's interest is in raising standards but leaving the terrain open for many different technological solutions to blossom. Large companies with lots of political clout may see the alternative to, say, CFCs as another chemical; or the alternative to cars running on leaded gas as cars running on lead-free gas. They may collude with governments to set standards that benefit their particular brand of environmental progress.

However, small companies less wedded to particular technologies may come up with quite different solutions through lateral thinking, rather than building on their existing product base. They may find answers in mechanical processes rather than chemical ones or in biotechnology rather than engineering. It is important to foster this inventiveness, rather than suppress it.

The idea of building an industry around government regulation is an uncomfortable one for companies to stomach. Business schools rarely think that environmental policy is an important component of what managers are taught. The preferred areas of study are innovation in finance, marketing, and management, rather than the less visionary concept of how to make the most of government regulations. Generations of managers have therefore been trained to think of government regulation, if at all, as an incidental inconvenience rather than a central fact of corporate life that might be turned to an advantage. "There's no single required course on business regulation in the United States," asserts Paul Portney of Resources for the Future. "I'd bet my mortgage on it." Most managers therefore think of environmental regulation as something to fight. A characteristic of American small companies that have spotted environmental niches is how often they turn out to be run by former regulators, often "graduates" of the Environmental Protection Agency. They understand how to turn environmental rules to their corporate advantage, rather than struggling against them.

Environmental Influences on Competitiveness

National environmental policies affect international trade in two distinct ways. First, governments that set high environmental standards (or impose steep environmental taxes) on processes will drive up the costs for companies, which may then threaten to decamp to other countries with lower standards. Second, one government may set environmental product standards that its own industries may be best placed to meet. That will help to keep out rival products.

As governments impose tougher standards on their own industries, they will increasingly be lobbied noisily by companies pointing out that they are in danger of losing foreign markets to dirtier companies. Environmental legislators will retort that strict environmental policies are good for industry and bring the promise of larger markets abroad. Can both perceptions be right?

They can, but not equally. Consider two points. First, such debates tend to blur the line between the products companies make and the processes they use to make them. Companies that take the lead in making green products will find plenty of eager customers abroad. But when governments force companies to employ greener processes, they will drive up the costs. Companies may also, serendipitously, find that the technologies they develop to bring down the costs of complying with high environmental standards for processes have a lively overseas market. But that will not always be the case, if only because green processes are often specific to a particular industry or even to a particular plant.

Japan and Germany, two countries whose industries have long been required by government to invest in green technology, illustrate the way tough environmental rules can pay off. They are both big and growing exporters of pollution-control equipment. Japan allocated a staggering average of 14% of industrial investment to pollution control in the 1970s. As a result, it found itself technologically well ahead of other countries, selling plant for scrubbing flue gases to European countries. Germany, during that decade, devoted only 5% of investment to environmental spending. Since then, its air-quality standards have risen. German manufacturers have developed desulphurization equipment, which they now sell to Japan. By contrast, Britain's first flue-gas desulphurization plant on a coal-fired boiler is not due to be commissioned until 1993. Britain's ratio of exports to imports in environmental technology declined from 8:1 to 1:1 in the 1980s.

In the United States, which introduced little environmental legislation between the mid-1970s and the Clean Air Act of 1990, 70% of the air-pollution equipment sold is produced by foreign companies.[1] As regulators insist on best available technology, even if made abroad, one country's advance will bring rapid growth in world demand for pollution-control equipment. OECD studies of the impact of environmental regulations on economic activity show that regulations may sometimes force old plants to close faster than they might otherwise have.[2] But they also create new industries, new jobs, and new markets. Investment in pollution-control may go hand in hand with modernization, and may spur innovation in industries where the pace of change has previously been slow. Spotting the benefit in individual industries is easier than seeing the overall picture: the costs of regulation are easy to identify, the benefits more indirect and diffuse. For most companies the costs of environmental regulation of their processes are tiny compared with other considerations such as labor costs and proximity to markets. Although more is spent on pollution-control in America, Japan, and a few European countries than anywhere else, these costs are usually small relative to total capital investment and operating costs. In no country are pollution-control expenditures by government and industry together more than 3% of gross national product; in most industrial countries, the average falls below 2%.

While some industries will gain world market share because of tough environmental regulations, others will lose. In industries where the costs of environmental regulation are higher, some companies undoubtedly shut down or move to less regulated markets. That generally means moving to a third world or developing country, rather than to another industrial one. The richest countries are those that have the toughest pollution controls; and the most successful industrializing countries are becoming fiercer about pollution, especially toward foreign firms.

A bigger threat than a loss of investment is that of competition from producers based in countries with weaker regulations. Such competition may be strongest with semiprocessed products such as steel or chemicals, where the corporate customer cares more about the quality and cost of the product than the circumstances in which it was produced. It is notable, for instance, that hardly any nonferrous smelters were built in industrialized countries in the 1980s. When developed countries import finished goods, they often find it hard to keep out products that incorporate banned materials such as PCBs (polychlorinated biphenyls). But such goods are likely to sell best at the bottom end of the market. At the top of every market, customers will continue to pay a premium for products whose suppliers can offer some sort of pledge that they do as little environmental harm as possible.

Comparing environmental standards is difficult. What matters is how standards are enforced, and this may be hard to measure. Raymond Kopp and two colleagues from Resources for the Future found that policies on air and water varied little among OECD countries, and were converging.[3] Differences were greater for hazardous waste mainly because no European country had legislation as rigorous as America's Superfund. European countries also tend to define hazardous waste more narrowly: Britain lists 31 substances and France, 100, compared with some 500 on the list published by the EPA. Because environmental policy in Europe will increasingly be dictated by the EC, and because policymakers on each side of the Atlantic tend to emulate one another's successes, the convergence is likely to continue.

Much greater differences exist between the old industrialized countries and the new. The most thorough examination of how these differences affect competitiveness was carried out by Jeffrey Leonard in *Pollution and the Struggle for the World Product*.[4] Leonard scrutinized the overseas investment patterns of American companies and concluded that only a small number of American industries had been driven abroad by environmental regulations. They fell into three categories. There were manufacturers of some highly toxic products that had not yet developed safer substitutes or changed their technologies to meet American standards for health and safety at work. These included makers of asbestos, benzidine-based dyes, and some pesticides for whom regulations had disrupted or halted production in the United States. Then there were basic mineral-processing industries such as copper, lead, and zinc whose relocation abroad had been encouraged by requirements in some countries that minerals mined in a country be processed there too. A third group consisted of chemical companies, which, said Leonard, had gone abroad to produce or purchase "intermediate" organic chemicals to process in the United States.

Leonard found some signs in the investment and trade figures that there were moves abroad in two sectors—chemicals and minerals-processing—where pollution abatement spending as a proportion of all new plant and capital spending was between one-and-a-half times and double that for the manufacturing industry as a whole. But he argues that the industries most likely to flee to escape pollution controls are those with dying markets. They are the ones with the least incentive to install expensive pollution-controls or to develop substitutes. Healthy, growing industries—even the makers of polyvinyl chloride and acrylonitrile, feared by environmentalists but in solid demand in the mid-1980s—stayed put. They adjusted to environmental controls instead of escaping them.

The industries fleeing environmental regulation went to a handful of places. Apart from Japan and the rich countries of Europe, the bulk of all overseas direct investment by the chemicals and metal-processing industries went to Ireland and Spain in Europe and to Mexico and Brazil in the third world (see Table 14.1). Such Faustian bargains were explained by an old Irish politician who said, "All my life I've seen the lads leaving Ireland for the big smoke in London, Pittsburgh, Birmingham, and Chicago. It's better for Ireland if they stayed here and we imported the smoke." In the 1970s, Ireland regarded its looser pollution rules as a potential attraction for American companies; Spain made a special pitch for chemical and metal-processing firms; Mexico attracted footloose small companies across its border, like pesticide manufacturers and companies using asbestos for textiles and building supplies.

Often, tighter regulation in developed countries is followed by a brief period before substitutes appear; such emigrant companies take advantage of these windows. Eastern Europe's sloppy prerevolutionary environment rules seem to have helped it to sell cheap chemicals to America. As American regulations have cut off the market by banning the chemicals as well as tightening standards on chemical manufacturers, new markets have opened in the third world. More recently, according to Leonard, industrializing countries have begun to bargain more fiercely with incoming multinational firms. People in developing countries are more likely to complain if they think a foreign company is polluting than a local one. In 1989, for instance, ICI was forced to close a plant in southern Taiwan making methyl methacrylate after local fishermen complained that a subcontractor was dumping waste acid near the coast. Occasionally, a company may make an investment and then be forced by local environmental opposition to shut a plant, as Raybestos Manhattan was forced in 1980 to shut a plant making asbestos brake pads in Ireland's County

Cork. More often, though, tough regulations are weakly enforced, or are enforced on multinationals but not on local companies or subcontractors, who may therefore "launder" multinational muck.

Environmental Challenges to Free Trade

As industry worries more about the impact of various environmental standards on competitiveness, international organizations will worry about their impact on trade. Two of the main

Table 14.1 Direct Investments by American Chemical and Mineral-Processing Industries in Rapidly Industrializing Countries, 1980 and 1984 ($m)

	Chemicals		Mineral processing	
	1980	**1984**	**1980**	**1984**
TOTAL by American companies outside Canada, Japan & industrialized Europe[a]	6,633	6,533	2,160	1,757
TOTAL in under-industrialized Europe[b]	1,362	651	115	118
TOTAL in Ireland and Spain	1,250	621	98	113
% total under-industrialized Europe in Ireland and Spain	91.8	95.4	85.2	95.8
TOTAL in less-developed countries	4,462	4.275	1,652	1,390
TOTAL in Brazil, Mexico	2,094	2,021	952	1,095
Brazil & Mexico as % of total in less-developed countries	46.9	47.3	57.6	78.8

[a]Excludes Ireland, Spain, Portugal, Greece, Turkey.
[b]Includes Ireland, Spain, Portugal, Greece, Turkey.
Source: H. Jeffrey Leonard, *Pollution and the Struggle for the World Product* (Cambridge: Cambridge University Press, 1988).

international economic agencies, the OECD and the GATT, are studying the effect of environmental policies on trade.

To GATT, which sets the rules by which countries are supposed to play in world trade, the position is clear. Governments may impose national product standards—as long as they do not discriminate in favor of their own manufacturers. In the late 1980s, a GATT panel ruled that an American tax on certain chemicals, imposed to pay for cleaning up toxic waste dumps, was legitimate because it was levied at the same rate on domestic and foreign producers. A second American tax, on petroleum products, was imposed at a higher rate on foreign producers; the panel ruled against it.

With production processes, GATT believes in allowing each country to choose its own rules. But no country may then use trade weapons to force its competitors to apply the same standards as it chooses to. If one country allows the employment of child labor, another may not impose penalties on its products to compensate for any competitive advantage it may thus gain. The same rules apply to environmental standards. If one country chooses to stop its chemical companies from polluting the rivers, it may not penalize chemical imports from other countries that choose differently. Sometimes environmental economists see merit in that last point, arguing that different standards may be appropriate for some pollutants in different places. Smoke controls are essential in crowded cities, less so in open country.

Diverging Product Standards

The issue of different product standards has caused special problems within the EC. While GATT is interested in free trade, the EC is interested in trying to create a single market throughout its 12 members. National product standards notoriously obstruct free trade. The European Court of Justice made a landmark decision in 1979 to prevent West Germany from banning French crème de cassis (a black-currant liqueur) on the grounds that its alcohol content did not meet German regulations. A standard accepted in one EC country, the judgment implied, should generally be accepted in another. But environmental product standards are different. That was the implication of a decision in the court on a case, mentioned in Chapter 11, involving a law introduced in Denmark in 1981 which required that beer and soft drinks be sold only in returnable bottles, with a compulsory deposit. Brewers from other countries grumbled that the costs of recycling bottles might not be a burden on Carlsberg, Denmark's main brewer, and its many small local rivals, but wiped out the profit to be made by importers in Denmark's small market. In 1986, the EC Commission took the case to court, arguing that the Danes were imposing a disproportionate level of environmental protection.

In September 1988, however, the court backed Denmark. Its judgment, that in some circumstances environmental considerations should take precedence over free trade, has had important consequences. It encouraged the Dutch to propose financial incentives for motorists who bought cars that would meet the EC's deadline for exhaust emissions ahead of the deadline, which had been set only after prolonged wrangling among EC countries. The Dutch decision blew a hole in an elaborate compromise. In part because it was clear that the European Court might uphold the Dutch decision, and in part because elections to the European Parliament were looming, EC ministers hastily agreed to a tighter timetable and to tougher exhaust standards. The court decision also led the Germans to introduce a package-recycling scheme and a ceiling of 28% on the proportion of one-trip drinks bottles that can be sold. Under the recycling scheme, German retailers are increasingly likely to stock only products certified as recyclable or biodegradable by a German company, set up by German manufacturers for the purpose. And the low quota of nonrefillable containers on which the law insists will protect not just the environment but also Germany's many small brewers, which will find it easier to comply than will large international companies like Continental Can.

Germany is more adept than most countries at the use of environmental standards for dual-purpose protection. When, in the late 1980s, Germany set limits on residues of chlorinated organics in papers, its own producers could generally meet the standards but Canadians could not. In fact, Canadians expected similar limits in their domestic market and quickly switched to low-chlorine techniques. The big German car manufacturers are now installing plants to recycle cars; when they have finished, foreign car manufacturers should not be surprised if Germany makes car recycling compulsory.

Come what may, multinational companies will increasingly find themselves facing different environmental product standards in different countries. The best way to reduce the impact of such standards on trade is to make them international rather than national. Companies will therefore lobby governments to harmonize on standards that they can meet. As a result, the environmental standards set in the largest markets will tend to spread to smaller ones. California's standards on car emissions have, after a lapse of time, become America's; Germany's packaging laws threaten to become Europe's. The EC negotiations on controls on car emissions were long stalled by an argument between, on the one hand, those countries whose car industries specialized in big cars and were already fitting catalytic converters to the cars they sold to America, and, on the other hand, those that tended to sell smaller cars, on which catalytic converters were less economical. The emission standards that the greener EC countries wanted Brussels to set (including, predictably, Germany) could be achieved only by fitting three-way catalytic converters and sophisticated fuel-injection equipment. They would discourage the development of the fuel-efficient, lean-burn engine with an oxidation catalyst, which Britain hoped would be a better, less expensive answer. The main drawback to the lean-burn engine was that it was still on the drawing board. In any event, it was not the attitude of Europe's car manufacturers that broke down opposition to standards requiring three-way converters. But since that decision, the British government has been lobbied hard by Johnson Matthey, a British company, which is the world's largest manufacturer of autocatalysts, to bring in tax incentives to encourage motorists to switch early to catalytic converters. The EC debate showed that in order to win industrial backing for tougher standards, it may be necessary to back one technology against another: existing technologies are a less expensive basis for environmental reform than those that are still bright ideas.

Chlorofluorocarbons present an even more striking example of congruent interests in green standards. In September 1987, the countries that signed the Montreal Protocol agreed to cut CFCs by half by the end of the century. That was a brave move, since commercial alternatives to CFCs had not yet been developed. A year later Du Pont, the world's main manufacturer of CFCs, announced it would go much further and stop making CFCs by the end of the century. The industry's support for the protocol was crucial to its success. Mexico, the first country to sign it, is one of three third world countries in which Du Pont makes CFCs; Brazil, the most populous signatory, is another. When, early in 1990, the American government refused to commit new capital to help third world countries switch to alternatives to CFCs, it was the producers and users of CFCs in America who protested loudly enough to get the decision reversed.

Why did industry take this line? One possible motivation for Du Pont's initial decision to abandon CFCs was referred to earlier: the company may have feared being sued by people who contracted skin cancer and blamed it on the damaged ozone layer. But Du Pont, and other big producers and users of CFCs, are investing immense sums in developing substitutes. *Managing the Environment* quotes a manager from ICI, one of the first companies to develop such substitutes, as saying, "The risks involved in this investment are horrendous. We are going out with a product which is less efficient than the one we are replacing, costs five times as much, and the only reason is because of the environmental imperative. We've never been in a market quite like it before."[5]

Profits from increasingly scarce CFCs will accrue to the manufacturers; so will profits on the substitutes. Users will carry most of the costs of adapting. Having invested over $3 billion in developing substitutes, the large chemicals companies now have powerful incentives to make sure that the ban on CFCs is watertight. Their representatives were influential bystanders at the second conference of parties to the Montreal agreement in London in 1990, at which the main challenge was to increase the number of third world signatories. A major issue for India was the amount of technical assistance that Western companies would provide to make CFC substitutes in India. Both Du Pont and ICI were encouraged by their respective governments to try to pacify the Indians. Given India's cavalier attitude in the past toward intellectual property rights, both companies are wary of giving India the technology to make CFC substitutes or even of selling it, at least until they can be sure that India will not pinch the technology and export it. A more probable option is a joint venture, which would allow the Indian government to take a share of future profits. Both companies have a vested interest in making it as easy as possible for third world countries to acquire technologies for using CFC-substitutes and in getting Western governments to foot the bill.

Makers and users of CFC substitutes also have a strong interest in making sure that the schedule for the Montreal agreement leaves them time to earn a decent return on their enormous investment. This is the flip side of the companies' vigorous support for the protocol. It creates a potential problem. The two main groups of substitutes now under development, known collectively as hydrofluoroalkanes (HFAs), both have problematic environmental side effects. One group, the HCFCs, are essentially CFCs in which some of the ozone-damaging chlorine is replaced by hydrogen. The remaining chlorine would do some damage to the ozone layer, though much less than CFCs. HCFCs are easy to use in air-conditioning, refrigeration, and foam-blowing. But some of the greener countries (which generally do not have chemical companies developing CFC substitutes), want limits to the use of HCFCs written into the Montreal Protocol. The other compounds, HFCs, are CFCs in which all the chlorine is replaced by hydrogen. They are likely to be used mainly in refrigeration and leave the ozone layer unscathed. But they add to the greenhouse effect—not as much as CFCs, but enough to worry environmentalists. Manufacturers of CFC substitutes point out to governments that the cost to society of phasing out CFCs will depend largely on how quickly the change has to take place and how confident users can be that new technologies will not have to be quickly replaced. A study carried out by the U.S. Department of Energy in 1989 reckoned that to phase out CFCs by the end of the century would cost $19 billion to $34 billion in equipment write-offs, assuming (too pessimistically) that no commercial recycling market were to develop.[6] If limits are placed on CFC substitutes, the costs will be higher. Users will stick with CFCs for longer, in the hope that other substitutes will come along before the ban eventually bites. Manufacturers may charge more for substitutes to insure against limits on the time they have to recoup their development costs. The argument over curbing the growth of CFC substitutes shows that environmental protectionism has its drawbacks. Better, though, to have a protocol on CFCs in exchange for protecting the market for substitutes than no protocol at all. And better for manufacturers to win an international agreement, forcing competitors to adopt the same standards, than for individual countries to move alone. The agreement reduces the risks to manufacturers that are developing CFC substitutes; the development of substitutes, in turn, reduces the costs to society of banning CFCs.

Diverging Process Standards

Environmental standards for processes will pose a rather different threat to free trade. In countries where pollution-control rules are strict, companies will increasingly complain that they face unfair competition, both at home and in third markets, from other countries with looser standards. A new form of protectionism may spring up: bans on imports of goods made by dirty processes, using suspect materials.

Countries may hesitate to use trade barriers to protect the jobs of their workers, arguing that to do so raises the prices that everyone pays for goods in the shops for the benefit of a smallish section of the population. To keep out, say, Bangladeshi shirts may keep American or British shirtmakers in business but means that American and British poor have to pay more for their shirts. Environmental protectionists feel no such scruples. They will argue that sound environmental policies benefit the whole community—and future generations. So they will find it easy to persuade governments to keep out products from dirty countries. Setting tough standards will be the first step. The next step, though, may be the imposition of environmental tariffs, introduced under pressure from regulated companies as environmental rules tighten.

Already the United Nations Environment Program has discussed the possibility of introducing a levy on dirty trade and using the proceeds to pay for environmental programs. In the United States in 1990, during negotiations of a free-trade agreement between the United States and Mexico, Sen. David L. Boren of Oklahoma introduced a bill in Congress to put a tariff on goods coming into the United States from countries with weaker environmental standards. He proposed a charge equal to the amount per unit that companies in such countries were estimated to save by operating under a laxer regime. The idea is not new. It was considered by Jimmy Carter when he was president; he was dissuaded when his advisers pointed out that other countries such as Sweden, with even stricter environmental standards than the United States, might retaliate.

Arguments over different standards can take unexpected forms. In 1990, Mexico complained to GATT about American legislation banning imports of tuna from countries that killed more dolphins than American tuna fishermen were allowed to. America argued that the rule was important for the conservation of dolphins. Mexico retorted that it was intended rather for the conservation of the American tuna fishers. GATT officials argued that the case appeared, at least on the surface, to be a classic example of one country attempting to impose its own standards on another.

Environmental Protectionism

The clash between national environmental standards and free trade will become more important as countries give more attention to global environmental problems. Rich countries will be tempted to use trade sanctions to foist environmental virtue on others. In 1991, America threatened to ban imports of some natural products, including pearls, from Japan unless Japan took tougher measures to protect the endangered hawksbill turtle. Here, no protection, real or imaginary, of an American industry was involved; the United States was using the threat of trade sanctions to change Japan's environmental policy. Japan did not protest to GATT (where it would probably have been heard sympathetically, as GATT's rules deplore the use of trade sanctions as threats). Instead, it agreed to speed up the end of imports of turtles.

Such tactics may increasingly be used against third world countries that are seen to be damaging their environments. For instance, the Netherlands is proposing to ban from 1995 imports of tropical hardwoods harvested in unsustainable ways.

More ominous, though, is the precedent set by the Montreal Protocol to phase out CFCs. It includes provisions for countries that comply to ban products containing CFCs from other countries and even products whose manufacturing process involves the use of CFCs. That may yet set an awkward precedent for the embryonic treaty on global warming. If products manufactured with CFCs can be banned, why not penalize countries that fail to curb their consumption of fossil fuels? Free traders will fret. Yet environmental trade barriers in such situations may have a logic of their own. GATT rightly objects if one country seeks to impose its standards on another, arguing that the state of a country's environment is its own affair. But what if one country's neglect of environmental policy harms other countries? Then, surely, it is legitimate for its neighbors to take an interest. When only the national environment suffers, dirty countries can reasonably retort that what they do with their own rivers and hillsides is nobody else's business (though just wait for the environmental protectionists to reply, in turn, that their concern is for the dirty country's future inhabitants). When the environment of other countries suffers, though, the logic of green protectionism is stronger. It may be the only way that one country can put real pressure on another to make sure its companies shoulder the costs they would otherwise impose on the global environment.

Countries that agree to curb planet-threatening pollution have few ways to discourage free riders, those less virtuous countries who benefit for free from the self-restraint of others. Environmental protectionism offers a double benefit: a way to discourage free-riders, and a way to win the backing of clean companies by ensuring an international return on their investments. In that way, environmental protectionism may amount to much the same as offering a special subsidy to clean companies, not just to those in the country that sets the standards, but to those that try to export to it. They all enjoy a protected market.

The main theme of this book has been that cleaning the environment requires government intervention. That can be done in both cost-effective and expensive ways. Some intervention is deeply harmful. Some is expensively unnecessary. But some is essential and has already made the industrial countries nicer places to live in than they might otherwise have been.

Companies must make sure that government intervention is conducted in ways that reward the cleanest and greenest. Industry's ingenuity can reduce enormously the costs of tackling environmental problems: by inventing substitutes for CFCs, by developing energy efficiency, by finding sustainable uses for rain-forest products, by reducing the rubbish heaps of the world, and by inventing simple, reliable forms of contraception. Harnessing that ingenuity by the skillful design of environmental policies is the challenge for governments. Together, wise government and inventive industry could be a formidable alliance for a greener world.

A Checklist for Companies

How should the sensible company chairman turn the ideas in this book into action? Here are a few suggestions to begin with:

1. Put the most senior person possible in charge of environmental policy. A member of the board should have clear responsibility, and there should be a well-defined management structure. All the golden intentions in the world are pointless unless the chairman cares and is known to care.

2. Draft a policy, then make it public. Make it clear. Include targets, with numbers and dates; this will not be possible unless you also follow the remaining suggestions.

3. Measure. Nothing concentrates the mind like numbers. In particular, discover what wastes you are creating and what energy you are using.

4. Institute a regular environmental audit to check on what is happening. While an outside consultant may be a help with the first three steps, this one can be done in-house. Pay particular attention to the follow-up: there is no point in knowing what is wrong if nothing is done to fix it.

5. Consider ways to reduce the range of materials you use that could do environmental harm. Do you really need so many toxic chemicals?

6. Think about the materials in your product. If you had responsibility for disposing of it when your customer threw it out (and one day, legislators may well dump that burden on your firm), could you do so? In an environmentally benign way? If not, consider changing the design and materials you use.

7. Remember that you may be able to make a business opportunity out of disposing of your product when the customer has finished with it. If your customer brings back used paint drums or old refrigerators, it offers a chance to build a new link—and to make your customer dependent on you in a new way.

8. If you invest in a country where environmental standards are low, do not expect them to stay that way. If one country finds a way of forcing companies to clean up, others will follow. Better to assume that standards everywhere will rise than to risk an expensive and disagreeable surprise.

9. Accept that environmental regulations will tend to converge upward. What is compulsory in the most energetically environmental markets (California, Germany, Scandinavia) will probably reach your home market. If you accept the highest standards before they are made compulsory, you steal a market advantage.

10. Remember that greenery is often a proxy for quality—in the eyes of your customers, your workers, and your managers. A truly green company is unlikely to be badly managed. Conversely, a well-managed company finds it relatively easy to be green.

References

Introduction

1. D.H. Meadows et al., *The Limits to Growth* (London: Earth Island, 1972).
2. Nicholas Ridley, "Policies Against Pollution," (London: Centre for Policy Studies, 1989), p. 9.
3. Quoted in John Kay and Aubrey Silberston, "Green Economics," *National Institute Economic Review* (February 1991), p. 50.
4. Garret Hardin, "The Tragedy of Commons," *Science,* vol. 162 (1968), pp. 1243–1248.
5. World Commission on Environment and Development, *Our Common Future* (Oxford: Oxford University Press, 1987).
6. Project 88—Round II, A Public Policy Study sponsored by Sen. Timothy Wirth and Sen. John Heinz (Washington, DC, May 1991), p. 1.
7. Project 88: "Harnessing Market Forces to Protect Our Environment," a public policy study sponsored by Sen. Timothy Wirth and Sen. John Heinz (Washington, DC, 1988).
8. David Pearce, Edward Barbier, and Anil Markandya, *Blueprint for a Green Economy* (London: Earthscan Publications, 1989).

Chapter 1

1. David Pearce, "Global Environmental Change: The Challenge to Industry and Economic Science," 35th Fawley Foundation Lecture, University of Southampton.
2. "Are the Costs of Cleaning Up Eastern Europe Exaggerated? Economic Reform and the Environment" (London: Centre for Economic Policy Research, Discussion Paper 482, 1990).
3. IBRD (World Bank) and IMF, Development Committee, "Environment, Growth and Development," Paper No. 14 (Washington, DC, August 1987).
4. David Pearce and Kerry Turner, *Economics of Natural Resources and the Environment* (London: Harvester Wheatsheaf, 1990).
5. OECD, *Environment and Economics* (Paris, 1984).
6. *World Conservation Strategy* (Gland, Switzerland: International Union for the Conservation of Nature, 1987); World Commission on Environment and Development, *Our Common Future* (London: Oxford University Press, 1987).
7. John Pezzey, "Economic Analysis of Sustainable Growth and Sustainable Development" (Washington, DC: IBRD Department of Environment, Working Paper No. 15, 1989).

8. David Pearce, Edward Barbier, and Anil Markandya, *Blueprint for a Green Economy* (London: Earthscan Publications, 1989).
9. Quoted in Pezzy, "Economic Analysis of Sustainable Growth and Sustainable Development," p. 67.
10. Partha Dasgupta and Karl Göran-Mäler, "The Environment and Emerging Development Issues," paper prepared for the plenary session of the World Bank's conference on development economics, April 1990.
11. Ibid.
12. Tom Nash, "Green about the Environment," *Director,* (February 1991), p. 42.
13. Dennis Anderson, "Environmental Policy and the Public Revenue in Developing Countries" (Washington, DC: IBRD Department of Environment, Working Paper No. 36, 1990), p. 15.
14. Quoted in Ibid.
15. Comment by George Jaszi, quoted in Henry Peskin with Ernst Lutz, "A Survey of Resource and Environmental Accounting in Industrialized Countries" (Washington, DC: IBRD Department of Environment, Working Paper No. 37, August 1990).
16. Robert Repetto et al., *Wasting Assets: Natural Resources in the National Income Accounts* (Washington, DC: World Resources Institute, 1989).
17. Peskin with Lutz, "A Survey of Resource and Environmental Accounting in Industrialized Countries."

Chapter 2

1. Quoted in Per-Olav Johansson, "Valuing Environmental Damage," *Oxford Review of Economic Policy,* vol. 6, no. 1 (Spring 1990), p. 46.
2. G. Pennington, N. Topham, and R. Ward, "Aircraft Noise and Residential Property Values," *Journal of Transport Economics and Policy,* vol. xxiv, no. 1 (1990), pp. 49–60.
3. This chapter draws on Jeffrey A. McNeely, *Economists and Biological Diversity, Developing Incentives to Conserve Natural Resources* (Gland, Switzerland: International Union for the Conservation of Nature, 1988).
4. C.M. Peters, A.H. Gentry, and R. Mendelsohn, "Valuation of an Amazonian Rain Forest," *Nature,* vol. 339 (June 29, 1989).
5. David Pearce and Kerry Turner, *Economics of Natural Resources and the Environment* (London: Harvester Wheatsheaf, 1990).
6. C. Starr, *Science,* vol. 165, no. 1232 (1969), quoted by Paul Slovic, "Perceptions of Risk," *Science,* vol. 236 (April 17, 1987), pp. 280–285.
7. Michael Gough, "How Much Cancer Can EPA Regulate Anyway?," *Risk Analysis,* vol. 10, no. 1 (1990), pp. 1–6.
8. Bruce Ames, Renae Magaw, and Lois Swirsky Gold, "Ranking Possible Carcinogenic Hazards," *Science,* vol. 236 (April 17, 1987), pp. 271–280.
9. Environmental Protection Agency, "Environmental Investments: The Cost of a Clean Environment" (Washington, DC, December 1990).

10. P.R. Portney, "Economics and the Clean Air Act," *Journal of Environmental Protection,* vol. 4 (1990), pp. 173–178.
11. Environmental Protection Agency, "Unfinished Business: A Comparative Assessment of Environmental Problems" (Washington, DC: Office of Policy, Planning and Evaluation, February 1987); and Environmental Protection Agency, *Reducing Risk: Setting Priorities and Strategies for Environmental Protection* (Washington, DC: Science Advisory Board, SAB-EC-90-021, September 1990).

Chapter 3

1. Robert Repetto, "Skimming the Water: Rent-Seeking and the Performance of Public Irrigation Systems" (Washington, DC: World Resources Institute, Research Report No. 4, 1986); Mark Kosmo, "Money To Burn? The High Costs of Energy Subsidies" (Washington, DC: World Resources Institute, 1987); Robert Repetto, "Paying the Price: Pesticide Subsidies in Developing Countries" (Washington, DC: World Resources Institute, Research Report No. 2, December 1985).
2. Quoted in Repetto, "Skimming the Water," pp. 4–5.
3. Ibid., p. 18; ibid., p. 17.
4. Ibid., p. 18.
5. Kosmo, "Money to Burn?", pp. 11–17.
6. Joanne C. Burgess, "The Contribution of Efficient Energy Pricing to Reducing Carbon Dioxide Emissions," *Energy Policy,* vol. 118, no. 5 (June 1990), pp. 449–454.
7. P.S. Nicola, "The Politics of Energy Conservation" (Washington, DC: Brookings Institution, 1986). Quoted in Kosmo, "Money to Burn?", p. 29.
8. "Energy Efficiency Strategy for Developing Countries: The Role of ESMAP," background paper for ESMAP's annual meeting, Paris, 1989, p. 2.
9. Philip Fearnside, "Brazil's Balbina Dam: Environment versus the Legacy of the Pharaohs in Amazonia," *Environmental Management,* vol. 13, no. 3 (1989).
10. Burgess, "The Contribution of Efficient Energy Pricing to Reducing Carbon Dioxide Emissions," pp. 449–454.
11. U.S. Department of Agriculture, *Agricultural Resources—Cropland, Water and Conservation—Situation and Outlook Report* (Washington, DC: Economic Research Service, 1987); U.S. Department of Agriculture, *The Second RCA Appraisal* (Washington, DC: USDA, 1989).
12. OECD, *Agricultural and Environmental Policies: Opportunities for Integration* (Paris, 1989).
13. National Research Council, *Alternative Agriculture* (Washington, DC: National Academy Press, 1989), p. 42.
14. Repetto, "Paying the Price," pp. 12–15.
15. Ibid.

16. Quoted by Alan Winters in "The So-called 'Non-Economic' Objectives of Agricultural Support," in OECD, *Economic Studies,* no. 13 (Winter 1989–90), p. 257.

17. Ibid.

18. Florentin Krause, Wilfrid Bach, and Jon Kooney, *Energy Policy in the Greenhouse* (London: Earthscan Publications, 1990).

19. Hans P. Binswanger, "Brazilian Policies That Encourage Deforestation in the Amazon" (Washington, DC: IBRD Department of Environment, Working Paper No. 16, 1989).

20. Dennis J. Mahar, "Government Policies and Deforestation in Brazil's Amazon Region" (Washington, DC: IBRD, 1989).

21. R. Paris and I. Ruzicka, "Barking up the Wrong Tree" (Manila: Asian Development Bank, Environment Office, Occasional Paper, May 1991).

22. David Sawyer, "Taxes Good, Subsidies Bad," *Financial Times* (July 31, 1990).

23. Dieter Helm and David Pearce, "Assessment: Economic Policy Towards the Environment," *Oxford Review of Economic Policy,* vol. 6, no. 1 (1990), pp. 1–16.

Chapter 4

1. Tom Tietenberg, "Economic Instruments for Environmental Regulation," *Oxford Review of Economic Policy,* vol. 6, no. 1 (1990), pp. 17–33.

2. Michael Cameron, "Transportation Efficiency: Tackling Southern California's Air Pollution and Congestion," The Environmental Defense Fund and the Regional Institute of Southern California, 1991.

3. Project 88, "Harnessing Market Forces to Protect Our Environment," a public policy study sponsored by Sen. Timothy Wirth and Sen. John Heinz (Washington DC, 1988).

4. Scott Barrett, "Environmental Regulation: Market Solutions," unpublished paper.

5. World Bank, "Poland—The Environment," unpublished paper (Washington, DC, June 1989).

Chapter 5

1. Quoted in William Fulkerson, Roddie R. Judkins, and Manoj K. Sanghri, "Energy from Fossil Fuels," *Scientific American* (September 1990), p. 85.

2. Marc H. Ross and Daniel Steinmeyer, "Energy for Industry," *Scientific American* (September 1990), p. 49.

3. IEA/OECD, *Energy Conservation in IEA Countries* (Paris, 1987).

4. J. Goldenberg et al., *Energy for a Sustainable World* (Washington, DC: World Resources Institute, 1987).

5. World Bank, *Financing of the Energy Sector in Developing Countries* (Washington, DC, April 1989).

6. Yu Joe Huang, "Potentials for and Barriers to Building Energy Conservation in China," *Contemporary Policy Issues,* California State University, July 1990, pp. 157–173.
7. William Chandler, ed., *Carbon Emission Control Strategies* (Baltimore, MD: World Wildlife Fund, 1990).
8. IBRD internal document, "Poland and the Environment," June 1989.
9. Mark Kosmo, "Money to Burn? The High Costs of Energy Subsidies" (Washington, DC: World Resources Institute, 1987).
10. M.J. Grubb, *The Greenhouse Effect: Negotiating Targets* (London: Royal Institute of International Affairs, 1989).
11. Jerry A. Hausman, "Individual Discount Rates and the Purchase and Utilisation of Energy-Using Durables," *Bell Journal of Economics,* vol. 10 (1979), pp. 33–54.
12. M.J. Grubb, *Energy Policies and the Greenhouse Effect* (London: Royal Institute of International Affairs, 1990), p. 132.
13. Amory Lovins, "Four Revolutions in Electricity Efficiency," *Contemporary Policy Issues* (July 1990), pp. 122–141.

Chapter 6

1. Walter V. Reid and Kenton Miller, "Keeping Options Alive: The Scientific Basis for Conserving Biodiversity" (Washington, DC: World Resources Institute, 1989), pp. 50–51.
2. Ibid., pp. 41–45.
3. Jeffrey A. McNeely, *Economists and Biological Diversity, Developing Incentives to Conserve Natural Resources* (Gland, Switzerland: International Union for the Conservation of Nature, 1988), p. xi.
4. Edward Barbier et al., *Elephants, Economics and Ivory* (London: Earthscan Publications, 1990).
5. David Pearce, "An Economic Approach to Saving the Tropical Forests," in Dieter Helm, ed., *Economic Policy Towards the Environment* (Oxford: Basil Blackwell, 1991).
6. Ibid.

Chapter 7

1. This chapter draws extensively from the *Oxford Review of Economic Policy,* vol. 6, no. 1 (1990), especially from the articles by Partha Dasgupta, Scott Barrett, and Karl Göran-Mäler.
2. Scott Barrett, "Ozone Holes, Greenhouse Gases and Economic Policy," London Business School, July 1989.
3. Peter H. Sand, *Lessons Learned in Global Governance* (Washington, DC: World Resources Institute, 1990).
4. Barrett, "Ozone Holes, Greenhouse Gases and Economic Policy."

5. Florentin Krause, Wilfrid Bach, and Jon Cooney, *Energy Policy in the Greenhouse from Warming Fate to Warming Limit* (London: Earthscan Publications, 1990).
6. Alan Manne and Richard Richels, "Global CO_2 Emission Reduction—The Impacts of Raising Energy Costs," *The Energy Journal,* vol. 12, no. 1 (1991), pp. 87–107.
7. Robert Williams, "Will Constraining Fossil Fuel Carbon-Dioxide Emissions Really Cost So Much?" (unpublished).
8. W.D. Nordhaus, also in "To Slow or Not to Slow: The Economics of the Greenhouse Effect," Yale University Department of Economics, 1990, mimeo.
9. David Pearce, "Economics and the Global Environmental Challenge," *Millenium Journal of International Relations,* vol. 90, no. 3 (December 1990), pp. 365–388.
10. Michael Grubb, *The Greenhouse Effect: Negotiating Targets* (London: Royal Institute of International Affairs, 1989).

Chapter 8

1. Paul E. Gray, "The Paradox of Technological Development," in Jesse H. Ausubel and Hedy E. Sladovich, eds., *Technology and Environment* (Washington, DC: National Academy Press, 1989), pp. 192–204.
2. Quoted in Jesse H. Ausubel, "Regularities in Technological Development: An Environmental View," in Ausubel and Sladovich, *Technology and Environment,* p. 72.
3. Quoted in Partha Dasgupta, "Exhaustible Resources," in Laurie Friday and Ronald Laskey, eds., *The Fragile Environment* (Cambridge: Cambridge University Press, 1989), pp. 123–124.
4. Ibid., p. 124.
5. Robert Repetto, "The Concept and Measurement of Environmental Productivity: An Exploratory Study of the Electric Power Industry," paper for Towards 2000: Environment, Technology and the New Century, conference sponsored by World Resources Institute and OECD, Annapolis, 1990.

Chapter 9

1. John Elkington and Julia Hailes, *The Green Consumer Guide* (London: Gollancz, 1988). Published in America as *The Green Consumer: You Can Buy Products That Don't Cost the Earth* by John Elkington, Julia Hailes, and Joel Makover (New York: Viking Penguin, 1990).
2. Abt Associates Inc., "Consumer Purchasing Behavior and the Environment" (Cambridge, MA, November 1990).
3. Mintel International, "The Green Consumer," London, 1989.
4. ENDS, "Eco-Labeling Plan Gets Broad Backing," Report 177 (London, October 1989), pp. 25–26.

5. Quoted in Jaclyn Fierman, "The Big Muddle in Green Marketing," *Fortune*, June 3, 1991, p. 91.
6. "Green, Greener, Greenest? The Green Consumer in the UK, the Netherlands and Germany," survey by Brand New Product Development Ltd and Diagnostics Market Research Ltd, London, September 1989.
7. Peter H. Sand, *Lessons Learned in Global Environmental Governance* (Washington, DC: World Resources Institute, 1990).
8. *Managing the Environment* (London: Business International, 1990), p. 155.
9. Marc Epstein, "What Shareholders Really Want," *New York Times*, April 28, 1991.

Chapter 10

1. Franklin Associates Ltd, "Characterization of Municipal Solid Waste in the United States: 1990 Update." Prepared for the U.S. Environmental Protection Agency, Washington, DC, 1990.
2. Project 88—Round II, A Public Policy Study sponsored by Sen. Timothy E. Wirth and Sen. John Heinz. (Washington, DC, May 1991), p. 43.
3. C. Lehrburger, *Diapers in the Waste Stream: A Review of Waste Management and Public Policy Issues* (Sheffield, MA, December 1988), quoted in U.S. Congress, Office of Technology Assessment, *Facing America's Trash: What Next for Municipal Solid Waste?* (Washington, DC: National Academy Press, 1989), pp. 116–117.
4. See ENDS, Report No. 185, June 1990, pp. 16–18.
5. Michael Weisskopf, "Administrative Costs Drain 'Superfund,'" *Washington Post*, June 19, 1991, pp. A1 and A14.
6. "Environmental Risks and Corporate Credit Quality," Moody's Special Comment, Moody's Investor Services, New York, April 1991.

Chapter 11

1. P. Bardos et al., "Market Barriers, Materials Reclamation and Recycling," Warren Spring Laboratory, Department of Trade and Industry, 1990.
2. Richard M. Titmuss, *The Gift Relationship: From Human Blood to Social Policy* (London: Allen & Unwin, 1971).
3. Joel P. Clark and Frank R. Field III, "Recycling: Boon or Bane of Advanced Materials Technologies? Automotive Materials Substitution," paper presented at Towards 2000: Environment Technology and the New Century, a symposium sponsored by World Resources Institute and OECD, Annapolis, 1990.
4. Environmental Protection Agency, "Methods to Manage and Control Plastic Waste," report to U.S. Congress (Washington, DC, 1990).
5. Project 88—Round II, a Public Policy Study sponsored by Sen. Timothy Wirth and Sen. John Heinz (Washington, DC, May 1991), pp. 50–52.

6. U.S. Congress, Office of Technology Assessment, *Facing America's Trash: What Next for Municipal Solid Waste?* (Washington, DC: National Academy Press, 1989), p. 318.
7. Ibid., quoted on p. 198.
8. Project 88—Round II, pp. 54–60.

Chapter 12

1. Quoted in *Managing the Environment* (London: Business International, 1990), p. 130.
2. Ibid., pp. 133–137.
3. OECD, *The Promotion and Diffusion of Clean Technologies*, Paris, June 1987.
4. Quoted in *Managing the Environment*, p. 89.
5. Robert Herman, Siamak A. Ardekani, and Jesse H. Ausubel, "Dematerialization," in Jesse H. Ausubel and Hedy E. Sladovich, eds., *Technology and Environment* (Washington, DC: National Academy Press, 1989), pp. 61–62.
6. See the Industry Council for Packaging and the Environment (INCPEN), "Packaging and Resources," London, 1990, p. 6.

Chapter 13

1. International Chamber of Commerce, "Environmental Auditing," Paris, 1989.
2. R.H. Gray, "The Greening of Accountancy: The Profession after Pearce" (London: Chartered Association of Certified Accountants, Research Report No. 17, 1990).

Chapter 14

1. Michael Porter, "America's Green Strategy," *Scientific American* (April 1991), p. 168.
2. OECD, *Environment and Economics*, Paris, 1984.
3. Raymond J. Kopp, Paul R. Portney, and Diane E. De Witt, "International Comparisons of Environmental Regulation," *Resources*, no. 11 (Fall 1990), pp. 10–13.
4. H. Jeffrey Leonard, *Pollution and the Struggle for the World Product* (Cambridge: Cambridge University Press, 1988).
5. *Managing the Environment* (London: Business International, 1990), p. 14.
6. Putman, Hayes & Bartlett, Inc. "Assessment of the Impacts Associated with a Total CFC Phase-out," study for the U.S. Department of Energy (Washington, DC, 1989).

Index